To Wayne –

It's always great to see you.

Best Regards.

Jim

I Have Slipped The Surly Bonds Of Earth And Danced The Skies

Personal
Aviation and Architectural Anecdotes
&
Life Story

Jim Warner

Deeds Publishing
Marietta, GA

www.deedspublishing.com

All pictures, unless otherwise noted, are from the personal collection of the author.

Cover design and layout by Ali Grasty and Jeff McKay

Printed in the United States of America
Published by Deeds Publishing, Marietta, GA

First Edition, 2008

Books are available in quantity for promotional or premium use. For information write Deeds Publishing, PO Box 682222, Marietta, GA 30068 or www.deedspublishing.com

ISBN 978-0-9776018-6-8

DEDICATION

To my wonderful family

and many loyal friends

who have made my life

anything but dull.

TABLE OF CONTENTS

PART I

*"There I Was,
Flat on My Back
at 9,000 Feet ..."*

JIM WARNER, CDR USNR RET.
FORMER NAVAL AVIATOR

Jim Warner... Personal Aviation Anecdotes

ANECDOTES

Flying is made up of a great many small incidents and a small number of interesting ones. An anecdote must, therefore, unless it would become tedious, be extremely selective, discarding all the inconsequential incidents in one's life and concentrating on those that have remained vivid in one's memory.

an-ec-dote (an ik dot) **n.** [Fr. <ML. *anecdota* < Gr. anekdota, neut. Pl. of *anekdotos*] **1.** unpublished little known facts of history or biography.

PREFACE

It was a dark and stormy night, Halloween 1923, when I was born at Gantt's Quarry, Alabama, in a little unpainted Alabama Marble Company house up on rock piers (sob) about fifty feet from a marble quarry. When I was three, Dad, an estimator for the company, was transferred to Chicago where we lived near Lincoln Park, a few blocks from the Loop, in a high rise apartment building overlooking Lake Michigan. When I started school, we moved just west of the Windy City to the little town of Glen Ellyn where I had to walk two miles round trip to school in three feet of snow (sob).

During the Great Depression, the company transferred Dad to Birmingham, where I spent my happy teenage years in the suburb of Homewood.

I joined the Navy V5 Program in November '42 and was called to active duty in March '43 after my first co-op quarter at Georgia Tech. I earned my wings at Pensacola in October '44 and was selected to be an instrument flight instructor at NAS Whiting, returning to civilian life in December '45. I studied architecture at Georgia Tech and graduated in December '49.

I returned to Navy active duty in December '52 and was stationed at NAS Quonset Point, Rhode Island, in Utility Squadron Two. I returned to civilian life in December '54.

In the active Naval Air Reserve from March '46 to December '66, I became squadron commander of my reserve squadron and retired as Deputy Wing Commander with the rank of Commander and 3,100 flying hours.

(Everything related here is unembellished and remembered without "advantages", but as clearly as if it all happened yesterday. I'm afraid it only shows how undistinguished my Naval service was. I didn't have the opportunity to kill anybody in the wars, except myself while flying.)

CONTENTS

1
YELLOW FOOTPRINTS (1942)

While I was on my first Georgia Tech Co-Op work term, I was walking down the street in Birmingham one morning when I came upon some yellow footprints on the sidewalk. I followed them right around the corner into the Navy recruiting office. What the heck! I took the screening test for the Naval Aviation Cadet flight training program, V5. I passed, but had to get my parents' permission to enlist. Mom and Dad didn't want to sign the papers, but I told them I was going to have to "go" sooner or later so let me go where I wanted to go. I had seen the original movie *All Quiet on the Western Front* when I was just a kid and it made an indelible impression on me. Anything to stay out of the infantry. They finally gave in and signed the papers. It probably saved my life. I would have been just the right age for Omaha Beach.

The next step was going to the Naval Aviation Cadet Selection Board in Atlanta, in the Capitol Cadillac show room and repair shops across the street from the Biltmore Hotel on West Peachtree. GM was making tanks and torpedo bombers that year, not Cadillac's. The mental and physical tests got serious here. The minimum weight for the program was 124 pounds. I weighed 123 pounds, but the Navy made an exception for me. I guess they needed pilots pretty badly. Later, in flight training, my cadet buddies kidded me telling me that the reason 124 pounds was the minimum was because, if you bailed out and weighed less than 124 pounds, the chute wouldn't open. Luckily, I passed all the tests.
Those who passed were sworn in (it was November 4, 1942) and sent home to wait for orders to report for flight training. I went back to work at the TCI Steel Mill in Ensley. When my work term was up, I had not been called yet. The head of the Steam Engineering Department where I worked was a great guy. He said I could continue on a second work term until I got my orders. The orders came to report on March 4, 1943 for Flight Prep at University of South Carolina in Columbia.

I can remember, as if it were yesterday, walking down the woods path to catch the *Edgewood 39* trolley car to World War II, with Mom waving goodbye from the front steps.

2
ON MY WAY

"Where am I goin'? I don't know. When will I get there? I ain't certain. All I know is I am on my way."

Paint Your Wagon

I got off *Edgewood 39* at 3rd and 20th and walked thirteen blocks to the Terminal Station to get the train to Atlanta where I was to report for active duty at the naval Aviation Cadet Selection Board. I had nothing but confidence in the future, regardless of what lay ahead. I was on my way.

When I got to Atlanta, I walked to the Biltmore Hotel on West Peachtree Street, where the newly arrived cadets were assembled to be processed. We filled out forms, signed up for a $10,000 GI life insurance policy, and a bunch of other stuff. That evening, we were taken to the Atlanta Terminal Station and put on a Pullman car to Columbia, South Carolina – first class. It was the last time I ever slept lying down when transferring from one training base to another.

The first phase of training was called "Flight Prep", a three-month phase during which we had athletics and courses in dead reckoning navigation, athletics, aerology, athletics, Morse code-blinker-semaphore, athletics, aircraft engines, athletics, military drill, and athletics. We never laid eyes on an airplane.

I was in the 3rd Battalion. Who should I run into but my childhood buddy, Robert Atchison. He was in the 2nd Battalion. I went to Camp Cosby one year with Robert and his brother, Roy. The three of us checked out a .22 and went off into the woods to shoot at targets. I was the only one of the three of us who survived the war. Robert crashed on a carrier landing in Tokyo Bay and Roy was a Marine lieutenant shot by a Jap sniper on a by-passed island in the Pacific – both killed after the war was over. Forever young.

3
THE SUMMER OF '42

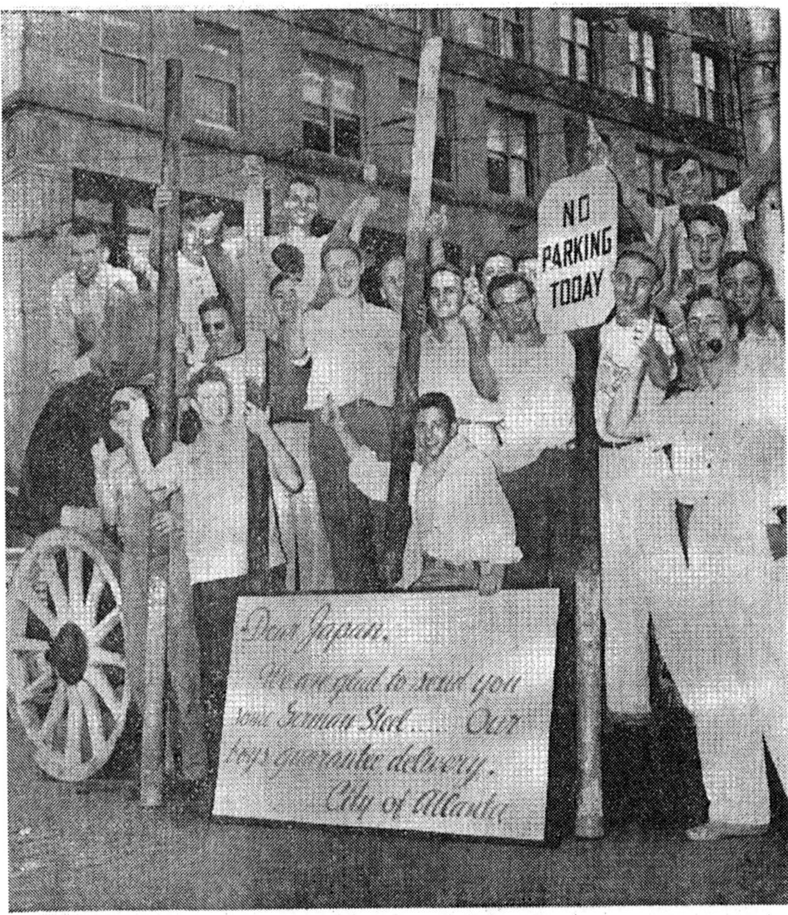

JOIN MARCH TO VICTORY—The nation's call for scrap metal brought out many odd pieces, but Georgia Tech came near topping the list here in Atlanta when they marched to Five Points Monday with the steel goal posts from Grant Field. The goal posts will be replaced by wooden uprights. Here the patriotic lads pose with their booty before turning it over to the salvaging committee.—Journal Photo.

4
"WHAT DID YOU DO IN THE WAR, DADDY?"

Q: Why do I think about the past so much?
A: Because the past was more interesting than the present.

During my 23 years flying, I flew the TBM, F6F, Corsair, A-26, and the F8F Grumman *Bearcat* plus several lesser aircraft. Total all types = 3,038 hours.

I had three years active duty in WW II, two years active duty during the Korean War (but not in Korea), and eighteen and a half years with the Naval Air Reserve. I was the Commanding Officer of a Reserve squadron, an Assistant Wing Commander (Admin) and retired with the rank of Commander.

During my 41 years in architecture, I worked for five architectural firms before I started my own firm, from which I retired thirty years later.

5
WHAT, ME WORRY?

6
FIRST SOLO

I soloed in a J3 Piper Cub at Albert Whitted Airport in St. Pete, Florida, which was not a bad place to learn to fly. One good thing about the Piper Cub - if something went wrong, you could always ride the biggest piece down. My first instructor was Mr. Lindsey - "mean-as-a-snake" Lindsey. He looked just like Lee Van Cleef, the mean as a snake Western movie villain. If he didn't like the way you were flying, he would unexpectedly throw the stick rapidly back and forth from side to side to beat your knees.

We had to have a minimum of eight hours of instruction in the air to solo (more hours, if necessary - within limits). After we soloed, the rest of the training was alternating dual and solo flights. Not a single cadet in our group had to have more than eight hours to solo, and most of us had never been near an airplane before.

Landing north, we approached over the water. One day in my approach over the water, I had too much airspeed. Lindsey would sit so you couldn't see the airspeed indicator and you had to fly by the sound of the wind (by the seat of your pants, so to speak). He grabbed the controls and shouted (he always shouted), "You want to dive it? We'll dive it!" He went into a steep nose dive, and all I could see was water. He pulled out at the last minute and made a perfect landing. I was impressed, but would have preferred to be impressed some other way.

Coming in for a landing at the end of my eighth hour, there was another Cub in the take off position. I didn't see (read "notice") it. Mr. Lindsey yelled, "GO AROUND!". When I landed after going around, he told me to let him out. When he got out, he stuck his head back in the cockpit and said, "I'm getting out. You're not safe to fly with," and I took off on my first solo. It was August, 10, 1943. And, as they say, "The rest is history".

My instructor in the next phase, which consisted of spins, stalls, practice dead stick landings and stuff like that, was Mr. Mathews. He was a really nice guy.

We were practicing dead stick landings near a St. Pete golf course. The practice did not take you all the way down to landing. It was just to see if you could have made it without hitting something. Mathews cut the power and I headed for a nice wide fairway. When it was obvious that I could make it, he hit the throttle, and we started a climbing turn to the left. He was headed right for a water tower. I thought he was going to give me a thrill. He said, "What are you doing?" I said, "I thought you had it!"

Adding power without changing trim (Cubs didn't have trim tabs – didn't really need them) causes the plane to climb and turn left if no one has the controls. Another lesson learned.

7
ARE WE THERE YET?

I had my first night flying at NAS Memphis, in an open cockpit Stearman, in the winter of '43-'44. The way it worked, after your first night solo, six planes in a 500 foot landing pattern would fly touch and go landings while six other planes chased each other around the field at 1,000 feet. It got lonesome flying around all by yourself on a cold black night, chasing the plane ahead of you when all you could see was the little white light on its rudder. When the period was half over, the six planes in the upper circle swapped places with the six planes in the landing pattern.

Night touch and go landing patterns can be dangerous. On the climb out there is a tendency for the cadet to drift to the right so that when he makes his turn onto the downwind leg he could be heading straight for the plane that is climbing out behind him. On one occasion this resulted in a midair collision, killing cadets Scwabb and Watson. I remember viewing the wreckage in the hangar. There was one brown shoe amongst the tangle of metal and fabric. It's strange how sudden collisions almost always result in the victim's shoes coming off.

On one night flight with an instructor, I forgot to set the altimeter on zero before we look off. The traffic pattern being at 500 feet, it was important to set the altimeter at zero feet so you would know when you got to 500 feet. On the climb out I realized that I had made a mistake, so I just kept climbing until the instructor shouted, "You're too high!" through the Gosport (a rubber tube that ran from a canvas thing over the instructor's mouth through two rubber tubes connected to the cadets helmet – one way conversation only, instructor to cadet). Then I would lose some altitude until he shouted, "You're too low!" I continued trying this solution until he quit shouting. I then assumed I was at 500 feet, so I set the altimeter at 500 feet.

8
THE CHECK RIDE

After "Preflight" at Athens, Georgia, the next phase of flight training was "Primary" (referred to by cadets as "E-Base" – "E" for "Elimination from flight training") at Memphis, Tennessee, flying N2S Stearmans, an open cockpit biplane, the winter of '43-'44. The Stearman was, and still is, a beautiful airplane. There were several stages in the syllabus. There was "A" Stage for just learning to take off and land the Stearman. "B" Stage was precision landings, "C" Stage aerobatics and "D" Stage formation flying and formation take offs. Then there was the first experience with night flying.

My instructor was Ensign Ed Brown from Birmingham. I found out fifty years later, during a visit with him in Birmingham, that I was his first student. I was not a brilliant student pilot, but progressed fairly well under his patient instruction.

The precision stage involved "slips to the circle" landings and "S" turns to the circle. The circle was painted on the runway and was about 30 feet in diameter. We also flew Pylon 8's. This involved flying figure 8's around two pylons on the ground about 100 yards apart. The object was to fly a track on the ground that was a perfect 8, allowing for wind drift by varying the bank depending on the wind direction and velocity.

At the completion of this stage I got a "down" check, because my slips were not precise enough. The slip to the circle involved making the approach purposely too high. To lose the excess altitude and hit the circle, you dip one wing to lose the altitude and use opposite rudder to stay on the wind line (the line down the middle of the runway). You neutralize the controls just before you reach the circle so you land in a three point attitude.

When you got a "down" you had to go before a board of three instructors to be granted what was called "Squadron Time". I went before the board and they decided I might be worth saving, so they granted me the extra time, two additional instruction flights after which you had to fly two "ups" to stay in the flight program. They asked if I wanted another instructor, and I told them I wanted Ensign Brown to continue as my instructor.

Ed took me up and concentrated on slips. He would pick out the top of a cumulus cloud and I would practice slips to the top as if it were the circle on the field. He would coach me in how to do it perfectly.

It came time to fly the two ups. The first was with a LT Shelton, noted to be a hard nose check pilot. On the climb out to the assigned operating area the routine was to climb at 60 knots and make standard rate (three degrees per second) 90 degree turns every 60 seconds. The afternoon of the check ride was a beautiful, clear as a bell, day with very smooth air. My climb out was perfect. That gave me some confidence.

The first things I had to do were the "slips to the circle". They were perfect. Then to the pylons. Again everything went great. Shelton was looking at me in the mirror over his instrument panel. He looked puzzled. After the pylons he told me to go back to the field to do more slips. I thought this was odd, since I had done them perfectly.

When we got back to the main field he asked to see my dog tags. Very strange. About that time Ensign Brown walked up and said, "How'd my boy do?" At that, Shelton turned to the schedule board and put a down arrow by my name. Brown asked why. Shelton said, "His slips are so good they're dangerous. He doesn't fly like a student," ENS Brown said, "You can't give him a down, if he was that good!" LT Shelton just rubbed his LT collar bars, and that was it.

> *"The only real objective of a check ride is to complete it and get the bastard out of sight"*
> *-unknown*

It seems that earlier that month some instructors played a trick on Shelton. They had another instructor impersonate a cadet on a check ride, maybe to observe his methods. He had wanted to see my dog tags, because he thought I was an instructor. Believe it or not.

Since the down meant that I couldn't fly the two required ups to stay in the program, I figured I was going to be a Seaman Second at Glenview. I didn't sleep much that night. Next morning I was relieved that Shelton had changed the down to an up. I went on and flew an up on the second check ride, and that's how I was able to retire as a Commander.

9
HOW'D MY BOY DO?

10
IS THAT THE SAME HELMET AND JACKET ON THOSE CADETS?

CONTINUING TRAINING—Five Alabamians who recently completed primary flight training have been transferred to Pensacola, Fla., for intermediate training. They are, left to right: From Birmingham, James E. Warner, Jr., son of Mrs. J. E. Warner, 910 Saulter Road; Paul Tidd, son of Mrs. M. J. Robinson, 2325 Steiner Avenue, and Thomas M. Seale, Jr., son of Mrs. T. M. Seale, 919 North 39th Street; from Tarrant, Ralph G. Zorn, son of Mrs. John M. Zorn, 1233 Waverly Street; from Ensley, William H. Warren, son of Mrs. Ola M. Warren, 2000 Avenue I.

Mr. & Mrs J. E. Warner,
910 Saulter Road
Birmingham, Alabama

Dear Mr. & Mrs Warner:

I am enclosing a little clipping which I believe you will want to put in your memo-book.

With every good wish for your son, I am,

Sincerely,

Bob Wharton.

Encl.

RHW/mc

11
COOKS AND BAKERS SCHOOL

After three month at Athens Preflight, the fun started. We were sent to St. Petersburg, Florida, for what was called WTS, War Training School. Sort of an odd name since we were learning to fly in a Piper Cub (". . . and a beautiful thing it was, but not much use in a fight".)

Occasionally a Russian Mine Sweeper would dock near Albert Whitted Airport, which was right on Tampa Bay (it was the airport from which the first commercial flight was flown in the early days of aviation.) The epaulets on a cadet's uniform had a single star. Stripes were added as you advanced in rank – if you advanced in rank. When Russian sailors passed us on the street they would salute. They must have thought that we were very young brigadier generals.

We ate at the nearby Merchant Marine Cooks and Bakers School. They had a two week course. The food was not all that great the first week, but by the end of the two weeks it was pretty good, especially the baked goodies. The next two weeks started with a new class, and we had to get used to the first week cooking all over again.

St. Pete was great, almost like summer camp. Athletics was fun. We worked out on a baseball field that was used by the New York Yankees for Spring training and frolicked on the beach with Mac McMahan (the biggest guy I ever knew), "Fighter" Williamson (he wanted to be a fighter pilot worse than any cadet I ever knew – he probably got torpedo bombers when he got his wings), "Tojo" McClellan (he had slanting eyes, his father having been an Army officer in the Philippines), Glenn Pugh and Henry Livingston (killed later in flight training), Lou Helms (who lives in California and with whom I am in touch after 63 years), and "Razor" Warner (I was a 125 pound weakling).

12
"FOLLOW THE LEADER" CAN GET YOU IN TROUBLE

At Barin Field our air to air gunnery was conducted on four gunnery ranges that extended south into the Gulf from the barrier island that runs East and West at the Gulf end of Mobile Bay.

Cadets at Barin were assigned to a "Flight" with which they flew together on most of the training exercises. I was in Flight 628 with Phil Lindsey, Elmo Parker, Bob Scales (a future Eastern Captain), Bill Smith, Bob Warner (future architect –Yale) and me (future architect – Georgia Tech).

On air to air gunnery flights, we took turns leading the flight and turns towing the target. The tow plane would orbit at the head of the assigned range until the flight arrived and identified itself. Sometimes more than one flight was assigned to the same range. Leading the flight one day, I was approaching a tow plane at the head of our assigned range to I.D., when another formation was approaching to I.D., just ahead of my flight. To give the other flight some time, I took mine in a 360 turn to be in position to make my approach to the tow plane, if it turned out to be ours.

When a flight approached to identify, the flight leader put his formation in column (line astern, as the Brits say) – each plane directly behind and stepped down below the plane ahead. The leader flew directly under the tow plane to check the side number. This guy flew slightly over the tow plane so each plane in the column came closer and closer to the tow plane. The pilot of each plane in a column formation has his eyes glued to the plane in front of him, and is unaware of anything else.

As I came out of the 360 I saw the last plane hit the tow plane (it happened to be Lindsey in our tow plane). It all seemed to be in slow motion. One plane went into a grave yard spiral and the other into a spin. It seemed like forever, but both cadets bailed out.

Lindsey hit the water, got his pararaft out and waited for a PBY to pick him up. When the PBY taxied over to pick him up, one of the wing floats hit him and knocked him back into the water. Before all this happened, Lindsey was a quiet, nondescript sort of laid back guy. After surviving the mid-air collision, he was a changed person, very out going, and a sociable fun loving guy - a complete personality change.

13
IF YOU TOUCH ME THERE AGAIN, I'LL SCREAM

"Bloody Barin" was one of the seven training bases in the Pensacola Training Command – Chevalier (Mainside), Corry, Saufley, Bronson, Ellison, Whiting and Barin.

At Barin we went through the phase of training called "Final Squadron" which was air to air gunnery, strafing, dive bombing, over water navigation, and night formation flying. It was the last phase of training before we got our wings, with a high accident rate.

Barin had two runways separated by hangars, administrative buildings, and the parking area for about three hundred SNJ's. Both runways ran north and south. If the wind was from the east or west, you got to hone your crosswind landing technique. The traffic pattern was 500 feet down the middle between the two runways and a peel off to an approach to the runway from which you had taken off.

For night operations the runway lights consisted of three pairs of flare pots on each side of the runway, spaced about fifty feet apart. We were supposed to land between the first two pairs of flare pots. Returning from a night formation hop, I made a good approach and landed right at the end of the runway. As the roll out slowed, I started a right turn to get on the first taxiway. Even though it was dark, I glanced over my shoulder out of habit, and all I could see was a large spinning propeller fast approaching. Some knucklehead had landed hot and long and was just about to hit me. Because I was starting to turn, his prop chewed my tail off. If I had continued my roll out straight ahead, his left wing would have hit my rudder and thrown his prop into the cockpit.

There ain't no justice. The accident board gave me one-third blame, the knucklehead one-third blame and the landing signal officer (he gave you a red light if you were making a wheels up approach) one-third blame. My share of the blame was for turning off on the first taxiway instead of the second which led directly to my parking spot – a damn technicality. It was the early turn off that saved my life.

I protested to no avail. I got eight hours marching with a rifle after chow, eight demerits and eight nights in O&R removing and replacing (and removing and replacing, and removing and replacing, and remov . . . etc . . .) eighteen sparkplugs from a crashed SBD. If you got twenty demerits during your entire flight training, you were washed out. They were the only demerits I ever got. I guess they were worth it.

14
THE TREE! THE TREE!

The last phase of flight training at "Bloody" Barin Field, near Foley, Alabama, was where we learned air to air gunnery, strafing, dive bombing, six plane formation night flying (it made you pay attention), and more aerobatics.

It was called "Bloody" Barin because of the high cadet fatality rate. Before I got there they were losing almost a cadet a day. One of the cadets was the nephew of the famous radio personality, Walter Winchell. Winchell raised so much hell in Washington about it that the Navy tightened up on the safety program at Barin, and the cadet fatality rate dropped to about one cadet a week.

On what I think was my last check ride before getting my wings, I had, as often was the case, a tough check pilot. Everything seemed to go well during the check until the very end. I was coming in short on my landing approach. Just inside the fence there were two scrub pines, one on my left and one on my right. It looked like I was going to hit one of them. I was looking at the one on my right, just as the right wing tip grazed the top of it. The check pilot said, "You came pretty close to that tree!" Apparently he was watching the tree on the left. What the check pilot doesn't know can't hurt you.

15
WHAT WAS THAT THING?

One clear, calm evening after chow (I use the term loosely), a bunch of us cadets were standing around outside the chow hall shooting the breeze. Suddenly, very high in the western sky a small dot raced across the sky, faster than anything we had ever seen in the air. We had no idea what it was. None of us had ever heard of a jet plane.

Years later, I was relating this to my friend, Bob Harris. It turned out that Bob was a test pilot flying out of Eglin Field, just east of Pensacola. Bob said, "Jim, that was probably me." It seems Bob was one of the two test pilots at Eglin testing the first jet fighter. Small world!

Bob had been in the China-Burma-India Theater flying P-40's and shooting down Japs. Ironically, after the war, Bob went to work for General Electric, living in Japan selling GE jet engines to, of all people, the Japanese.

16
NIGHT FLYING AT BLOODY BARIN

At Barin Field, during "Night Flying" we flew solo in assigned sectors at assigned altitudes; and in the advanced stages, we flew in six plane formations (in two Vee's) chased by an instructor who would rather be somewhere else. We had no running lights, only the flare from our exhaust stacks plus good night vision. The tighter you held your position, the more quickly you could detect movement of the plane on which you were flying, making it easier to hold your position.

There were no runway lights at Barin. When we landed, we had no landing lights on the SNJ's we were flying. There were three flare pots lined up, spaced about 100 feet apart on each side of the runway.

We were told to be aware of a phenomenon known as "auto-kinetic hypnosis". When flying tight formation and staring at a single source of light, it can appear to oscillate, causing vertigo and loss of control of the airplane.

While at Saufley Field flying the SNV Vultee "Vibrator", one of my roommates was Bill Warren from Birmingham. One day he got an overdose of sun and had such a bad case of sunburn that he couldn't even wear a shirt, much less strap on a parachute. That night he was scheduled for night flying. Getting sunburned is a misdemeanor in the Navy. If he didn't fly that night he was in trouble, so I volunteered to take his hop and sign his name to cover for him. As I walked through the dark to the airplane I thought to myself, "Gee, I'll probably get killed, like in the movies".

After overcoming the initial fear of night flying, usually acquired while flying Stearmans at night in Primary at Memphis, night flying can be very pleasant. The air is usually smooth, you can see other planes and their direction of flight can be determined by the green and red wingtip and white rudder navigation lights (unless you are at Barin Field where there ain't no light), and you can find airports more easily by their rotating beacons. When flying at night over a cloud layer you can see the glow of city lights lighting up the top of the clouds – kinda spooky.

I was lucky flying for Bill Warren that night, nothing happened, and I lived to fly another night.

17
GETTING THE BIRD

After "Bloody Barin" we went to Pensacola Mainside (Chevalier Field) for a two week course in Naval Customs and Traditions, plus a check out in the "Dilbert Dunker". The Dilbert Dunker in the movie *"An Officer and a Gentleman"* looked like, and probably was, the same one we used.

We went to the tailor shop in the San Carlos Hotel (long gone now) in Pensacola to order our officer uniforms. We got a $250 uniform allowance with which to buy Aviation Greens, Blues, Khakis and a really neat grey trench coat. Our cadet whites still fit and only had to have Ensign shoulder boards added. That's a lot of uniforms for $250. In the fall of 1944 at Mainside, 300 cadets were commissioned and designated Naval Aviators every Tuesday and every Thursday – every week!

I got my wings (The Bird) on October 3rd, 1944 and got orders to Ft. Lauderdale for Operational Training in torpedo bombers (TBM's like George H. W. Bush flew). My orders included 30 days leave prior to reporting. The next day I was informed that my orders had been changed, and I was to "report without delay" to Instrument Flight Instructors School (IFIS) at NAS Atlanta (now DeKalb Peachtree Airport) "Without delay" means what it says – right NOW! I caught the train for Atlanta that night.

18
HORN! WHAT HORN?

Being an instrument flight instructor at South Whiting Field in the Pensacola training command during WW II has always bothered me. I missed the big show. I frequently think of the words of Henry V addressing his troops who were outnumbered five-to-one before Agincourt in Shakespeare's Henry The Fifth, "... And gentlemen in England now a-bed shall think themselves accurst they were not here; and hold their manhoods cheap whiles any speaks that fought with us upon Saint Crispin's day". The Battle of Midway was Saint Crispin's Day of WW II, I missed that.

NAS Whiting at Milton, Florida, was twenty miles north of Pensacola. Whiting was two separate fields joined by hangars with administration buildings between them. North Whiting was for multi-engine training, and South Whiting was for instrument flight training. The instrument syllabus consisted of basic instrument blind flying, recovery from unusual attitudes, precision timed turns, climbs and descents plus low frequency radio range navigation (flying the "beam"), all under the hood. Actually we were teaching cadets two things: If you believe your inner ear, it will kill you. If you believe your instruments, they will save your life. It was just that simple.

We were flying SNJ's with the instructor in the front cockpit and the cadet under the hood in the rear cockpit. A typical instruction flight was one and a half hours in our operating area, which was north of Whiting as far north as Brewton, Alabama, and as far east as the Eglin Field restricted area.

This story involves one particular flight. Whiting had the longest traffic pattern on the planet. After a flight, we entered the traffic pattern at Crestview, Florida, 42 miles east of Milton and 30 miles north of Destin.

Any questions so far? We flew the 42 miles west along a railroad track to Milton where we turned north toward Whiting. This was over a small grass field called Milton "T" field. Milton "T" was the geographic point over which we lowered the landing gear (a poor squadron practice – if flying to another airfield where there was no Milton "T" field to remind you to lower the gear you might do something stupid – and make a wheels up approach).

On this particular flight, the cadet asked me a question on the intercom right over Milton "T" as I was about to lower landing gear. I answered his question and flew on, having been distracted enough to forget to lower the landing gear. That was my first mistake.

When I reduced power turning final in my approach to landing, I couldn't figure out why I couldn't slow up. I was in the straightaway when I realized my wheels must be up. I didn't even hear the warning horn. I was too distracted by the airspeed problem.

I wasn't about to take a wave off and go back to enter the longest traffic pattern on the planet, so I did the practical thing. I dumped the landing gear lever as I flared in a three point attitude. It must have been a beautiful sight to see. The wheels became fully extended the moment they touched the runway, and I landed in a perfect three point attitude. I was impressed.

The squadron executive officer was not impressed. He happened to observe this act of superb airmanship out his office window. Soon I found myself standing at attention (I was just a simple Ensign) in front of his desk. All I could say was the standard, "No excuse, Sir".

I was issued a bicycle, two red flags, and a bottle of water. For a week I was to give each plane in the approach a "Roger" if the wheels were down, or a wave off if they weren't. If the wind changed, I had to peddle like crazy to get to the end of the new duty runway.

I got a great tan.

...and then there was the time there was a riot in the Chiefs' barracks the night Ensign Warner had the duty.

...and the night I had the duty when the German P.O.W. escaped.

19
HOW TO LAND AN SNJ... FROM THE BACK SEAT

George Richard "Sandy" Sander and I followed each other around most of our lives. We were both instrument flight instructors in Flight 3 at Whiting Field in the Pensacola Training Command way back in 1945. Flight 3 was one of eight Flights in Squadron VN3D8. We had about 16 pilots instructing in the SNJ. The skipper was LT Jackson, a Georgia Tech grad.

Instrument flying is partly imagining the attitude of the plane relative to the horizon when you can't see it. A few months after I got in Flight 3, the brass figured if a cadet could fly the SNJ visual he could better visualize his attitude when flying on instruments. Basic consisted of precision landings and formation flying. So we were all made instrument and basic instructors. As basic instructors we sat in the back seat from which you could see almost nothing, especially when landing. That's when I got to know Sandy. He was already checked out in landing from the back seat and was chosen to check me out in doing it.. When you were landing from the back seat with a cadet in the front seat you could hardly see the runway.

Nobody got killed and then the war was over in August '45. All the Flight 3 pilots went home to start their life's work, whatever that was going to be. I went back to Tech and started over having flunked almost every course when I was co-oping before flight training. Just by chance, it happened that Sandy was in that freshman class, too. While he was going through IFIS (Instrument Flight Instructors School) at NAS Atlanta (now PDK), he met Betty Jane Watson who lived with her folks on Rumson Road, two doors from the park in Garden Hills, less than a block from where we live now. They got married after the war and that explains how Sandy wound up at Georgia Tech.

It was good to see a naval aviator friend from Pensacola. I was majoring in Architecture and Sandy was majoring in Civil Engineering. The GI Bill paid $105 per month plus fees and tuition. Rent in the Tech married student housing, in the old Nurse's barracks across the street from Lawson General Hospital, was $35 per month. To supplement the $105, Sandy and I signed up for the Naval Air Reserve, commonly referred to as the "Ready Reserve", flying out of NAS Atlanta. We were both ensigns and were assigned to "FASRON (Fleet Aircraft Service Squadron) 52". We got $50 a month for flying one weekend per month. We were rich, $155 per month, plus we got to fly (which we would have done for nothing). The Georgia Tech Married Student Housing was near the Naval Air Station. Every time we went flying on a drill weekend Betty Jane made sure Sandy was wearing his good luck charm.

When FASRON 52 was first organized, it was anything but organized. Normally before flying an airplane, a pilot has to study the pilot's manual and take a written test. In those early months of the reserve at NAS you didn't have to prove you could fly. You just signed for any plane and took off, a pair of gold wings on your chest was all that was required. We'd check out a Twin Beech or an SNJ and fly somewhere like Chattanooga or Knoxville, just to get a cup of coffee. As the years passed it got much tighter.

After graduation (Class of '50), by pure chance Sandy and I went to work for Smith & Hobbs, a small A&E firm in the Peters Building at Five Points. We were still in the same squadron flying Corsairs when I moved to Brunswick and until I volunteered for active duty in 1952 to escape from Abreu & Robeson Architects.

When I returned to civilian life in 1955, my pay billet in FASRON 52 had been held open for me, and I went back to flying with Sandy. I became squadron commander with Sandy as my executive officer. When I moved up to Wing staff, Sandy became the squadron commander.

I retired from flying after 23 ½ years, with the rank of commander. Sandy stayed active and retired as a captain with 30 plus years. He now lives just around the corner, four houses from our house – sixty years after checking me out in the back seat.

Small world.

20
THEN THERE WAS THE NIGHT THERE WAS A "RIOT"

When I was a lowly cadet I was in awe of Chief Petty Officers. The CPO's ran the Navy, and they ran it well. There is a great story about three Ensigns who were taking an examination. One of the questions was, "How would you raise a 30 foot flag pole?" The first two Ensigns wrote out a very long and detailed answer – how to dig the hole, how deep, how to mix the concrete, how to handle the long steel pole, etc. The first two Ensigns flunked the question. The third Ensign got a 4.0. His answer was: I'd say, "Chief, raise that flag pole".

One night I was SDO on the Dog Watch at Whiting, a brand new Ensign. I got a report that there was, I quote, a "riot" in the Chiefs' barracks. I grabbed my hat and got my driver to get me there right away. When I walked in, all hell was breaking loose. There were drunk Chiefs everywhere. One was being thrown in the shower fully clothed. There was whisky, bowls of ice cubes, and mix on all the dressers. They were totally ignoring my presence. After all, I was just an Ensign. What was going on was not really a "riot". It was the celebration of a guy making Chief. Lucky for me, there was an older and sober Chief amongst the celebrants. He apparently had a fatherly feeling toward green Ensigns, so, as if by magic, he stopped the "riot" single handed. No Ensign ever had that much power.

21
WHERE IS THAT GUY?

When I was stationed at Whiting Field as an Instrument Flight instructor from December 1944 to December 1945 I was in "Flight 3" of eight Flights in Squadron VN3D8. Each Flight had about 20 pilots. The pilots from time to time stood Squadron Duty Officer (SDO) watches. Ensigns usually got a "dog watch' from 2am – 6am, if I remember the hours correctly. RHIP (Rank Hath It's Privileges) and Ensigns had very few privileges.

At Whiting there was a German P.O.W. camp, holding Germans from the Afrika Korps. They were very handsome, tanned, disciplined soldiers. Ironically, they were frequently guarded by a skinny teenage white hat reading a comic book with an unloaded .45 on his hip. I wonder what those Krauts thought.

On one of my dog watches I got a report that a German P.O.W. had been seen loose on the base. A muster of their barracks revealed that no prisoner was missing, yet there was a prisoner loose on the base. I called out the Duty Section to issue side arms and start a hunt for the German. It was ridiculous – regulations prevented personnel from carrying loaded firearms on the base, so the duty section had to stand in line to sign out for the bullets.

I got a driver and a Pontiac station wagon to be driven all over the landing field area (very rough terrain when not on the runways) with nothing but the headlights to light the area. We found nothing. Every time this "escapee" was sighted, they took another muster at the P.O.W. barracks. Still there was nobody missing. It seems, they found out later, the elusive German had escaped from a different P.O.W. camp at another installation and had "broken into" Whiting trying to find food and clothing. Too bad. I never got my Congressional Medal of Honor for fighting the Germans.

22
JUST AN OLD SOFTY

During WWII, I had the good fortune to be an instrument flight instructor at NAS Whiting Field in the Pensacola Training Command instead of finding a watery grave in the Pacific Ocean. The instrument squadron at Whiting was Squadron VN3D8. There were eight "Flights" with about twenty instructors each. I was in Flight 3. The Syllabus was basic instrument flying, radio navigation, flying precision patterns with standard rate turns (three degrees per second), changes of altitude at 500 feet per minute and recovery from "unusual attitudes" all flying blind "under the hood".

The cadets flew with different instructors on each hop. It was our custom in Flight 3 to give a cadet an "Incomplete" on a check ride, if we thought he wasn't flying well enough to get an "Up". We would discontinue the check ride and continue the period giving extra instruction on his weak point. The cadet would then be rescheduled for a check ride. Illegal, but we never gave a cadet a "Down" in Flight 3.

After some months, the "powers-that-be" decided that the cadets would be better able to visualize the attitude of the plane relative to the horizon (the secret of blind flying) when under the hood, if "Basic" was added to the Syllabus. Basic included precision landings, night flying and formation flying in the SNJ, the same plane they flew under the hood. So we became Instruments Flight Instructors <u>and</u> Basic Flight Instructors.

I had a cadet who was to solo in the SNJ shooting precision landings on an outlying field. When I felt he was safe to solo, I got out to watch his landings. After a couple of landings I realized I had been wrong. He wasn't safe to solo the "J". Before I could motion him over to tell him I would have to give him a "Down", he taxied over and stopped. I jumped up on the wing, and before I could say anything he said, "Mr. Warner, I don't think I'm ready to solo. You better give me a "Down".

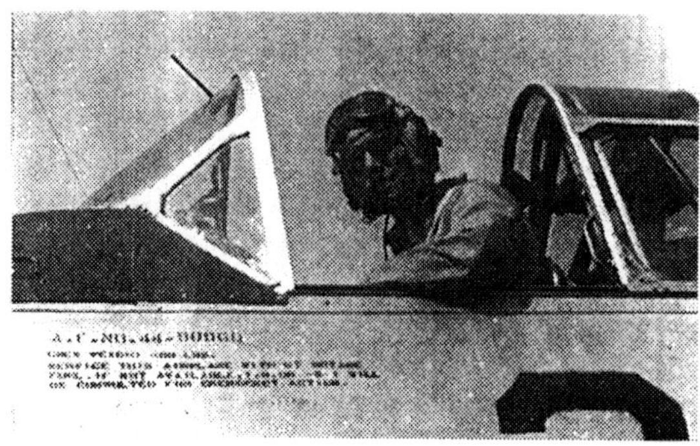

23
THE BENT WING

The first high powered Navy fighter I flew was the F4U Vought Corsair, the one with the gull wing. It had a 2,000 Hp (Horsepower) Pratt and Whitney radial engine. At first they were built by Vought then later also by Goodyear Tire and Rubber Company (believe it or not). We called it "the Bent Wing". The prop was so big that the wing was "bent" to shorten the landing gear so it would be strong enough for carrier landings.

The first models killed a lot of Marines being checked out in them at Quantico, Virginia. There was a lot of torque from the huge prop and the left wing had a habit of stalling out before the right wing stalled on the landing approach. The designers added a spoiler to the right wing to make it stall at the same time as the left wing – almost.

In the Reserve I was transitioning from the SNJ with a 550 Hp Pratt and Whitney radial engine to the Corsair, a fairly big jump for me. I remember on the first take off I looked back to see if I was on the wind line and was amazed that I could hardly see the runway, I was going so much faster than I ever had before.

My squadron mate, Gordon Lawless, checked out in it just before I did. When he taxied back to the chocks I jumped up on the wing and asked, "How was it?" He looked up at me and then looked at his right hand on the stick and, mocking tension, he pried his fingers loose with great effort. Of course he was really very happy.

After a few orientation hops, I decided to see how the Corsair handled in a spin. I pulled it up in a stall and the left wing dropped off into the spin. I got it out after three very vicious turns. I don't think you were supposed to do intentional spins in the "Bent Wing".

24
WHY ARE THEY CALLED WHISKEY SOURS?

It was the Summer of 1949. The squadron checked in at NAS Atlanta to start that year's two weeks training duty. We checked in on a Saturday, moved the squadron on Sunday and were operating 100% on Monday at NAS Opa Locka, Miami, Florida.

After our first day operating, the pilots hit the beach for Liberty. We went to a bar in a less than high class section of town. All the waitresses were too fat – and ugly. The other guys ordered drinks. Since I had never had a drink (I was 26 years old), I didn't order one. Being the good old buddies they were, they didn't want to see me sitting there with nothing to drink.

It was suggested that I order a beer just to be sociable. It tasted awful. Someone suggested that I try a whiskey sour. I ordered one. They tasted good – all seven of them. From then on the evening was a blur. Cyd Bugden and I wound up at a famous strip joint, The Red Barn. I assumed we were still in Miami. I think I had some more whiskey sours.

They had a stripper. She was beautiful. I fell in love with her. I even bought her a whiskey sour. When it was time for the place to close, Cyd refused to leave. He must have been drinking whiskey sours, too. We were finally kicked out and headed back to the BOQ.

I remember lying down on the big leather sofa in the BOQ lobby in my khaki's, shoulder boards and all. I also remember the other pilots heading for the flight line the next morning. I didn't fly Tuesday for medical reasons.

(Let the record show, this was two years before I met Betty).

25
I FEEL BETTER NOW, BUT I FORGOT HOW TO START IT

26
GOODBYE, MR. ABREU

Working for architects Abreu & Robeson in Brunswick had its drawbacks. There were no breaks. The only time I got to take a break was when the bloodmobile came to town.

During the eighteen months I lived in Brunswick, I commuted to my Navy drill weekends on the Friday night train from Brunswick to Atlanta and on the Sunday night train from Atlanta back to Brunswick – sat up on the day coach both ways (sob).

On one of my drill weekends, Mr. Abreu asked me to drive Mrs. Abreu's new Cadillac to Atlanta where she was staying in their Philip Schutze designed house on West Paces Ferry at Habersham. He told me, "It takes five hours to drive to Atlanta. I can make it in four. I want you to make it in six".

Just before Betty and I were to be married in June '52, I thought I had better ask for a raise. One day Mr. Abreu was in town, a fairly rare occurrence, and I asked to see him in his office. He was at his desk going over some papers. He didn't look up when I came in. I got my courage up and said, "Mr. Abreu, Betty Geiger and I are getting married next month. I was wondering if I could get a raise." Without looking up he asked, "How much are you making now?" I said, "Seventy-five dollars a week." Still looking at his papers he asked, "How much raise do you want?" I gulped and meekly said, "Five dollars a week?" After a moment's thought he said, "No, you're not worth it" (he was probably right). That was the end of the meeting. He never once looked at me – so Betty and I got married on seventy-five dollars a week.

I felt it would be safer to volunteer for the Korean War than to work for Abreu & Robeson – so I did, but that's another story.

27
OFF TO RHODE ISLAND

I hit the road for Rhode Island with my fingers crossed. I had traded up to a 1946 used Oldsmobile that used more oil than gas and wouldn't go over 55 miles per hour. I drove for twelve hours the first day, and eleven hours the second day. I watched the oil pressure gauge, not the gas gauge. I stopped for oil when I saw the oil pressure start to drop, even when I didn't need gas.

I made it to Providence and spent the second night there. The third day I checked in to VU-2 – beat the hell out of Korea. I checked in with the Squadron Duty Officer and got a room at the BOQ where I would stay until I could find housing for Betty.

The VU-2 mission was to provide aircraft services for destroyer training exercises which involved towing targets for destroyer five-inch deck gun firing practice, providing aircraft for the CIC schools at Newport and Boston (where shipboard fighter director officers were trained to direct fighter intercepts), photo missions photographing destroyer surface firing exercises (photographing hits on a target sled towed by a sea-going tug), ship radar calibration, coordinating submarine torpedo firing exercise, making simulated attacks on destroyers from various directions and altitudes to train ship's gunners to pick up targets and train their guns when under aerial attack – and other fun stuff.

VU-2 was under operational control of COMDESLANT and the administrative control of UTWINGLANT. Our operating area was south of the shipping lanes for the ship exercises and between Block Island and Martha's Vineyard for the CIC work. A training exercise was referred to as "Event # - - -". We had about twenty pilots and three ground officers. The typical daily flight schedule, which as Squadron Flight Officer (Schedule Officer), it was my duty to prepare, based on COMDESLANT training requirements. It involved about twenty flights every day. I had a great time flying the F6F, TBM, A-26, and the F8F Bearcat. It was much more fun than slaving over a hot drawing board all day.

28
WHAT? ME WORRY?

29
THEM WAS THE GOOD OLD DAYS

When reporting for active duty (Dec.5, 1952), I got a 30 day refresher at NAS Atlanta (PDK) in the F4U Corsair (during the 30 days, Betty and I lived at the old Piedmont Hotel), and then I was assigned to VU-2 (Utility Squadron 2) at NAS Quonset Point, RI. Sure beat going to Korea. The Squadron mission was to provide aircraft services under the operational control of COMDESLANT at Newport, RI. Our operating area was at sea, south of the shipping lanes. We did CIC fighter interceptor training with ships, mostly destroyers. We towed targets for the destroyers' firing exercises, did "Battle Problems", radar calibration for the ships, photo work (photographing hits and misses) for the destroyers firing at a sled, located lost dummy torpedoes for subs out of New London, and other fun stuff.

In the winter we sent a detachment to Puerto Rico to work with the destroyers that went south to train in better weather than they had at Newport.

We flew F6F Hellcats, TBM Avengers, F8F Grumman Bearcats and JD's (the Douglas B26, later designated the A26). I draw this comparison: the Hellcat was like a Buick, the Corsair was like a Cadillac and the Bearcat was like a Maserati. I got 120 hours in the F4U, 500 in the F8F, 120 in the F6F, 180 in the TBM and 160 in the JD. I returned to unexciting civilian life back to the drawing board in Atlanta in Dec.'54!

30
SNEAKY, BUT EFFECTIVE

When first reporting to VU-2 at NAS Quonset Point, Betty and I made our courtesy calls to first the Skipper, Commander Soderholm, and then to the Executive Officer, Lieutenant Commander Charlie "Shakey" Fuller (a very nervous fellow).

Soderholm was a good skipper according to my newfound squadron mates, but he had a sneaky way of serving the drinks. He served them in aluminum "glasses" so the new pilot wouldn't know that the skipper was just drinking water while plying his visitor with alcohol. A very clever way to quickly find out what kind of new pilot had been assigned to his command.

The story goes that when Vinny Hughes, a feisty little pilot from New Joisey, paid his courtesy call, the skipper stayed cold sober while Vinny slightly overindulged. As he said his goodbyes at the front door he stumbled, and when Soderholm grabbed his arm to keep him from falling, Vinny said, "Watch it! I've never decked a skipper before!"

Fuller was less devious. He served the drinks in clear glasses. We had a nice visit. We met his teenage twin boys. As we were leaving he said, "I hope you have had chicken pox. The boys have it". I soon spent two weeks isolated in sick bay with the worst case of chicken pox the Medical Officer said he had ever seen.

Fuller was transferred to a jet squadron somewhere on the East coast and was killed in a midair collision with another jet. The new XO was Gerry Colleran, one of the finest officers I ever served under. He was a perfect role model.

31
EVERYBODY BACK IN THE WATER

The older I get the more I miss flying and the less I miss architecture. I like to think back on those flying day – makes me feel young again.

When I was at NAS Quonset Point we lived off the base. Our next door neighbors were Sally and Dick Bowers, a very nice couple. Dick was a LTjg Civil Engineering officer. One night over drinks he said he was taking a work party to "No Man's Land" to repair a target. "No Man's Land" is a little island about one mile wide by one mile long which was used for bombing practice, thus the name. It is about five miles southwest of Martha's Vineyard. I said, "Great. I'm checking out in the F8F tomorrow and I'll give you a buzz".

The next morning I headed for "No Man's Land" just in time to see the work party boat approaching the north shore of the island. I pushed over into a dive and headed right for it, I was going to give Dick a good show. I came roaring down toward the boat and every guy in the work party, except Dick, dove over the side into the water. They thought I was making a bombing run. Dick hadn't told them about our discussion the night before.

Dick Bowers was a little green when it came to Navy procedures. He was the base crash officer. If a plane crashed he would to take a work party to the crash site and bring the plane back where it would be meticulously examined in order to determine the cause of the crash.

An AD had crashed some distance from Quonset in a heavily wooded area in nearby Massachusetts. Dick took a crew to bring the wrecked plane back to the base. He examined the situation and decided the only way was to build a long road through the thick woods. That would require a lot and time and effort. Being a highly intelligent graduate of Yale – he buried it!

32
MY FIFTEEN MINUTES OF FAME

We had an air show at NAS Quonset Point. There were several flyovers and, since the Blue Angels didn't make it, four guys from one of the fighter squadrons flying F9F's put on the same kind of show. They were almost as good as the Blues. I was flying F8F Bearcats at the time and asked the Quonset operations officer if I could demonstrate an unrestricted T.O. (take-off) to 10,000 feet. He OK'd it, but because of the timing of the flyovers, I would have to make it quick and come right back and land. I said, "The crowd needs to see something more exciting than the take off. I'd like to do a roll on the break when I turn onto the down wind leg". He asked, "Can you do it?" I assured him I could (I had done rolls over destroyers we worked with a lot lower than our 500 foot traffic pattern).

When I think back on it, there was no way this guy could know if I could do it. He had never seen me before. Betty was watching from a friend's house near the field. I got to 10,000 feet in 120 seconds from "wheels up" (honest), came back and did the roll on the break. When I got home that night I asked Betty, "Did you see me?" She said, "No. I was changing Jimmy's diaper".

My fifteen minutes of fame and Betty was changing a diaper.

33
YOU DO THE MATH

7,000 lbs and 2,250 Hp / Lb per Hp / You Do The Math

34
GRUMMAN F8F-2 BEARCAT

The Ghost Squadron's F8F-2 Bearcat

By the last half of the Second World War, most new US fighter designs were much heavier and more complex than earlier fighters. When planning a replacement for their successful F6F Hellcat carrier fighter, however, Grumman chose to built as lightweight a design as possible around the most reliable large radial engine. The result was the F8F Bearcat, which was often called a "hot rod" by its pilots for its fantastic acceleration and climbing ability.

Using the well-proven Pratt & Whitney R-2800 engine, the first Bearcat prototype flew on August 21, 1944. After minor modifications, including the addition of a dorsal fin, early production F8F- 1s began armament tests and carrier qualification trials in early 1945. By May of 1945, the Bearcat was cleared for operations, with very few restrictions on its flight operations over its wide speed range. A total of 654 F8F- 1s were delivered, all fitted with the 2,100 hp R-2800-34W engine.

The Bearcat was the first US Navy fighter to feature a full "bubble" canopy, giving excellent all around vision. It was also fitted with so called "Safety Wing Tips", the outer 40 inches of which were designed to break off cleanly in case of the wing being overstressed in a dive or other maneuver. After several incidents where one or both wing tips tore off, this feature was eliminated from later production Bearcats.

Two squadrons, VF-18 and VF- 19 were equipped with F8F- 1 s, and training was expedited in order to get the new fighter into service against Japanese suicide attack planes in the Pacific. VF-19 was onboard the carrier USS Langley, enroute across the Pacific, when the war ended on August 16, 1945.

The final production Bearcat was the F8F-2, with a more powerful R-2800-30W engine of 2,250 hp and an automatic variable speed supercharger. The extra power required an extra foot be added to the vertical fin, and F8F-2s carried a heavier armament of four 20mm cannons. The F8F-2P was a photo-reconnaissance version, fitted with up to three cameras in the fuselage. By 1956, the last Bearcats were taken out of service and stored or scrapped, having been replaced by the new age of jets.

Specifications

One Pilot
One Pratt & Whitney R-2800-30W Engine

Length 27' 6"
Height 13' 10"
Wing Span 35' 6"

Twin-row 18 cylinder Air-cooled Radial
2,250 hp for Takeoff

Max. Weight 13,460 lbs
Empty Weight 7,650 lbs

Four 20mm Cannons
Up to Four 5-inch Rockets

Normal Fuel 185 gallons
Max. Fuel 335 gallons
(with 150 gal belly tank)

Max. Speed 455 mph @ 28,000 feet
Cruise Speed 185-220 mph
Landing Speed 105 mph

Normal Range 865 miles
Maximum Range 1,435

Initial Rate of Climb 6,300 ft/min
Service Ceiling 40,800 ft

35
FLIGHT SCHEDULE

DATE: 7 SEPT. 1954 TUES.

SDO: LTJG. G.D. LEFLER, USNR. SUNRISE: 0617Q
ODO: LT. J.E. WARNER/ LT. W.E. MACNAIR SUNSET: 1910Q

EVENT	TIME	PLANE	PILOT	AREA	MISSION	FREQ	ACTIVITY
201	0815 1145	F8F	MACNAIR	FALL RIVER	Z-56-CC 1-N-22	ch-11 ch-13	MARKET BREAK
201	0815 1145	JD	HAYES HEGOOD S.	FALL RIVER	Z-56-CC 1-N-22	ch-11 ch-13	MARKET BREAK
201	0815 1145	T BM	WILSON	FALL RIVER	Z-56-CC 1-N-22	ch-11 ch-13	MARKET BREAK
203	0815 1145	F8F	TURNER	BLOCK ISLAND	Z-56-CC 1-N-22	ch-7 ch-13	WINELIST
203	0815 1145	JD	SHROYER P.S.	BLOCK ISLAND	Z-56-CC 1-N-22	ch-7 ch-13	WINELIST
203	0815 1145	TBM	MORGAN	BLOCK ISLAND	Z-56-CC 1-N-22	ch-7 ch-13	WINELIST
213 ADIZ	0930 1200	JD	RAINES P.O.S.	N/W cor. 10	Z-2-G 1-N-11	7500 253.8	ISHERWOOD DD-520
217	0945 1145	JD	EMERSON P.S.	Vicinity Mike Bouy 21	IFF check & track 1-N-22	7540 254.8	COMDESDIV 201 (OCE) 4 ships in port.
	AM STANDBY PILOTS:			HATCH	SNYDER		
214 ADIZ	1230 1600	JD	BIRK P.O.S.	N/W COR. 10	Z-2-G 1-N-11	7500 253.8	ISHERWOOD DD-520
202	1245 1615	F8F	WARNER	FALL RIVER	Z-56-CC 1-N-22	ch-11 ch-13	MARKET BREAK
202	1245 1615	F8F	SNYDER	FALL RIVER	Z-56-CC 1-N-22	ch-11 ch-13	MARKET BREAK
202	1245 1615	TBM	HATCH	FALL RIVER	Z-56-CC 1-N-22	ch-11 ch-13	MARKET BREAK
204	1245 1615	JD	SCHULTZ P.S.	BLOCK ISLAND	Z-56-CC 1-N-22	ch-7 ch-13	WINELIST
204	1245 1615	JD	PUGSLEY P.S.	BLOCK ISLAND	Z-56-CC 1-N-22	ch-7 ch-13	WINELIST
204	1245 1615	TBM	EMERSON	BLOCK ISLAND	Z-56-CC 1-N-22	ch-7 ch-13	WINELIST
	PM STANDBY PILOTS:			TURNER	RAINES		

TIME	PLANE	PILOT	AREA	MISSION	
0800 0900		TONOLE	TRAINING BLDG.	LINK	
0830 1130	SNB	HERSTEIN AUTEN S.	LOCAL	INST.	1-A-2
1245 1545	SNB	CRAWFORD TONOLE S.	LOCAL	INST.	1-A-2
1810 2010	SNB	ROBINSON WARNER S.	LOCAL AREA	NV&GCA	3-A-1

NOTE 1 Oxygen masks will be carried in all type operational aircraft.

NOTE 2 Hard hats will be worn on take-off and landing in JD type aircraft.

SUBMITTED BY:

for J.V. Robinson
J.E. WARNER, LT., USNR.
FLIGHT OFFICER

APPROVED BY:

for J.V. Robinson
A.J. SCHULTZ, JR., CDR., USN.
COMMANDING OFFICER

36
LET'S SEE... UP IS DOWN... NO, DOWN IS UP... NO, UP IS DOWN... NO...

When I was in Utility Squadron Two at NAS Quonset Point, R.I., we flew the TBM, F6F, F8F and the JD (A26). We had to get two hours night flying plus two practice GCA approaches every month. My Exec, Gerry Colleran, and I frequently did our night flying together in Grumman F8F "Bearcats". At the end of the night flying period we would do the GCA's in turn, flying safety pilot for each other.

One night I was "chasing" him while he made a GCA. When he reached "100 feet and a quarter mile" he dumped wheels and flaps. I dumped 45 degrees full flaps so as not to overtake him. I went into an immediate violent 90 degree bank to the left. Realizing that only the right flap had extended, I quickly pulled the flap lever up – the right flap came up and the left flap went full down putting me in an immediate 90 degree bank to the right. Somehow the flaps had been "hooked up" cross ways by some mechanic when the plane was in for a maintenance check before I took it up that night.

I didn't have time to think at that altitude. I put the flap lever halfway down. The left flap came halfway up and the right flap went halfway down, and everything was under control again.

One might ask, "Why didn't you cycle the flaps before you left the chocks to see if they were operating properly?" The reason we didn't in the F8 was the flaps were more like dive breaks and only the underside of the wing was the flap. If cycled, the flaps could not be seen from the cockpit.

Sometimes I flew night flying alone in an F8. I used to fly south from Newport over that big black empty ocean for as long as I could stand it. Conquering fear is very important if you are going to fly airplanes. I love the adage, "There are some aircraft sounds that can only be heard at night".

37
YOU ASKED FOR IT

While on Detachment to Puerto Rico the Winter of '53-'54, I was towing a target for a destroyer about eighty nautical miles north of Vieques. I was making beam runs for a five-inch deck gun firing exercise. After every pass the ship would request that I make lower runs. I was happy to oblige.

At 200 knots and 2,000 feet of cable, the target droops about 350 feet below the plane's altitude. I thought, they want low, I'll give 'em low. On my next pass I really came in low. As I passed over the ship it radioed, "You just took away our radar antennae!"

"Fear is nature's way of spurring us to take action to prevent harm. But insufficient fear can lead us to complacency. If we can be scared out of our wits, we can be scared into them as well"
Author unknown

I never heard an official word about the incident. My guess is the skipper of the destroyer never reported it, since he asked for it.

One exercise we conducted with destroyers was what they called "radar calibration". The ship would vector us on different headings at different altitudes. During this procedure they could adjust their radar and find any blind spots.

I was working a destroyer about 100 nautical miles northeast of Vieques in a TBM on such an exercise. I was given a vector of "zero four five" (for landlubbers that's northeast.) I flew for quite a while with no further instructions from the ship. I was getting a long way from Vieques out over that big empty deep ocean. Hey, the Puerto Rico Trench is thirty-five-damn-thousand feet deep. Finally I picked up the mike and said, "Say something, even if it's *Goodbye*!" They quickly came up with a new reciprocal vector.

38
FIRE ONE!

Just north of Vieques is a little island which is little more than a pile of rocks. It was used by the submarines as a target for live torpedo firing exercises. It didn't sound like much of a challenge for a sub to fire at a stationary target, but I guess they had their reasons. Maybe it's the way they trained Ensign submariners.

During these events, I would fly a TBM over the rocks to make sure there were no Puerto Rican fishermen dumb enough to fish in an area known to be a target for live torpedoes. A TBM was used because it could stay on station for as much as six hours, and it seemed to me like it took a sub almost that long to get lined up on a stationary target for one shot. I can hear the skipper now, "Okay, Five hours is up. Fire One!"

I guess the word had gotten around among the fishermen, because I never did see one. It was all a complete waste of aviation gasoline.

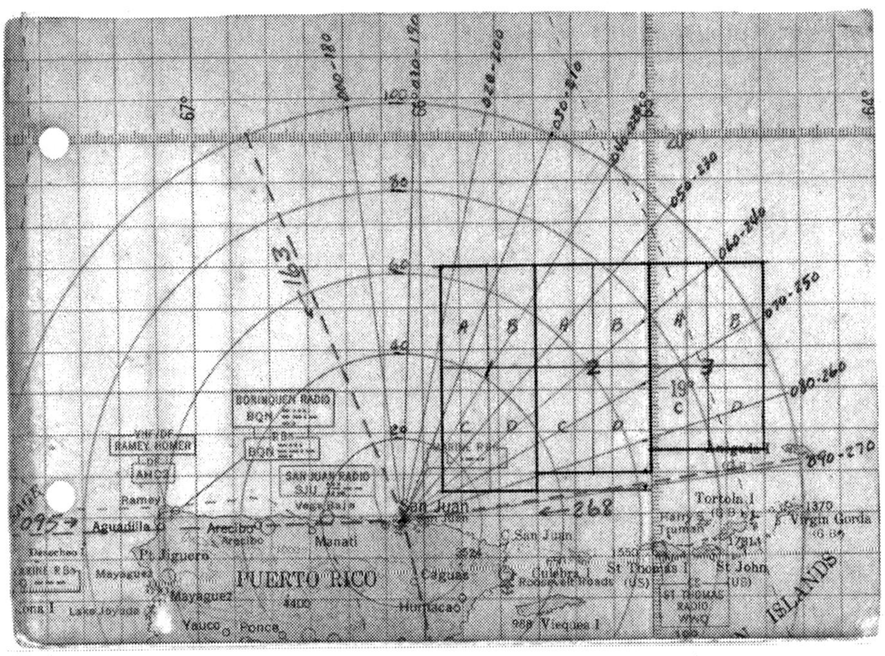

39
GET THAT MAN'S NAME!

Most of the exercises at Quonset involved just one plane, except the CIC School work which involved two F8F's and a TBM.

To break the monotony and have some fun at one another's expense, we invented "the Old Upsweep". Here's how it worked. If you were flying an F8 and spotted another VU-2 plane flying at a lower altitude and ahead of you, usually another F8 (we always knew it was one of us because no other squadron flew the F8), you would dive on it and pass about ten feet under at a much greater speed. When directly under, you pulled back into the beginning of a loop. You were going so fast that your reaction time, as fast as it was, was just slow enough that by the time you pulled back on the stick you were barely clear and immediately went up directly in front of your "victim". It had been done to me and it was really a shock. Your field of vision was suddenly totally filled with airplane. It was almost like you had a midair collision.

Johnny Butner was a Chief A.P. in the squadron who was transferred to another squadron at Quonset flying AD's. He was tooling around one day when he spotted one of our F8's, so he decided to say hello with "the Old Upsweep". The F8 pilot happened to have his hands off the controls while pressing his helmet against his ears to hear the radio. When he saw nothing but airplane suddenly in front of him he screamed, "MAY DAY! MAY DAY! MIDAIR COLLISION!

Just about then Johnny joined up on him in a nice tight wing position and stared into the face of – CDR Brown, the commanding officer of VU-2 (Brown was not comfortable in the F8 under the best of conditions, but I gave him credit for flying it at least once a month – among other things I was the schedule officer).

Pug was one of the two F8's involved in the exercise. The skipper ordered Pug to "catch that SOB and find out who had the nerve to pull a stunt like that". Pug told me that Johnny had a little head start but, even though he pulled metro power in an effort to catch him, Johnny beat him back to Quonset. Pug told the skipper, "I couldn't catch him". He knew it was Johnny, but never told the Skipper.

After Pug returned to civilian life, he became the Chief Pilot for Chrysler and hired Johnny Butner and Grady Lefler, both ex-VU-2 pilots.

40
"HEY, GUYS! ALBANY'S THAT WAY"

During my tour with VU-2 at NAS Quonset Point, '53 & '54, I was, among other duties, the Hurricane Evacuation Officer. During hurricane season in 1954, we had three Hurricane "fly-aways". Our evacuation base was Albany, NY.

The first hurricane was Hurricane Carol, a bad one. It went right up Narragansett Bay at high tide. Downtown Providence, R.I. was under nine feet of water. Thirty cars on the base at Quonset were washed into Narragansett Bay. Luckily, my 1950 Olds hardtop came through unscathed.

We flew the F8's, F6's and JD's to Albany, New York, on such short notice most of the pilots and crew members had no money and some had only their flight gear to wear when we got there.

I flew an F8 and felt very important when, what seemed to be the whole town turned out to see all our planes come in. We were quartered in the Ten Eyck Hotel, the best in town. The supply officer told us, whatever you need, food or drink, "Just sign the check. The Navy will pick it up and take it out of your pay later". (They never did). We were there three days while they cleaned up Quonset so we could land – best three day squadron party I ever attended. When I drove in the driveway at home, which was about a mile from the field, the house was covered with a spattering of leaves and dirt. The power had been off for three days. The power happened to go back on just as I drove in. Timing! Betty was not happy. She said, "You save the planes and leave the women and children behind in the storm".

The second fly-away was not so much a novelty to the citizens of Albany, and the crowds there to see us land were much smaller than the first time we flew in. We were quartered in the next best hotel in town, which wasn't too bad, but no Ten Eyck. Food and drinks were on our own this time.

The third fly-away was really a let down. Nobody showed up at the airport, and we were quartered in a third rate hotel. The supply officer was getting smarter. Having been spoiled by previous luxuries, all the pilots checked out and checked into the Ten Eyck at our own expense.

This third hurricane came closer to Albany than it came to Quonset. The pilots went to hear the Concertgebou Orchestra of Amsterdam at Renselear Polytech, a short bus ride from town. Nobody believed us.

41
WHAT WHISKEY?

When my tour in Puerto Rico was up, I was assigned to fly one of the JD's [A-26] back to Quonset Point. Our guys always flew from San Juan to Miami, refueled, RON (Remain over night), then flew to Quonset the next day. Everyone hauled a load of cheap booze (a fifth of V.O. in Puerto Rico was 85 cents). To clear customs with no sweat, they knew how to slip a bottle or two to the custom agents. Being a short timer, I wasn't up on the procedure, so I decided to fly direct to Glynco in Brunswick.

Betty and Jimmy were at Betty's folks in Brunswick while I was on detachment. Since the JD was a single pilot aircraft it didn't have a copilot. Three mechanics typically flew back with the pilot, two in the back and one in the jump seat beside the pilot. Not knowing the ropes, I passed the word among the men that I wasn't going to allow any booze on my airplane.

The next morning, one of the men going back with me said, "Mister Warner, there is something I need to tell you". I asked, "What is it?" He said he had some booze hidden in the plane. I said, "I told you guys – no whiskey on my airplane!" To which he replied, "They'll never find it." It was too close to take off time to do anything about it, since we had already been cleared by Agriculture (don't take any bugs back to the States).

My plan was to make landfall at West Palm Beach and fly up the coast to Brunswick. It was five hours over water. I was unable to make contact with any stations to which I was to make the routine position reports while en route. When I made the approach to the 1800 foot runway at Glynco, I was surprised at how short it looked. It was. At most fields we had from 5,000 to 10,000 foot runways. I put the JD down on the first foot of the runway and came to a stop at the very end. My mechanics had to be impressed. I know I was.

A jeep with an officer in it came rushing out to the plane. He said, "Who in the hell are you, and where are you from?" When a plane leaves for a destination an "inbound" is sent from the field of departure. Glynco had gotten no inbound on me.

I had to wait for a customs agent to come out from the city to check me out. I showed him my clearance from Agriculture. After inspecting everything, he didn't find a thing. I spent the night, and the next morning I loaded Jimmy's high chair into the bomb bay and took off for Quonset.

My Mom and Dad happened to be in Brunswick that day and they got to see their little boy fly the big airplane.

42
"HEY, GRADY. WHAT'S THE COURSE TO QUONSET?"

43
FANCY MEETING YOU HERE

Milt Pugsley was straight out of Central Casting. He looked like a fighter pilot and had the fighter pilot personality. Of all the pilots in the squadron, Milt was the most gung ho.

Pug and I were scheduled for a "battle problem" Event. We flew to the op-area at about 1,000 feet in a two plane section of F8F's, Pug on my wing. When I spotted the ship I started a diving turn to make a low pass to identify the ship by its side number. Expecting Pug to orbit at 1,000 feet while I confirmed the ship was the one we were assigned to, I came out of my diving turn right on the water, headed for the ship and did a barrel roll up over the ship, rolling out right on the water. Unbeknownst to me, Pug had followed me down and caught up with me just as I was upside down over the ship. Spectacular! The guys on that ship must have thought we were the hottest pilots in the Navy.

When we got back to Quonset after the battle problem with our ship, Pug said, "Gee, Warner, I had no place to go". Most pilots would've raised hell with me for not letting them know what I was going to do, but Pug thought it was great fun and laughed it off.

44
PUG AND ME

45
F8F BEARCAT RARE BEAR

A WORLD WAR II GRUMMAN F8F2 BEARCAT, CIRCA 1946

The Rare Bear is a World War II era Grumman F8F Bearcat. It has been restored, substantially modified and equipped with a Wright R3350 engine producing in excess of 4000 horsepower. This has allowed the Rare Bear to establish the Closed Course World Speed Record (528.3 mph) and 3000 Meter Time-To-Climb Record (91.9 seconds).

The Rare Bear was discovered as a severely damaged wreck in 1969 by Lyle Shelton. It had been abandoned next to a runway in an Indiana cornfield after a crash in 1962. The once proud airplane had been stripped by parts hunters, so Shelton found a fuselage, wing center section, landing gear and a right wing panel, but little else.

The pieces were trucked to Orange County, and restoration began. Volunteers donated their time and expertise to the task of locating impossible-to-find Bearcat parts, including a Wright R3350 - 2700 horsepower engine. The first flight was made on September 13,1969 from Orange County to the Chino Airport. Just a week later, the Bearcat appeared in its first National Championship Reno Air Race - sporting its first name "Able Cat", where it finished a respectable 5th (356.4 mph), despite the lack of preparatory and flight test time.

Bitten by the air racing bug and with their sights set on future races, the crew knew hard work and modifications were in order to make the airplane a winner. This lengthy preparation was rewarded in 1971 when the newly renamed "Phoenix I" tasted its first victory at Cape May, New Jersey, winning the event with a speed of 360.15 mph. The "Phoenix I" then went on to Reno that September to place 2nd, finishing only .32 seconds behind the winner.

In February of 1972 the airplane challenged and broke the long standing Time-to-Climb record by ascending 3,000 meters in a mere 91.9 seconds. 1974 - 1975 brought further wins in Miami, Mojave and Reno. With the plane grounded from 1976 through 1979, Lyle Shelton managed and directed the Mojave Air Races. In 1980, the Bearcat was brought out of the hanger, dusted off, and renamed for the last time. The name chosen was "Rare Bear", and what a rare commodity she is. The next few years proved to be frustrating. Much of the restoration work had to be done without the funding necessary to cover the costs of repairs and refurbishing. In order for Rare Bear to be competitive, a major sponsor had to be found.

This was accomplished in 1986. Wichita Air services provided the support for a thorough overhaul of the aircraft, hired a crew chief and secured a hanger for the team. Every restorable piece of the Bearcat was returned to its original condition. Those not available were individually manufactured and retrofitted. The extensive rebuilding project was completed in 1987, and it paid off as the Rare Bear flew the 3rd fastest qualifying time (452.90 mph) at Reno that September.

The winning tradition began in 1988 when the Rare Bear and her dedicated crew won both the Hamilton Air Races and the National Championships at Reno, where new qualifing and championship records were set. With victory fresh in their minds, the team never looked back. Lyle Shelton and his crew set their sights on capturing the 3Km World Speed Record for propeller driven aircraft - then 499.018 mph. Could the elusive 500 mph barrier be broken? A site for the challenge was scouted, and Las Vegas, New Mexico was selected for its high altitude and desert air. On Monday, August 21, 1989 the Rare Bear faced the challenge, sprinting the four legs of the course at an average speed of 528.33 mph - shattering the previous record by almost 30 mph! In September 1989 the Rare Bear (now hailed as "The fastest propeller driven aircraft in the world"), returned as defending champion to Reno. "Could the Rare Bear be beaten?" asked the headlines. The answer was a roaring "NO!" as she took the Gold Medal and victory once again. 1990 brought another challenge for the Rare Bear as she was fitted with a new three-blade propeller, the result of removing one blade and repositioning the remaining three.

Undaunted, the airplane not only won the race, but established a new Unlimited speed record of 468.20 mph. In 1991 the results were even more impressive, with a Gold win at over 481 mph, yet another Unlimited race record.

The Rare Bear is the crowd favorite. The plane's absence following the engine failure in the 1992 Reno final has reduced the degree of competition in the race, as evidenced by the lower winning speeds since 1995.

In 2006, the Rare Bear was purchased by Rod Lewis and has been undergoing a complete overhaul and inspection at the "Bear Cave" at the Reno Stead Airport, Reno, Nevada. Watch this web site for future developments.

Grumman F8F Bearcat

The Bearcat was a tremendous aerobatic aircraft, a fact recognized by the great Al Williams, who chose a Bearcat as his last "Gulfhawk." A production F8F could exceed 420 mph—Bearcats at Reno go much faster.

Rare Bear Grummman FBF-2 Bearcat Modification List		
	Stock Bearcat	**Rare Bear**
Weight, Lbs.	9000	8500
Wing Span, ft.	35	30.5
Flaps	Yes	No
Oil Consumption	0.5-5 gph	High
MPH, Closed Course	330	490
Top Speed @ 5000 ft.	370	540
Final Approach, Knots	85	120
Touchdown, Knots	65	110
Engine	P&W R-2800	Wright R-3350
Max HP	2400	4000+
RPM	2800	2900+
Boost Systems	ADI, Water Inj.	ADI, Water Inj. & NOx
Propeller	13.5 ft. dia. Aeroproduct	P3 Orion Ham-Std.
Fuel Consumption	300 gph @ 370 mph	600 gph @ 540 mph
Tailhook	Yes	No
Fuel Capacity, Gallons	180	180
Oil Capacity, Gallons	40	40
Armament	4x50 Cal.	Small Thermonuclear Device

46
WHAT? ME A LAWYER?

Our skipper at one time in VU-2 was CDR Brown. He was not a leader, he was always afraid he would make a wrong decision and not make Captain – a common problem with some skippers with the rank of Commander.

He called me into his office one day and told me, since one of my collateral duties was squadron defense council, he was sending me to Legal School at Newport, across Narragansett Bay from Quonset. I told him, I thought since I was a short timer, it would make more sense to send one of the other pilots who wanted to stay in the Navy. I guess that's why I never made Captain. Skippers don't like their decisions questioned. That didn't help my fitness report.

The next time he called me into his office (another one of my duties was squadron safety officer), he said, "Mr. Warner, we do not have a good squadron safety program." I said, "I know, but we aren't having any accidents." I shouldn't have said that!

Another reason why I didn't make Captain.

47
READY, NOW, SPLASH

The photo hop. Nobody liked the photo hop. The purpose was to conduct an exercise with one or more destroyers firing at a target (called a sled) towed by a sea-going tug to determine the ship's score. There was a camera on the towing vessel and we had a cameraman in the back of a TBM. Each camera had the time displayed on the film. The TBM circled the target at about 500 feet. The destroyers fired from three different distances, something like 1,000; 5,000; and 10,000 yards, I don't remember exactly. When the ship fired it would radio, "Fire" which gave the photographers time to get ready for the splash.

The problem was that at two of these firing ranges the projectile followed a trajectory that came under the plane's altitude, but at the third range the trajectory went up above the plane's altitude and then came down inside the circle we were flying. Most of the pilots didn't like that part of the exercise.

One of our pilots was Art Morgan, the weakest pilot in the squadron. He was afraid to fly the F8F, but was required to do so. We all had to stay qualified in the different type aircraft we had. He also didn't like to fly the dreaded photo hop and refused to do so. To disobey a lawful order is a court martial offense, but because we were short of pilots and needed all the help we could get, he got away with it.

When a pilot complained about a particular exercise he was scheduled to fly, Harry Hicks, our Operations officer and all around good guy, would put his arm around the pilot's shoulder, extend his other arm up 45 degrees, look skyward and with a smile on his face quietly say, "Go". Of course with that kind of send off the pilot would quit complaining and "go". Harry never wasted his time on Art, because he knew it wouldn't work.

48
IT WAS NOT MY INTENT . . . NOBODY'S PERFECT

One of our jobs at Quonset was providing aircraft under the operational control of ComDesLant for the CIC schools at Newport ("Winelist") and Boston ("Market Break") to train shipboard air controllers. A TBM as bogey would fly back and forth between Block Island and Martha's Vineyard. An F8F would be at each end of the course taking turns being vectored into position for a gunnery run on the bogey.

While one F8 made a run, the other would orbit until it was time to be vectored on the next intercept. Orbiting was very boring. One day I thought it would break the monotony if I did some aerobatics while waiting my turn. I was at about 8,000 feet and decided to do an Immelmann. An Immelmann is a half loop with a half roll at the top. Max Immelmann used the maneuver during World War I to get on the tail of an enemy plane flying in the opposite direction above him.

At the top of the half loop I ran out of airspeed – there I was flat on my back at 9,000 feet... running out of airspeed. I fell off into an inverted spin (The F8F Pilot's Manual PROHIBITS *intentional* and *unintentional* inverted spins). An inverted spin is when you are spinning upside down rather than right side up as in a normal spin. The recovery is the opposite from the normal spin recovery. If you don't know that, you make a big splash. We had a hop during flight training during which the instructor demonstrated an inverted spin recovery in a Stearman (piece o'cake – in a Stearman), and then the student made a recovery. I don't think they even teach normal spin recoveries now. Inverted spins were prohibited in the F8F for reasons I found out.

I did everything right. The F8 wasn't responding. Finally it did. I pulled out at 1,000 feet. Someone once wrote "Mastering the prohibited maneuvers in the Manual is one of the best forms of aviation life insurance you can get". Next time I did an Immelmann, I made sure I had plenty of airspeed.

*Footnote to this story: "The **Pour le Merite** gained international fame during World War I. Although it could be awarded to any military officer, the most famous recipients were the pilots of the German Army Air Service (Luftstreitkrafte), whose exploits were celebrated in wartime propaganda. In aerial warfare, a fighter pilot was initially entitled to the award upon downing eight enemy aircraft. Aces Max*

Immelmann and Oswald Boelke were the first airmen to receive the award, on January 12, 1916. Because of Immelmann's renown among his fellow pilots and the nation at large, the Pour le Merite became known, due to its color and this early recipient, as the Blue Max.

The number of aerial victories necessary to receive the award continued to increase during the war; by early 1917, it generally required destroying 16 enemy airplanes, and by war's end the approximate figure was 30."

49
WHAT'S THE NEXT BEST WAY?

Bob Shroyer had one of the most engaging personalities of anyone I ever met. He was also a classic gold brick. He would do anything to avoid a hop or stand the duty overnight in the office which was on the second deck of our hangar. There was a Warrant Officer in the squadron whom he would pay to stand the duty for him – very unprofessional, but nobody ever made an issue of it. I'm sure the skipper didn't know about it, but should have expected it. One thing I will say for him is he was one of the pilots who was not afraid to fly the F8F "Bearcat".

I was the squadron Flight Officer. My job, in addition to flying, was to make out the flight schedule providing aircraft for COMDESLANT training exercises with the destroyers. The schedule indicated who flew what type event in what type aircraft in what operational area for what ship on what frequency and at what time. I also had to make sure that each of us stayed current in all four type planes we flew (TBM, F6F, A26 and the good old SNB "Bug Smasher" so named because it never got over 10,000 feet.).

Shroyer posed a problem. He was low flight time pilot almost every month for one reason or another. I was discussing this with Robby Robinson, our laid back Operations Officer, my boss. He leaned back in his chair and said, "There are three things wrong with Shroyer. He's inept... inane and... IN... THIS... SQUADRON!".

While on an exercise at sea while we were on detachment to San Juan, Shroyer's F8 caught fire. He was about 80 nautical miles north of Vieques. It was never determined for sure, but it was probably an electrical fire. He bailed out. His first mistake was diving for the space between the wing and the tail instead of diving at the wing, which was the best way to avoid being hit by the elevator. You guessed it – he hit the elevator and broke his leg. So he's floating down with a broken leg.

He must not have been listening when we were told that when bailing out over water it is almost impossible to determine just when you are going to hit the water. There is nothing on the water to let your depth perception tell how high you are over the water when you get close to it. We were told that, as you approached the water, you should sit back in the parachute harness and unbuckle the leg straps. As soon as your feet hit the water, unbuckle the chest strap. You guessed it. He did just the opposite. Instead of unbuckling his leg straps first he unbuckled the chest strap, fell out of the shoulder harness and was then coming down head first held only by his legs, one of which was broken. When he did hit the water he couldn't reach the shroud lines and was being dragged through the water by the billowing chute, feet first. Somehow he finally got loose and got into his pararaft, with a broken leg and a nose full of water.

One of the planes on the same exercise circled looking for him. It is very difficult to find a relatively small object in so large a body of water. After quite a while he was located and Air Sea Rescue picked him up. When asked why he had not thrown out his dye marker so they could see him sooner he said, "I could see you guys".

About ten years after we were both off active duty in VU-2, Bob was passing through Atlanta and came by my office. He was selling mutual funds. Luckily I had just started my own architectural firm, and I didn't have the money to buy into whatever his con was. We did have a nice visit, and when he left I noticed he limped.

50
YOU NEVER KNOW WHO'S WATCHING

Most of our "battle problem" exercises (simulated attacks) were with destroyers, but on one such exercise, Don Hayes and I were scheduled for one with an AP (troop transport). We were in two F8's.

After we completed the exercise we decided to have some fun and put on a show for the ship's crew. We came down to about deck level and chased each other around the ship several times then headed home.

When we got back to the operations office, Harry Hicks, the Ops officer, said, "What did you guys do? There was an Admiral on that ship!" I thought, oh, oh, we're in big trouble now. Then Harry added, "The ship sent a message – 'Thanks for the excellent aircraft services.'"

Lucky for us, the Admiral enjoyed the show.

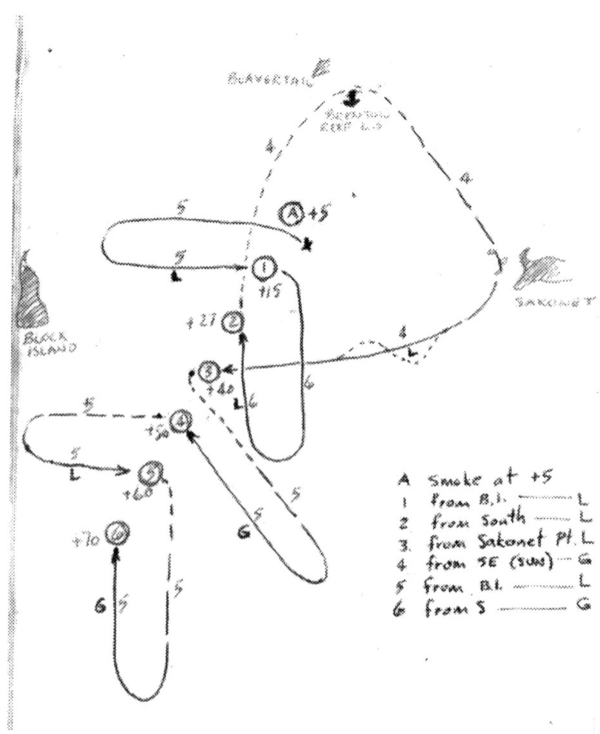

Battle Problem. From my knee pad ---
How else could I remember all that?

51
THE DAY I FLEW THE JET

About the time I was leaving VU-2 at Quonset Point, my two year tour being up in December 1954, the squadron was about to replace the F8F Bearcats with F9F Cougars. Since I was about to go back to civilian life and was all of 31 years old, I was not one of the pilots selected to start the transition from props to jets – a great disappointment to me.

I did get to fly a jet **once**. Our neighbor and friend was Paul Koch. He was a superb pilot assigned to O&R (Assembly and Repair) where various type planes were modified, given periodic checks and wrecked airplanes repaired. Paul was a test pilot who flew the planes when they came out of O&R.

One of the planes he tested was the "Sky Knight", a twin jet single pilot night fighter. He had a test flight coming up in one, and asked me if I'd like to ride along. Next to the pilot's controls was a jump seat for a radar man. We took off and Paul flew the tests after which he asked if I would like to fly it. BUT OF COURSE. He landed and we swapped seats. He took the jump seat and I took the controls.

I'd never been in a Sky Knight or any other jet before. Paul said, "Just hold the brakes and give it 100% power. If everything looks OK (he told me when everything looked OK), let 'er roll". It was so quiet and smooth – and easy – I was amazed. I flew around for a while and we headed back for the field. He told me what power settings and airspeeds to fly on the approach. The approach felt a lot like the JD approach. Landing was smooth and I was impressed with how well it handled – and that was the day I flew the jet.

Above: *The XF3D-1 on 30 Sep '48. The* Skyknight *was the first jet-powered night all-weather fighter. The last F-10 (post-1962 designation), configured for electronic warfare, was retired in 1970 after Marine service in Vietnam.*

52
PARTY TIME!

It was 1953-54 at NAS Quonset Point in VU-2. It didn't take much to cause a VU-2 squadron party. We had a beautiful O-Club with several special rooms with bars and space for a dance floor.

The really big party each year was on the eve of our Operational Readiness Inspection, the feared ORI. The Wing Commander, Commodore Fox (a very impressive officer who looked a little like Lord Mountbatten) came up from Norfolk with his staff of inspectors whose jobs were to see how dumb they could make our pilots look under simulated emergency situations in the air and on the ground.

The "ORI Party" was at the O-Club where the pilots and their wives (or girl friends) socialized with the Wing staff and Lord Mountbatten. It was very cordial and the booze flowed freely, to our regret flying the day of the ORI.

Then there were the other squadron parties. The one that I remember most clearly was one that I could not attend. It was on a Saturday night. I was the Squadron Duty Officer with responsibilities other than attending parties. My post was at the squadron office in the hangar watching over the airplanes and in charge of the Duty Section.

I got a report that the party had gotten out of control. It seems that Ensign Tonoly and Lieutenant Pugsley were chatting at the bar when one of them playfully threw a drink in the other's face. I don't know who was the throwee or who was the throwor. The other pilots took sides, with the end result that the room turned into a mess.

The next morning there was an Admiral on board who planned to inspect our beautiful club. Big trouble! I got all the guys who were at the party to go up to the Club and clean up the mess ASAP. I told them, "No matter how far along the clean up is when the Admiral shows up, tell him you just started".

They did get the place clean, and there was no word about it from the Admiral, but VU-2 was barred from the O-Club for six weeks.

53
WHO NEEDS MEDALS?

In 1953, I flew mostly the F8F Bearcat fighters, where if I screwed up nobody knew it. Some of my time was in TBM's and JD's. The TBM had two ordnancemen aft, and the twin engine JD (Douglass A-26) had two ordnancemen aft plus a plane captain in the jump seat next to the pilot. When I look back on it, I often wonder if the guys who flew with whomever they were scheduled to fly with thought they were flying with a hot pilot, a good pilot, a poor pilot – or a crazy pilot. In my opinion, these guys had nerve. While most of the pilots were having fun, they must have been sweating.

I remember one time when I was making a low run on a destroyer to check its side number before starting a training exercise, one of the men in the back picked up the mike and said, "Mister Warner, water is splashing on the bomb bay". I guess he rated me one of the crazy pilots.

When I was leaving the squadron to go back to the hum-drum world of architecture, the guys in the Line Crew presented me with a letter that read,

Mr. Warner;

Upon your separation from the Naval Service, we of the line crew wish you to know that we have enjoyed working with you during your tour in Utility Squadron TWO, and all of us are sorry to see you leave. As a token of our esteem, please accept this small token of our friendship and our best wishes to you and your family on your return to civilian life.

The Line Crew.

There followed 33 names at the bottom of the letter. Then they gave me a Waring Blender. Even though it was against regulations, I accepted it. The Wimbeldon trophy could not have looked better to me.

That letter means more to me than anything that ever happened to me in the Navy.

54
ROUND AND ROUND WE GO!

Luckily, the Bearcat had a wide landing gear. After a long day slaving behind a hot airplane engine in the summer of '53, I had just landed on runway 18 when the Quonset tower called and told me to expedite my turn off the runway – there was a P2V on final right behind me. Tower operators are taught at Tower school that the big airplanes get more respect than the little airplanes.

I unlocked the tail wheel and immediately turned off onto the nearest taxiway. I knew I was going too fast to turn off that soon, but when the tower speaks you listen – they can put you on report.

I never thought I'd see the day when I would ground loop an F8F. This was the day. As soon as I recognized what was happening, I didn't have to be a genius to recognize the beginning of a ground loop, I held the stick full back, gave it full opposite rudder and gave it full throttle (all 2,250 Hp). I think I lost count, but I made at least a 720 before I stopped it.

Then there was the day, after two 3 ½ hour hops slaving behind a hot engine, that I again heard the "soothing" (?) female voice of the Tower operator, "Go around! You are making a wheels up approach!!"

Now let me defend myself. On takeoff the F8 accelerated so fast that, if you didn't get the wheels up the moment you knew it would fly, the wheels would not fully retract and the wheel doors would not close – so after takeoff we always checked the wheels up "barber pole" on the wheels position indicator. A barber pole showing was what you wanted to see, the wheels were up and the wheel doors were closed. On the approach we would check the wheels position. No barber pole was what you wanted to see. The wheels were down and locked. Are you with me so far?

We have a situation here where half the time the barber pole is good, and half the time the barber pole is bad. After flying for seven hours in a tight little cockpit, it was natural that fatigue could become a factor and good and bad could get mixed up.

When I got in the operations office, the Exec, Gerry Colleran, told me that the Tower had put me on report. Being the good guy he was, he understood my excuse and took no disciplinary action. He, too, had flown lots of long hours in an F8. He also probably had some pull with the chick in the Tower.

Then there was the time I had a blowout landing a Corsair at NAS Opa Locka, Miami, on our annual Two Weeks Training duty Summer of '49 – but that's another story.

55
DID YOU SAY . . . SHARKS?

On winter detachment we flew the TBM's and the A-26's (We called them JD's) out of what I call old San Juan Airport, just one runway. It was before they built the bigger commercial airport east of the city in about 1956. Our runway, if I remember correctly, was Runway 8-26 and was about 5,000 feet long. I don't remember ever taking off on 26, we always took off on 8. Must have been the trade winds. Runway 8 started on the west end at the water's edge and ended on the east end at the water's edge – right over the shacks up on stilts over the water where the people dumped their garbage, etc., right in the water. The sharks loved the stuff. There were a lot of sharks! Not a good place to lose an engine on take off.*

On our approach to land we flew a left hand approach from the downwind leg around Moro Castle. It was very picturesque. The area around Moro Castle was a golf course and had sand greens. I had never seen sand greens and never saw any again.

Holland American Line ships anchored in the harbor near the south side of the runway. We used to sit on the balcony of the O-Club drinking Heinekens and admire the beautiful white cruise ships. Life was good.

** Sometime between THE WAR and "Korea," a commercial airliner lost an engine taking off on runway 8 and ditched amongst the sharks. An Air Force friend told me that he had taken off right behind the airliner, circled the crash site, and watched in horror as the sharks attacked the survivors.*

56
HOW WE GONNA 'SPLAIN THIS TO THE SKIPPER?

On another occasion, Don Hayes and I were flying our required monthly two hour night flying and GCA's in the SNB twin Beech. The SNB had four fuel tanks. The fuel selector valve had five positions: MAIN, Rt-aux, Lft-aux, NOSE and OFF. We normally left the nose tank empty and flew off one of the wing tanks and then the main. It was our habit to use the wing tanks first, wait for the fuel pressure to start to drop and then switch to another tank. The squadron had two SNB's. The tank selector valves were 90 degrees different.

Near the end of the period, Don was flying a GCA concentrating on our approach to an unlit runway, unlit to keep the duty runway clear. I was flying as copilot. We forgot (I forgot) that we were flying on one of the wing tanks which held only twenty five gallons. We were over the approach end of the runway when both engines quit cold. When both engines quit at the same time, it says, "Empty fuel tank!" loud and clear. Don two blocked the throttles, mixture and prop controls and shouted, "Emergency!" As if I didn't know!

I reached down and grabbed the fuel selector valve and immediately switched to the next position – Silence. I had switched to either the empty nose tank or to OFF. It was pitch dark and I couldn't tell which selector valve was in this particular SNB. More silence. I couldn't wait around too long, so I switched to the next position. To our great relief, both engines caught and, with everything two blocked, they just about jumped out of the wings.

When we landed we compared our thoughts about when the engines quit. It was interesting. Exactly the same thought had run through both of our minds, not, "We're gonna die!", but "How we gonna 'splain this to the skipper?"

And then there was the time...

57
THE DEFENSE RESTS

When I was at NAS Quonset Point for my two years of active duty during the Korean thing, I was, among my other collateral duties, the squadron defense council. My first court marshal involved an enlisted man who was on "trial" charged with being AWOL. I didn't know quite what I was supposed to do, but fate smiled upon me. To make a short story shorter, about the time the proceedings were almost over, one of my squadron mates, who was just sitting in to watch, passed me a note which read, "They haven't proved he ever left the barracks". The defense rests!

After that the skipper told me he was going to send me to Legal School at Newport, across Narraganset Bay from Quonset. At about that time the Navy was trying to get more pilots to "go regular Navy". Of the 21 pilots in the squadron, I was one of three short timers who were qualified. A college degree was required, and the other 18 pilots were guys who got their wings in WW II like I did, but stayed on active duty and didn't get out to take advantage of the GI Bill like I did. They would have given anything to "go regular Navy", but weren't qualified. None of the qualified short timers wanted to "go regular" and stay on active duty. We wanted to go back to civilian life and pursue our chosen professions.

I told the skipper I thought it made more sense to send a pilot who wasn't a short timer. He didn't make me go, but I think that got me a poor fitness report. Maybe that's why I never made Captain. At least I didn't have to get up at 5 a.m. to ride the crash boat to Newport. Hey, it was winter!

Later I had to defend a kid who was charged with desertion. That's serious stuff, so I got a short timer LCDR who was a lawyer in civilian life from one of the other squadrons to be my "assistant" defense council. I graciously let him do all the work, and he got the kid off on some kind of mitigating circumstances. That was the end of my legal career.

After the two years at Quonset I came back to my old reserve squadron and came out of "legal retirement". Once while I was Squadron Commander. One of the enlisted men in the squadron was caught stealing hub caps in the parking lot during a weekend drill. I had to hold a "Captain's Mast". It was an open and shut case. He didn't do time, but he wasn't in the Navy by the time we secured that day.

58
THE BRIDGE

I was watching TV News during lunch one day when the picture of a beautiful steel bridge came on the screen. It looked familiar. While I watched, it blew up and crashed into the water. It will be replaced by a bigger and better bridge according to the news report. It was the Jamestown Bridge across Narragansett Bay.

When I was in VU-2 at NAS Quonset Point, Rhode Island, flying Grumman F8F "Bearcats" during the Korean War, the Jamestown Bridge was where we entered the traffic pattern. Being in VU-2 was like being on Mister Roberts' ship, the *Reluctant*. The *Reluctant* was in the backwaters of the Pacific War, and VU-2 was in the backwaters of the Korean War, half a world away. When returning to base from our operating area outside the ADIZ (Air Defense Identification Zone), south of the COMDESLANT destroyer base at Newport, we entered the pattern with, "Quonset Tower, this is Anthony 47, over the bridge for landing".

The twenty three pilots in the squadron came from all over the country. Harry Hicks, Iowa; Vinney Hughes, New Joisey; Bill McNair, Massachusetts; Grady Lefler, Texas; me, Georgia; and so on. One of the two Ensigns was "Red Eyed Willie" Wilson from the town of Rifle, Colorado.

Red Eyed Willie became famous the day he called in, "Quonset Tower, this is Anthony 42, *under* the bridge for landing". Red Eyed Willie's performance was flawless, except for one little thing – the NAS Quonset Point legal officer was on the beach near the bridge and got his number.

I never found out how Red Eyed Willie was able to keep his wings after the court marshal. His defense must have been flawless.

"There are Rules and there are Laws. Men who think they can fly your airplane better than you make the Rules. The Laws (of Physics) are made by The Great One. You can suspend the Rules, but you can never suspend the Laws. If you deviate from a rule, it should be a flawless performance (i.e. if you fly under a bridge, don't hit the bridge)".

Author unknown

59
FAT, DUMB AND OBLIVIOUS

Almost all our F8F hops were just one plane going out on an Event alone. Sometimes two of us would be taking off at about the same time and would be side by side on the taxiway at the end of the runway, checking the mags. One day I found myself next in line to take off behind Art Morgan.

Art was not comfortable in the "Bearcat," but we all had to fly every aircraft we had to stay current in all types (F6F, TBM, F8F and A-26). He was cleared for take off by the tower and when he started to taxi onto the runway I saw an opportunity to make a formation take off as was our custom in such circumstances, so I said on tower frequency, "Formation take off?" His response was "Formation take off" which I interpreted as a yes. He had actually said, "No formation take off," and I didn't hear his, "No".

The duty runway was 36 which had the Naragannset Bay on the right side and planes from all the squadrons parked close aboard the left side. Art started his take off roll with me on his left wing. I realized later that he was unaware of my presence. He was not known to have "situational awareness". As he gathered speed, he didn't give it enough right rudder to compensate for torque and as we were about to reach take off speed, he started drifting to his left about to force me into the parked planes. The F8 was not ready to fly, so I gave the F8 full throttle and leapfrogged over to his right side. Thank goodness for those 2,250 horses in the R-2800 18 cylinder radial engine. I looked over my shoulder just as he became airborne on the left side of the runway where I would have been and watched him drift over all those parked planes, unaware of where the hell he was.

The gods, and the R-2800, were with me that day.

60
THE WRONG WINDOW

Sometimes, if the weather looked questionable and not good enough for flying an Event (training exercise) with a ship, the VU-2 operations officer would send up one of our own pilots on a "weather hop" in an F8F to make a quick check on the conditions. I didn't like to fly weather hops, because no matter which way I reported the weather conditions, not everybody would be happy with my report. The only good part was that it was kinda fun flying the F8 up there all by yourself.

Normally, the Quonset aerologists would hold all Events, if they considered the weather unsuitable. I was scheduled for a battle problem Event in an F8 with a destroyer about 60 miles south of the ADIZ (Air Defense Identification Zone). To find a ship, we would just fly the heading to the assigned op-area for the number of minutes it would take to cover the distance at 180 knots. That made it easy figure out in your head – 180 knots is three nautical miles per minute on the assigned heading for whatever the distance – can't miss.

On one battle problem exercise when I got to where the ship should have been it wasn't there, and the ceiling was down to less than 200 feet. I did a little square search and soon picked up the ship's wake. I followed the wake and when I got to the ship I reported, "Anthony 47 on station". Of course there was no way we could conduct a battle problem with less than a 200 foot ceiling. I just wanted the guys on the ship to know I was where **I** was supposed to be. They thanked me and told me to return to base.

When I got back I went up to Aerology and told the aerologist, "When you said the weather was O.K., you must have been looking out the wrong window".

61
LOST TARGET

We towed targets with TBM's and JD's (A-26) on destroyer five inch deck gun firing exercises. The JD was a great twin engine single pilot attack bomber rigged so that two ordnance men aft of the bomb bay could deploy a six foot diameter twenty-six foot long bright red nylon target "sleeve". The nylon sleeves came in very handy when we traded for mahogany in Haiti during winter detachment in San Juan. The target was attached to a quarter inch steel cable and was 2,000 feet behind and 200 feet below the plane. We made various patterned runs on the ships during the exercise.

The way it was supposed to work was the guns were radar controlled, but the ship's Gunnery Officer had to have visual contact with the target to make certain that the radar didn't "walk up" the cable and lock on the tow plane.

On one exercise, flying a JD, I felt the plane surge forward and knew that the ship had shot the sleeve off. I told the ordnance men to reel in the cable and stream another sleeve so we could continue the exercise. They said, "Mister Warner, we only reeled in a hundred feet of cable." I told them to go ahead and deploy another target. The gunnery officer probably blinked.

A miss is as good as a mile. I didn't want to abort the exercise and require the ship to steam all the way back to our operating area at 22 knots the next day when I could get there in 20 minutes at 180 knots.

62
COMMAND DECISION

Winter of 1953-54, I was on detachment to Puerto Rico. I was in Utility Squadron 2, and we flew out of the small San Juan commercial airport. It was just before the big new San Juan airport was built. On one occasion I was working with a submarine on a live torpedo firing exercise.

Just north of Vieques is a small island named Culebra – mostly rocks. The subs used the rocks for targets. My job was to fly over the target to make sure there were no fishermen in the vicinity. We also worked exercises with destroyers that had come to the area from Newport to operate in better weather than the winter weather out of Newport.

The next year we had a new skipper, CDR Schultz. The squadron home base was Quonset Point, R.I. The Wing Commander in Norfolk, Captain Fox, wanted the next detachment to operate from Roosevelt Roads on the eastern coast of Puerto Rico. Wing wanted our skipper's evaluation of moving to Roosey Roads. He took me with him to look the place over, since I had been on the last detachment.

When we landed at Roosey Roads, we both decided on the spot, before we even left the airplane, that the skipper would recommend using the old San Juan airport on the next detachment. It would have been a long ride in a broken down "publico" (taxi) to San Juan for liberty. Of course we were thinking about the men.

63
TAKE ONE APC AND CALL ME IN THE MORNING.

From the UTWGLANT NEWSLETTER 6-54

During the 14 flyable working days at Quonset point in the month of October, the twenty-one Utility Squadron TWO pilots, including the Commanding Officer, Executive Officer, and all department heads with the exception of the Maintenance Officer, who was not a pilot, flew a total of 1,048 pilot hours. This boils down to 49.9 hours per pilot and 74.8 hours per flying day. If anyone knows where Utility Squadron TWO can get some more pilots, please drop a note to the squadron's flight officer* c/o Quonset Point Dispensary, where he is undergoing treatment for a chronic ulcer.

*Me

64
WHAT A WASTE!

Whiskey was cheap in Puerto Rico in 1954. A fifth of V.O. cost all of 75 cents. Rum was even cheaper. A Cuba Libra at the O-Club cost ten cents, except on Friday when they were two for ten cents. As a result, every plane that went back to NAS Quonset from the VU-2 detachment in San Juan was loaded with cheap whiskey.

Harry Hicks and Vinney Hughes were flying back to Quonset in a JD with 22 cases of whiskey in the bomb bay. How they got through Miami Customs I'll never know. When they were off the coast of North Carolina it was getting dark and cold. Harry turned on the 180,000 Btu gas fired heater in the plane. Shortly after that, the heater caught fire. They were unable to extinguish it and decided they better ditch. Harry ditched in the mouth of the Cape Fear River. Harry, Vinney and the two ordnance men aft survived the ditching. As luck would have it, some men from a nearby lighthouse saw the plane go down, put out a boat and picked up the survivors.

I was the squadron safety officer and took Harry's accident report when he got back to Quonset. He stated in his report that he followed all the proper ditching procedures – reduce airspeed to about 90 knots and ditch slow, nose up, and tail low. Fine. He later told me, "Jim, that damn thing was on fire. I had to get us out. [He decided to ditch because they were at five or six thousand, the wind was from the west and they would have blown out to sea in the dark]. I hit the water at about 180 knots. When we hit, everything forward of the cockpit disappeared, but we managed to get out." He also told me about the 22 cases of whiskey that went down with the plane.

As safety officer, I was sent to Norfolk to be part of the accident investigation. Luckily, the plane was never recovered with the 22 cases of illegal whiskey on board. Just after the ditching a freighter put out to sea, passing over the approximate crash site. The ship drew enough water that, if the plane was where it went down, the ship would have scraped the wreckage. There was no contact with the wreck. I couldn't help but wonder what I would have had to say in any accident investigation report, if the plane had been brought up and the booze had been discovered. I could have had Harry court-martialed.

65
HOW I ALMOST "GOT A WING" IN A TBM

I flew F6F's, F8F's, JD's and TBM's at NAS Quonset Point. I almost "got a wing" in a TBM. We parked the TBM's very close to each other with the wings folded back. Sometimes there was one parked next to you, and sometimes there wasn't.

We were told that once you released the wings to unfold, the process could not be reversed while the wings were still unfolding. The wings folded back like the F6F, whereas the wings folded up on the F8F. JD wings didn't fold.

One day I was getting ready to leave the chocks and, looking to my left, there was no plane next to me. Being in a hurry, I failed to look to my right. I moved the control to spread the wings – and then looked to my right and was horrified to see another TBM smack dab next to me. I immediately moved the wing fold control to "fold" and miraculously the wings reversed and began to fold back.

That's how I almost "got a wing" in a TBM without "ground looping". It just goes to show – everything they say can't be done is like the song in Gershwin's *Porge and Bess*: "It ain't necessarily so...."

66
GO WEST, YOUNG MAN

VU-2 was a pretty small outfit. We had 21 officers, one of whom was not a Naval Aviator. The term aviator is important. Navy flyers are not pilots – they are "aviators". A pilot brings a ship into a harbor with which he is more familiar than the captain of a ship. An aviator flies airplanes. When people use the term pilot, they don't realize that they ain't talking about guys who fly airplanes.

We were lucky to have LCDR Van Bibber, our only non-aviator, as our Maintenance officer. He was almost a father figure and we knew that as long as he was in charge of keeping our planes in top flying condition, we had nothing to worry about.

He told us a story about when he was stationed in San Diego with a seaplane outfit that flew a lot of TransPac flights. Flying across the vast Pacific Ocean was pretty complicated back in those days. There were not many radio navigation aids and you had to do a great deal of complicated planning and have a very sharp navigator who was good at celestial navigation.

While launching one of these TransPac "flying boats" down the ramp into the water for take off, the plane was stopped on the ramp and the navigator stuck his head out of the plane and yelled, "Hey, Van! What's the course to Honolulu?"

To this day, every time I hear someone ask a dumb question, I think to myself, "What's the course to Honolulu?"

67
SIX CENTS A PACK

Harold "Squirty" Zell was in our wedding June 14, 1952, one of the two groomsmen. Six months later Ensign Zell found himself on an LST out of Norfolk, and LT Warner found himself flying round engines out of NAS Quonset Point.

He called me from Norfolk to let me know that his LST would be coming to Newport for some training exercises with one of the UDT outfits (that's Underwater Demolition Team to you landlubbers). I told him to let me know about when he would be in the area and I'd give him a buzz if I happened to have an F8F hop the morning he would be arriving.

I did have a hop just as his ship was approaching Block Island. I knew it was Squirty, because we almost never saw an LST in our area. I worked him over good. That night he came to dinner with us and we had a nice visit. He told me that when I buzzed the ship they were not up on "Fleet Common". That is a frequency that all ships monitor when underway so they can get emergency orders immediately or pick up any distress calls. His skipper thought my buzzing the ship was an attempt to communicate something urgent, when all the time I was having a ball. The communications officer caught the devil.

They didn't do too well on the UDT "war game" either. It seems that one night a frogman climbed over the side for a mock attack on the ship and the ship's sentry fainted.

When he came to dinner he brought me a present, a carton of Pall Mall cigarettes. He got them on his LST for sixty cents a carton. That's six cents a pack! With what they cost now, I'm glad I quit smoking back in 1967.

68
WRONG TARGET

One of our training exercises with the subs out of New London was to be on station with the sub during a dummy torpedo firing. The sub would fire a dummy torpedo at a target ship, any ship would do, with the torpedo set to go under the target ship. We would orbit the sub in a TBM. In case they couldn't find the torpedo when it quit running, we could spot it for them to pick up and re-use. In 1953 dollars, a dummy torpedo cost a bunch – at least $20,000.

On one such exercise the torpedo went crazy, circled around and hit the sub's propeller. End of exercise. The next day the exercise was rescheduled and, guess what, the same thing happened again.

On all the sub firing exercises I flew, I never saw a dummy torpedo before the sub did. On all those exercises, I wasn't needed.

69
IT DON'T GET NO BETTER THAN THAT!

It's Summer 1953. I take off from NAS Quonset Point in a Grumman F8F Bearcat, head south over Narragansett Bay, over the Jamestown Bridge and past Newport. I take up a dead reckoned heading to rendezvous with a destroyer at sea.

Soon I am out of sight of land. Me and the Bearcat, the ultimate prop fighter. 2,250 Hp in a 7,650 pound airframe! 3.4 pounds per Hp! I am snug in the tight little cockpit and feel like I am part of the Bearcat. It's just me, the empty ocean and a cloudless sky – suspended in space. Soon I spot the destroyer knifing through the blue water making thirty knots and a beautiful snow white bow wave.

Now the fun starts. I report on station and we begin a "battle problem" training exercise – just me and the destroyer playing games for about an hour, then the ship gives me a vector home to Quonset.

It don't get no better than that!

[A little background: During WW II, the Focke Wulf 190 was the best German fighter – better than the Messerschmidt 109. The Allies captured a Focke Wulf 190 intact. A Grumman rep and a Naval Aviator tested it and designed a Navy prop fighter (the Grumman F8F "Bearcat") that would outperform the FW 190. The Bearcat could get to 10,000 feet in two minutes from a carrier deck. It was intended to intercept Kamikazes. It never got into combat in WW II. The war ended before it was deployed in the Pacific. The souped up F8F "Rare Bear" holds the world land speed record to this day (528.33 mph and the world record climb rate 9,842 feet in 91.9 sec.) for props. The F8F was replaced in the 50's by the Grumman F9F Panther jet fighter.]

During a TV interview, Neil Armstrong was asked what his favorite plane was. He said he had never met a plane he didn't like, but his favorite was the Grumman F8F.

70
I'D FOLLOW HIM ANYWHERE

Commander Quinlan was the best skipper I ever had. He could fly better than anybody in the squadron. When flying wing on "Quinny", as we affectionately called him, you had a hard time keeping up with him. The following incident tells you a lot about the skipper.

Sandy had gone on a trip to Florida and brought back a potted palm about half the size of the Captain's palm tree in the movie *Mister Roberts*. We put it on the desk in the squadron office, and it became a fixture there.

One Sunday morning Quinny called all the pilots into the squadron office. He was not happy the way we were performing our various ground duties. He really read us the riot act. When he got through chewing us out he left the office, slamming the door behind him. A moment later the door opened slightly, he stuck his head in and said, "And don't forget to water my godamn palm tree".

I'd follow him anywhere.

71
JIM AND THE PALM TREE

72
CAMP COSBY

Camp Cosby was a great YMCA Summer camp not too far from Birmingham. I went there for two weeks two summers. Two weeks cost all of $10.00.

On the west side of the Camp Cosby Lake, on a ridge at the top of a steep hill, there were six cabins. Each cabin housed about ten campers. Every morning we would run down the hill to the lake and jump in naked, with our bar of Ivory soap, for our morning bath. One of the camp councilors was Tom Averett. It was the summer of 1940, during the Battle of Britain. We listened to Edward R. Murrow broadcasting from England on the radio.

Years later, in 1949, I was in a Navy Corsair reserve squadron. We were at NAS Opa Locka Florida for a two week training "cruise". Our squadron was there to support one of the NAS Atlanta attack squadrons flying AM attack bombers. The AM, built by Martin, was very complicated maintenance-wise, so complicated that only 180 were ever built and bought by the Navy. The Navy palmed them off on reserve squadrons.

I remember towing targets in a Corsair for the AM squadron air to air gunnery exercises. One of the AM pilots was – Tom Averett.

73
WHERE DID ALL THE COMMANDER JOHNSON'S GO?

Back in 1946 when the Ready Reserve was cranking up at NAS Atlanta, the station Operations Officer was a big no nonsense commander named Johnson. I was in Operations one day when the phone rang and he answered, with authority, "Commander Johnson!" There was a pause (it was a resident complaining about the planes flying over), then, "What color was the star on those airplanes!?" Another pause. "Well when you see one with a red star on it call me!" He hung up (with authority). Sadly, there are no more Commander Johnson's in the Navy these days.

Another time, I saw a Wave in Operations standing at the counter waiting for a flight out. She had put her little fru-fru dog on the counter. Commander Johnson glared at her and said, "Get your g-d--- mutt off my counter!" You can't do that anymore either.

74
CUBA LIBRES

VU-2 sent a Detachment to San Juan every winter to provide aircraft services for the COMDESLANT winter destroyer training exercises. I was on the 1954 Detachment. The squadron was already there and Bob McCullough and I were going to fly down in a JD. He was pilot and I rode in the jump seat next to him.

We flew to Miami, and then on to San Juan the next day. CDR Brown was C.O. and remained at Quonset. LCDR Harry Hicks was S.O.P. (Senior Officer Present) in San Juan. The detachment, thanks to Harry, was a happy ship operation. He put the Duty Sections on a "24 on, 24 off" schedule. The crew loved it. Aircraft availability was close to 100%.

When the word got back to Brown, I heard that he was very unhappy about it. It was certainly not the way he would have done it. I don't know how Harry managed to keep the system going against Brown's wishes, but he did. Harry was that kinda guy. The pilots had it good, too. We usually flew one hop a day and had the other half of the day off.

One day we flew to Haiti with a load of red nylon targets to trade for mahogany. We rented a cab for $2 for the whole day. We went by a place where there were a bunch of Haitians carving out mahogany trays and other stuff. The place, coincidently, was owned by a retired Naval Aviator who had at one time been a utility pilot.

We had two vehicles available for pilot transportation. One was a closed pick up type truck fitted with wire over the windows for use by the Shore Patrol and a van-like milk truck with no doors, like the UPS trucks are today. I always got a kick out of being driven down to the flight line like a bunch of drunken sailors being taken to the brig by the Shore Patrol.

The O-Club at San Juan was very nice. Cuba Libres were ten cents, except on Friday when they were two for ten cents (the O-Club at Gitmo was even better. They were five cents all the time). Bob and I used to sit on the San Juan O-Club balcony drinking Heinekens, watching the white Holland American Line cruise ships dock. Bob and I trained Heneroso, the bartender, to fix us two Cuba Libres when we held up two fingers when the destroyers were in port on weekends and the bar was crowded. If he didn't get a tip he would say, "No leche por los ninyos" (no milk for the children).

I knew things were going to be good when Bob and I first arrived. As we pulled into the chocks, a Chief Petty Officer walked up in front of the JD, smiling from ear to ear, holding a tray with two Cuba Libres.

75
WIND? WHAT WIND?

Late one Sunday on a drill weekend, Sandy and I were taxiing out in two Corsairs for a little formation flying and cloud hopping. We were checking the mags when the tower called and told us to return to the line. They didn't say why. When we got to the line they told us we were to sign out an SNB and take a chief petty officer to Indianapolis where he was to attend some Navy technical course starting on Monday morning.

Sandy rounded up the chief while I hastily made out the flight plan and calculated our ETA at Indianapolis. Sandy was the pilot and I was the co-pilot. The weather was deteriorating and soon after take off we were flying over an under-cast as it got dark. It was an interesting sight seeing the clouds glow as we would pass over a big city with all its lights on. We got to Indianapolis with no problem, let the chief out, refueled, I filed the flight plan calculating our ETA at NAS Atlanta, and we took off for home.

Along about Knoxville, the weather was bad all the way to Atlanta. I figured we didn't have enough fuel to make an instrument approach and make it to an alternate if we missed the approach at NAS, so we landed at Knoxville and checked into the BOQ for the night. As I sat there drinking a beer from the "honor system fridge" in the hall (25 cents), I was puzzled that we had enough gas on the trip to Indianapolis, but not enough on the trip home.

It all became clear to me when I filed the flight plan for Atlanta the next morning. There had been a strong head wind from the south that I had not taken into account when I was hastily figuring our ETA.

76
MOONRISE

During night flying one night on a Reserve weekend, the sky was clear except for a haze layer up to about 3,000 feet. I was headed north, just tooling along, when I looked over my right shoulder. I couldn't believe my eyes. The moon was just coming up. The moon looked huge, orange and about five times normal diameter. The top of the haze layer looked like the earth's horizon and the moon, rising above the true horizon clearly visible through the haze, gave the illusion that this monstrous orange ball was rising up out of the earth. It was if I was in outer space looking at this wonderful sight. It gave me a real shock, especially since I was up there in the dark all by myself.

I had a similar shock one day flying out of NAS Quonset Point in an F8F. I was bored orbiting between Block Island and Martha's Vinyard, waiting my turn for the Newport CIC School to vector me on a Bogey intercept. There was a total overcast. I rolled out of the orbit and looked over my left shoulder and, having no reference to the sun, I thought I was headed west, looking south, when in fact I was headed east, looking north. There before my eyes, islands appeared to have popped up out of the sea. It scared me until I realized what had happened. I was headed west, not east, and the islands that had "popped up" out of the sea were Martha's Vinyard and Nantucket.

77
PHOTO LINE CREW LETTER

Mr Warner;

Upon your seperation from the Naval Service, we of the line crew wish you to know that we have enjoyed working for you during your tour in Utility Squadron TWO, And all of us are sorry to see you leave. A s a token of our esteem, please accept this small token of our friendship and our best wishes to you and your family on your return to civilian life.

The Line Crew.

Anderson
Biglin
Bryan
Voeghringer
Newkirk
Hickman
Welton
Greenwalt
Mixner
Jones
Daley
Connolly
Sears
Mc GarrigleD
Darrow
Peterson

Perrotti
Chandler
B arry M
Wagner
Thorrington
Mancuso
McKeough
Tomczyk
Zimmerman
Walsh R.
Walsh G.
Barry D.
Mitschka
Cariker
Parry
Tuhey

78
OPERATION LAST FLIGHT - "READY FOR INSPECTION"

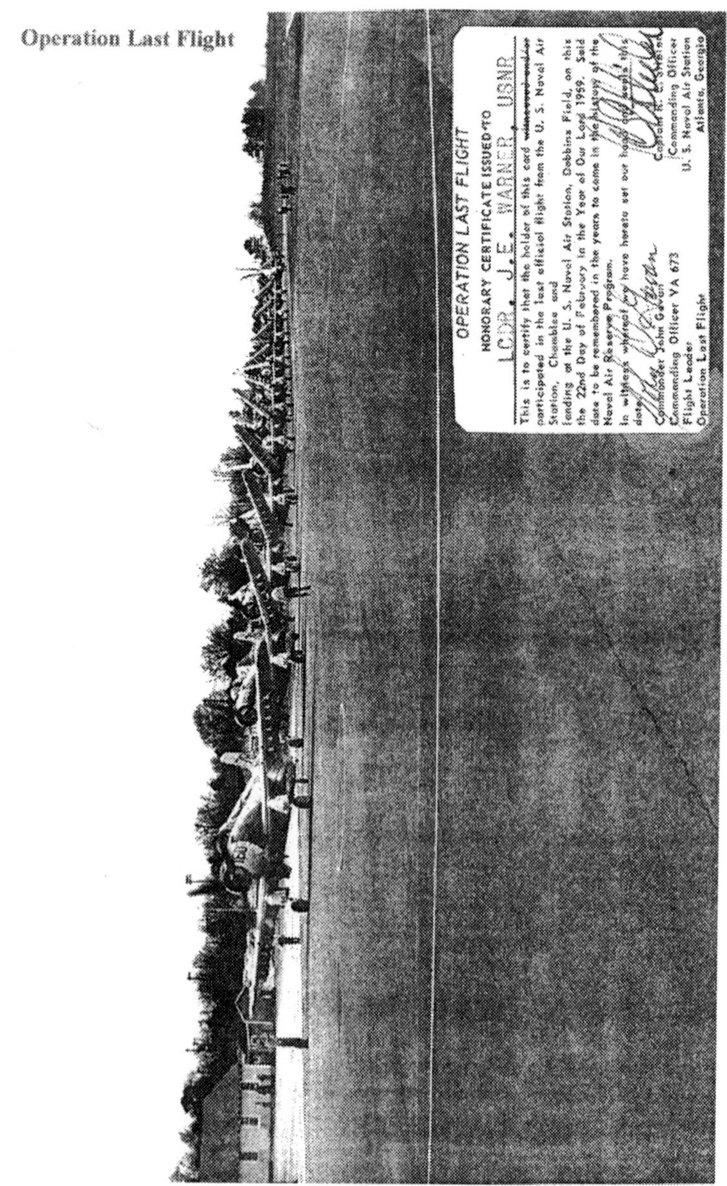

OPERATION LAST FLIGHT

HONORARY CERTIFICATE ISSUED TO

LCDR. J. E. WARNER, USNR

This is to certify that the holder of this card participated in the last official flight from the U. S. Naval Air Station, Chamblee and landing at the U. S. Naval Air Station, Dobbins Field, on this the 22nd Day of February in the Year of Our Lord 1959. Said date to be remembered in the years to come in the history of the Naval Air Reserve Program.

In witness whereof we have hereto set our hands and seals this date.

Commander John Galvan
Commanding Officer VA 673
Flight Leader
Operation Last Flight

Captain R. [illegible]
Commanding Officer
U. S. Naval Air Station
Atlanta, Georgia

Operation Last Flight

79
I NEVER SAW SO MANY AVIATORS TOGETHER, AND NOBODY WAS DRINKING

I am a member of the Georgia Chapter of the Silver Wings Fraternity. We have 180 members in the chapter. I was chapter president in 2002. To qualify for membership, you have to have soloed at least 25 years ago. If over 50 years ago, you get a little gold star on your name tag. Members are from military, general aviation and people (associate members) who just love airplanes. About 50 members meet every Wednesday for lunch and a program. When we don't have an "outside" speaker, some of the guys will come to the mike and tell of some of their flying experiences. The WWII pilots have the best stories.

"Silver Wings" doesn't refer to the color of your wings, Navy gold wings and AF silver wings, it refers to hair color. If you soloed at about 18, by the time you qualified for membership you would have gray hair, if you weren't bald.

The uniform is casual. I went to my first meeting in suit and tie. They thought I was the guest speaker.

A typical weekly meeting starts with the guys standing around comparing their physical ailments and the ravages of age.

You hear stuff like: "I'm gonna get a new knee next week"; "Joe will be out of the hospital tomorrow"; "The open heart surgery wasn't so bad"; "I need to get these cataracts operated on"; "Does your pacemaker have a defibrillator? Mine does"; "Nice cane"; "I got my hearing aid at the VA last year". Stuff like that.

Then when we sit down at the table (eight guys per table) a remarkable thing happens. The conversation is about only one thing – flying.

You hear stuff like: "You Navy guys were crazy to take off from something that might not be there when you got back"; "We couldn't stay with the bombers all the way 'til we got the P-51's"; "When the *Princeton* was sinking I had to jump from the flight deck eighty feet to the water"; "Yeah, the B-24 looked like the box the B-17 came in"; "When I bailed out I broke both legs and wound up in a German hospital". Stuff like that.

80
PEBBLES

When we meet at the Silver Wings fraternity every Wednesday, we usually have a guest speaker. On those occasions when there is no guest speaker one of the guys will come up to the mike and tell of some of his experiences during the war.

Gene Smith was a member who flew B-24's out of Africa and later Italy. On one mission on the way to the target when the German fighters attacked, his radioman's arm was shot off. He had to stay in formation and couldn't turn back to get the radioman to a hospital, so they put the parachute on the wounded airman and threw him out of the plane over enemy territory, hoping someone on the ground would find him and help him.

That night the Germans broadcast a message that they had picked him up, got him to a hospital and he was going to survive.

On a later mission, Gene was shot down and wound up in a Stalag Luft (that's Kraut for Air Corps P.O.W. camp). The camp was run by the Austrian army in Poland. He said the Austrians were fairly decent to the P.O.W's. As the Russians came closer to Germany, the camp was moved west toward Germany.

On the march, Gene had a machete tied to his leg under his greatcoat. The Austrians didn't worry about it because it was used to cut wood for fires at rest stops. Soon they approached an S.S. check point. Gene didn't have time to get rid of the machete and knew that the Germans would shoot him on the spot when they found it on him.

Thinking fast, he reached down and picked up a few pebbles. When he got closer to the check point he cradled the pebbles in his cupped hand close to his chest and kept softly saying, "Don't take my pebbles. Please, don't take my pebbles". The other P.O.W's glanced at Gene, pointed at their heads and shook their heads as if to say, "Poor guy. He's nuts". The S.S. let him through the check point without searching him.

Having survived the war, Gene went to Georgia Tech on the GI Bill and later started an engineering company that specialized in solving unusual engineering problems. What else would you expect from a smart guy like that? He wasn't so nuts.

81
JOHN JAMGOCHIAN AND THE "BLACK BOX"

Flying in the reserve was really fun and games. We got paid for four "drills" per week end per month plus two weeks active duty each summer. More than one squadron would meet on any one weekend. John Jamgochian was in one of the outfits that met on my drill weekend. He used to joke about times I had towed targets for his squadron that he missed during air to air gunnery hops. Lucky for me he missed me, too.

John was a remarkable fellow. He invented and developed several aviation aids while employed at Lockheed after graduating from Georgia Tech. His greatest contribution to aviation was the conception and development, for Lockheed, of the Black Box flight recorder that is so helpful in crash investigations.

My close friend and ex-squadron mate, Gordon Lawless, was in flight training at Pensacola with Jamgochian. He told me about one of Jamgochian's famous "adventures".

During the final phase of flight training at "Bloody" Barin, we had to make a three leg navigation hop over the Gulf and return, hopefully to the point of departure. On one of these hops "Jam" and two other cadets waited for a formation of three more cadets to join them at the warm up spot at the end of the runway. They finally got tired of waiting and told the tower they would meet the other three at the first turning point over the Gulf. After waiting for a long time at the turning point, they did a square search for the others. They had no luck with the search so they decided split up and fly independently north back to Barin.

Jam made landfall somewhere along the coast and was lost. He found a long straight highway and made a perfect landing. He would have to notify the base, so he taxied along the highway, which became curved and tree lined, to see if he could find a phone somewhere. He finally came to a little country store where he shut down and called the base. He had to hold the phone away from his ear when his instructor screamed, "TRUE NORTH!"

An instructor was sent out to fly the plane back to Barin. When he saw the curved road and big trees with Jam's plane parked by the store he was reported to have said, "How did you ever land here?" He didn't know that Jam had not landed there, but had taxied there.

Sadly, Jam was killed October 15, 1997 when his engine quit on take off from McCollum Field near Marietta and, instead of landing straight ahead, he turned to avoid crashing into a crowded shopping mall and spun in.

82
FLAT HAT-ING

"Flat Hat-ing" is against the rules in the Navy. Flat Hat-ing is flying very low and buzzing friends or relatives. It is fun, exciting and dangerous. It can get you killed.

In the 60's I was flying AD's in the reserve. Lauren Goldsmith and I worked in Heery's architectural firm then. Lauren flew all weather jet interceptors out of New England when he was in the Air Force. He was often heard to say, "Man was not meant to fly." I figured he would appreciate a buzz job on one of my drill week ends. I buzzed his house one Sunday morning where Roswell Road crosses the Chatahootchie River. After one very low pass, I suddenly realized there was another AD on my tail. He either wanted to play or was going to get my number and report me. Just to be safe, I pulled up and climbed into the sun so he couldn't get my number.

During flight training at Pensacola during the war there was a lot of flat hat-ing, especially during night flying when it was hard to see a plane's number, which made it less likely to be turned in. One sport was to fly between the projector and the screen at a drive-in movie. Another great sport was flying a few feet above the railroad tracks at night toward an oncoming train and turning on one landing light. All that is strictly contrary to good air discipline, but in wartime, pilots need to be a little crazy.

In ground school we had "Sense Books". "Formation Flying Sense", "Night Flying Sense" and other flight related subjects. The books told you what to do, and what not to do, if you wanted to live to get your wings so you could die for your country. There was an example in the "Flat Hat-ing Sense" book illustrating the futility of flat hat-ing when trying to impress a person who knew nothing about flying. It seems a cadet's girl friend and her mother came to Pensacola to visit him. They stayed in the San Carlos Hotel, the only hotel in town, a four story building. The cadet wanted to impress his girl and buzzed the hotel in an SNJ. Somebody got his number and turned him in.

At his court martial, the trial counsel asked the girl friend's mother, "Madam, in your opinion, was this young man flying too low?" She promptly answered, "Of course not. He never once got below the third floor."

83
"MUHHHHTH ... ER"

One day on a drill weekend back in the late '40's, three of us were flying cross country formation from NAS Atlanta (now PDK) to Auburn. I was flying wing on Bob Turney. As formation leader, he was doing the navigating and we were just following along like good wingmen.

We were about half way there. Bob kept looking around like he was lost and looking for landmarks. He unfolded a chart and would look at the chart and then look for a landmark. This routine went on for several minutes. I could see a concerned expression on his face (we liked to fly tight formation). He kept looking from the chart to outside the cockpit then back to the chart, back and forth, for something that looked familiar.

Bob looked very young for his age, like a baby faced sixteen year old. Pretty soon he folded the chart, put it away and picked up the mike and slowly said, "Moooooother."

It was then that I realized we were all lost.

84
BIO FOR TALK AT THE SILVER WINGS FRATERNITY

It was a dark and stormy night on Halloween 1923 when Jim was born at Gantt's Quarry, Alabama, in a little unpainted Alabama Marble Company company-house up on rock piers (sob) about fifty feet from a marble quarry. An appropriate start for one who grew up to be an architect. When Jim was three, his father, an estimator for the company, was transferred to Chicago and moved to Glen Ellyn where Jim entered grammar school.

During the Great Depression, the company transferred his Dad to Birmingham where Jim happily spent his teenage years and attended Phillips High School from 1937 to 1941.

Jim volunteered for the Navy V5 program in 1942, earned his Navy wings at Pensacola in 1944, and returned to civilian life in 1945. During WWII he was an Instrument Flight Instructor. He volunteered to return to active duty in 1952. He served without distinction during both WWII and Korea. Between WWII and Korea he studied architecture at Georgia Tech, graduating in 1949. In the Naval Air Reserve, he was Commanding Officer of FASRON 52 and retired as Assistant Wing Commander with the rank of Commander and 3,080 flying hours.

Jim got his architectural license in 1955, started the firm of Warner & Summers, Architects, in 1964, sold the firm in 1993 to three senior members of the firm and became unemployed.

He has survived two open heart operations, right and left coratid artery rechannelization, four cardioversions, acupuncture for a torn rotator cuff and an elbow operation to repair an old war wound – he fell off a bar stool in the officers' club.

Jim is married to the former Betty Geiger of Brunswick, Georgia, whom he asked to marry on the second date. A year later, in June 1952, they were married and are living happily ever after. Betty takes good care of Jim and watches him with an eagle eye to make sure that he doesn't drink tee many Martoonies.

85
I WANT TO BE A NAVAL AVIATOR

The following is a letter written by a fifth grader, and has been published in several newsletters:

> "I want to be a Naval Aviator when I grow up because it's fun and easy to do. Naval Aviators don't need much school. They just have to learn numbers so they can read the instruments. I guess they should be able to read maps so they can find their way if they are lost. Naval Aviators should be brave so they won't be scared if it's foggy and they can't see, or if a wing or motor falls off they should stay calm so they'll know what to do. Naval Aviators have to have good eyes so they can see through clouds and they can't be afraid of lightning or thunder because they are closer to them than we are.
>
> The salary Naval Aviators make is another thing I like. They make more money than they can spend. This is because most people think airplane flying is dangerous, except Naval Aviators don't because they know how easy it is. There isn't much I don't like, except girls like Naval Aviators and all the stewardesses want to marry them, so they always have to chase them away so they won't bother them. I hope I don't get airsick because, if I do, I couldn't be a Naval Aviator and would have to go to work.

86
AIR FORCE PILOTS LIE

"One thing about Air Force pilots is that they lie a lot. You simply can't trust them at all. We had an argument start one night at the Belvedere Inn across the gate at Pax. A bunch of our guys were arguing with some Eagle drivers from Langley about who was better at what, and which airplane was better. Well, we decided to settle it next morning in the restricted area over the bay. This is where we found out how much Air Force pilots lie! We agreed to meet nose to nose at 35 thousand and settle it once and for all. Don't you know those sneaky bastards showed up at 40 thousand. What a bunch of lying sneaky low lifes those Air Force types were, showing up with a five grand altitude advantage! If we hadn't been at 45 thousand, those lying Air Force scumbags would have had us for breakfast!!!"

Admiral Holliday

87
THERE ARE RULES AND THERE ARE LAWS

"There are Rules and there are Laws. Men who think they can fly your airplane better than you make the Rules. The Laws (of Physics) are made by The Great One. You can suspend the Rules, but you can never suspend the Laws. If you deviate from a Rule, it should be a flawless performance (i.e. if you fly under a bridge, don't hit the bridge)".

Author unknown.

88
HIGH FLIGHT

"Oh, I have slipped the surly bonds of earth

And danced the skies on laughter silvered wings;

Sunward I've climbed, and joined the tumbling mirth

Of sun-split clouds – and done a hundred things

You have not dreamed of – wheeled and soared and swung

High in the sunlit silence. Hov'ring there,

I've chased the shouting wind along, and flung

My eager craft through footless halls of air ...."

Up, up the long, delirious, blue

I've topped the wind-swept heights with easy grace

Where never lark, or even eagle flew –

And, while with silent, lifting mind I've trod

The high untrespassed sanctity of space,

Put out my hand, and touched the face of God.

HIGH FLIGHT
John Gillespie McGee

89
THE NAVY HYMN

"Eternal Father, strong to save,
Whose arm hath bound the restless wave,
Who bidd'st the mighty ocean deep,
Its own appointed limits keep;
Oh, hear us when we cry to thee,
For those in peril on the sea".

At Athens Pre-Flight in the fall of 1943, I was in the 35th Battalion, Platoon 35J1A. There were three battalions. Every Sunday, all three battalions marched into chapel in our sharp blue uniforms, the same uniform worn by Annapolis Midshipmen. Before being seated, we stood at attention and sang the first verse of the Navy Hymn. It was very impressive. I was nineteen years old. Sixty five years later, when I hear the Navy Hymn it brings a tear to my eye.

90

How do I know that my youth is all spent?

Well, my get up and go, got up and went.

But in spite of it all, I'm able to grin,

When I think of where my get up has been.

91
WHERE PILOTS GO WHEN THEY DIE

A place where a guy can buy a cold beer for a friend and a comrade whose memory's dear;

A place where no doctor or lawyer can tread, nor management type would ere be caught dead;

Just a quaint little place, kind of dark, full of smoke, where they sing loud and love a good joke;

The kind of a place where a lady could go and feel safe and protected by the men she would know.

There must be a place where old pilots go when their paining is finished, and their airspeed is low,

Where whiskey is sold, and the women are young, and songs about flying and dying are sung.

Where you'd see all the fellows who had flown West before, and they'd call out your name as you came through the door. They would buy you a drink, if your thirst should be bad,

And relate to the others, "He was quite a good lad!"

And then through the mist, you'd spot an old guy not seen in years, though he taught you to fly. He'd nod his head and grin ear to ear,

And say, "Welcome, son, I'm pleased that you're here. Relax with a cool one and a well deserved rest – this is Heaven, my son – you've passed your last test".

92
TIME IN TYPE

[Type A/C - Flight Time / Number Built - Number Airworthy 2006]

N2S 90 hours / 10,000 – 1,000
SNV 33 / 11,537 – 50
SNJ 984 / 17,000 – 350
SNB 505 / 9,388 – 250
T34 34 / 1,300 – 120
T28 22 / 2,232 – 150
TBM 180 / 9,836 – 42
F6F 120 / 12,275 – 7
F8F 500 / 1,266 – 10
F4U 120 / 12,571 – 28
AD 100 / 3,180 – 19
A26 160 / 2,466 - 40
Other 190

Total Flight Time 3,038

First flight:
Aug 10, 1943 J3 Cub
at Albert Whited Airport, St. Petersburg, FL.

Last flight:
Jun 28. 1964 SNB
at NAS Atlanta, Marietta, GA

93
TYPE AIRCRAFT FLOWN

N2S Stearman

BT-13 Vultee "Vibrator"

T-34 Beech Bonanza (w/ modified empennage)

North American T-28

Twin Beech SNB

North American SNJ

Douglas A-26 (Navy JD)

AD-2 Douglas Skyraider

F4U Chance Vought Corsair

F6F Grumman Hellcat

TBM Grumman Avenger

F8F Grumman Bearcat

94
TYPE AIRCRAFT FLOWN

N2S Stearman

BT-13 Vultee "Vibrator"

T-34 Beech Bonanza (w/ modified empennage)

North American T-28

Twin Beech SNB

North American SNJ

Douglas A-26 (Navy JD-1)

AD-2 Douglas Skyraider

F4U Chance Vought F4U Corsair

F6F Grumman F6F Hellcat

TMB Grumman Avenger

F8F Grumman F8F Bearcat

95
IN RETROSPECT

In retrospect, (Hell! Every thing is in retrospect now), I marvel at the very active fun life I have enjoyed, especially the flying years, and how lucky I was to get the chance. I flew some of the best and hottest prop single seaters of the period. There was lots of horsepower and no co-pilot to make snide remarks.

Today the jets are so air conditioned, clean, quiet and easy to fly compared to the good old radials. When you started a radial there was a lot of smoke and clatter. Sometimes they caught fire. If you followed the pilot's handbook, it probably wouldn't start. You had to hold your mouth right. To start a jet, you just flick a few toggle switches.

Every time I see a big new jetliner I say to myself, "Show me how to start it. I'll fly it."

96
EPILOGUE

As I look back on my life, I was no different than most kids my age when I volunteered for WW II. I was just going with the flow. I am constantly aware that I could just as easily have wound up dead on Omaha Beach. I have come to the conclusion that there is no "mystery of life". It's really very simple, and can be summed up in five words – THE LUCK OF THE DRAW.

The average Navy pilot, despite the sometimes swaggering exterior, is very much capable of such feelings as love, affection, intimacy and caring. These feelings just don't involve anyone else.

CARTOONS FROM ENVELOPES OF LETTERS SENT HOME DURING FLIGHT TRAINING

NOW WE GOTTA GIT YOU CADETS IN GOOD SHAPE. LET'S SEE YA PUT SUMPIN IN IT. A LITTLE HARD WORK IS GOOD FOR YA. LET'S SEE YA HUSTLE!

?
!
HOOD
the "SCREAMIN' EAGLE"

(MIDDLE MAN IN A RIGHT ECHELON TIGHT FORMATION)

(INSTRUMENTS SQUADRON)

OVER WATER NAVIGATION CALLS FOR QUITE A WARDROBE!

DARK!
AINT IT?
NIGHT
FLYING
TOONITE

THOSE GUYS IN MY FLIGHT ARE JUST GONNA HAFTA AIM AT THE SLEEVE TARGET INSTEAD OF TH' TOW PLANE!

PART II

Have T-square, will travel

CONTENTS

Advice to Young Architects.

Warner Summers Ditzel Clients.

Building Types.

February 4, 1964 – December 31, 2003.

States of Registration

The Darkest Years of My Life Were Spent at Georgia Tech – Some surviving cartoons from the student paper *The Technique*

1
GET OUT OF TOWN

After I got out of Tech, in December 1949, (you don't graduate from Tech – you "get out") I worked for a small A&E firm, Smith and Hobbs, in the Peters Building near Five Points. My schoolmate, Van Vanover, got me the job and I went to work the day after graduating. When the Korean War started Van was recalled to active duty in the Air Force. The construction business began to slack off, and business at Smith and Hobbs also slacked off. Cleve Cail and I were the only architectural draftsmen, and it was obvious that the firm could not keep us both. I was single and Cleve had a wife and two kids; therefore, each day at lunch time Cleve and I would go to a different architectural firm to seek employment – for me.

One day we went to Griff Edwards's office in the Leows Grand Theater building. (The premier of *Gone with the Wind* was in the Loews Theater). The office was empty except for George Hampton eating his lunch at his drawing board. This was before Griff and John Portman teamed up and set the world on fire. I asked George if Griff needed a draftsman. He said no, but he thought Abreu and Robeson might need one.

The next day I went to Area and Robeson's office. Matt Jorgensen was in the reception area. I asked him if they needed someone. He said, "Mr. Abreu (pronounced "Uh-bray'-uh") is here today. I'll let you talk to him". Everyone in Atlanta incorrectly pronounced it "A-broo", so, I was not aware that I was talking to the big guy. He asked me, "How would you like to work in a bachelor's paradise?" I asked, "Where's that?" He said, "Sea Island." (That's where he lived – the office was in Brunswick). All my friends were in Atlanta and I was reluctant to leave, so I said, "Can I think about it?" Abreu said, "Yes, I'll give you five minutes".

This was a crossroad in my life. I had always gone with the flow, following the line of least resistance. I didn't know anyone in Brunswick. I thought to myself, I've always done it the easy way. This time I'll do it the hard way. I told him I would go.

Just think how different my life would have been, if I hadn't taken that fork in the road. I would never have met Betty. I asked her to marry me on the second date. Fifteen months later, we were married and lived happily ever after.

(Abreu was a colorful character. Robeson was a very talented, mean person)

2
GOODBYE, MR. ABREU

Working for architects Abreu & Robeson in Brunswick had its drawbacks. There were no breaks. The only time I got to take a break was when the bloodmobile came to town.

During the 18 months I lived in Brunswick I commuted to my Navy drill weekends on the Friday night train from Brunswick to Atlanta and on the Sunday night train from Atlanta back to Brunswick – sat up on the day coach both ways (sob).

On one of my drill weekends, Mr. Abreu asked me to drive Mrs. Abreu's new Cadillac to Atlanta where she was staying in their Philip Schutze designed house on West Paces Ferry at Habersham (now "The Southern Center for International Studies"). He told me, "It takes five hours to drive to Atlanta. I can make it in four. I want you to make it in six".

Just before Betty and I were to be married in June '52, I thought I had better ask for a raise. One day Mr. Abreu was in town, a fairly rare occurrence, and I asked to see him in his office. He was at his desk going over some papers. He didn't look up when I came in. I got my courage up and said, "Mr. Abreu, Betty Geiger and I are getting married next month. I was wondering if I could get a raise." Without looking up he asked, "How much are you making now?" I said, "Fifty dollars a week." Still looking at his papers he asked, "How much raise do you want?" I gulped and meekly said, "Five dollars a week?" After a moment's thought he said, "No, you're not worth it" (he was probably right). That was the end of the meeting. He never once looked at me – so Betty and I got married on fifty dollars a week. I had $10 in my pocket and owed Rich's about $300 for classical records.

I felt it would be safer to volunteer for the Korean War than to work for Abreu & Robeson – so I did, but that's another story.

3
THE SUMMER OF '63

In the summer of '63 I had been working with Heery and Heery for six years. George Heery was a great guy to work for. He gave you all the responsibility you were willing to take, and he never spoke an unkind word to me (even though there were occasions when he would have been justified). When I first went to work there in the fall of '57 he was very up front about the fact that it would always be a father and son partnership. That was OK with me, but as time went on, I realized that I would never be a partner, and when I was 50 and asked for a raise, what would I do if he said no?

I found myself doing projects for Heery that I was capable of doing on my own, but I felt the need for a partner. Alex Summers was George's administrative guy. I was in charge of production. George had trained us well. Alex seemed like a good fit as a partner. He was the most intelligent guy in the office, and I was going to need all the help I could get.

That summer of '63 I sat on the beach at St. Simons and pondered all this (it was the last two week vacation I ever got during my working years) and decided to approach Alex. When I suggested that we open our own office, he said yes.

We had an agreement with George that when our contract came up for review we would renew it, negotiate it, or terminate it. We were required to give two month's notice if we were leaving. Before we went in to talk to him we agreed not to talk to him separately, and we were leaving even if he tripled our salaries. He didn't.

We gave the two month's notice and continued working 100% for George until we left (on good terms), and did no moonlighting. We hit the streets cold. I had no savings, three kids, a mortgage* and – and no clients. I was 40 years old.

We rented a beat up unit at 5 Baltimore Place and proceeded to clean it up and get it in shape to serve as an architectural office. We entered the cold cruel world on February 4, 1964, and, as they say, the rest is history.

On the first day we were in business, we were walking down Forsyth Street near Ham Stockton's recently opened men's store. Just before we got in front of Ham's shop, a big bird "let go" and it hit Alex on his left shoulder. Alex, being a graduate of Davidson before he studied architecture at Tech exclaimed, "I've been shat upon!"

When we got to Ham's shop, we decided we would each buy a new suit as a gesture of confidence in the future. The big bird and the Ham Stockton new suits were good luck for us.

* The mortgage was on the 1,000 square foot house we bought for $11,500 with a G.I. Loan in 1955. It was one mile west of NAS Atlanta (now PDK).

4
I WAS NEVER INTO BASEBALL

I was never into baseball. I've been to two professional baseball games. The first was when we lived in Chicago and Dad, who loved baseball, took me to Wrigley Field when I was about four years old to see the Cubs play. The second was while I was at Tech, and I went to see the Atlanta Crackers play in the old ball park across from Big Sears (now City Hall East). Watching baseball on TV is for me, to repeat an old cliché, like watching paint dry. Some would compare it to flying – "long hours of boredom punctuated by moments of stark raving terror".

What I'm leading up to is small world stuff. After Alex and I opened our office, Ronald Gann came to our rescue. He was our first client. I had met Ronald when a bunch, fifteen to be exact, of Atlanta guys got together to form "Lazyfare". The idea was to build "a shack at the lake" on Lake Lanier, at Flowery Branch. I wasn't a native Atlantan, but was invited to join because I could draw the plans for the "shack" free. It turned out to be a much nicer place than a shack, so we could get a construction loan at Gainesville Savings and Loan cosigned by fifteen up and coming young men.

Ronald was the head of the C&S Trust Real Estate department. He had a client who owned a roofing business and needed a structure to cover roofing materials. The location of this structure was to be right field home run distance from the Atlanta Crackers' ball park.

It was just after the firm started in February 1964. I went out to the site to check it out one really cold and windy afternoon. This was a big deal. The structure was to be approximately 18 x 24 with a roof and one wall. I told you it was a big deal. Having recently worked on large projects for Heery, it was quite an adjustment to draw the plans for this "unusual" project.

Ronald was a good client. He sent the $60 check almost in return mail. If we hadn't needed the money, we would have framed it and put it on the wall in the front office, but we cashed it. We needed the money.

5
STARTING OFF WITH CLASS

Our first big job was Hennessy Cadillac on Piedmont Road, just over a mile from where I live now. Back in 1965, the only Cadillac dealer in the state was Capitol Cadillac across from the Biltmore Hotel on West Peachtree. It was the Capitol Cadillac show room that was used by the Naval Aviation Cadet Selection Board to test candidates for the Navy V5 flight training program. It was there that my Naval career started.

Bob Hennessey was in Detroit with "GM Motors Holding", whatever that was. He convinced the right people there to let him open another Cadillac dealership in competition with Capitol Cadillac. He somehow made connection with Pat Dinkins, a contractor friend of ours. He wanted Pat to build his new dealership. We had done some design-build projects with Pat, and we would design Hennessey's new building, if the deal went through.

You couldn't find two nicer guys to work with. Bob flew us to Akron to look at a dealership he thought had a better traffic flow in the service area than the usual Atlanta dealerships had. We studied the building and agreed with Bob that it worked very efficiently. With Pat in the picture, the design was practical cost-wise and we made it a better looking dealership than any other in Atlanta at that time.

When we got the property plat, we discovered that the real estate agent had sold Bob a piece of land with 15 feet less depth than was shown. Piedmont Road had been widened and the Realtor, Jim B---n, had never told Bob that the plat showed more land than there was. In spite of that, our plan worked and the building was built with <u>zero</u> construction problems.

The fledgling architects now had their first prestige project. The building is even more prestigious now. Mark Hennessy and his brothers have since added several different car manufacturer dealerships, Honda, Mazda, Lexus, Pontiac, Land Rover, Porsche and GMC Truck, throughout metro Atlanta, and they have recently converted the original Cadillac building to their Jaguar and Rolls Royce dealership. You might say my architectural career started off with class.

I wrote Mark a letter congratulating him and his brothers on what they had built. He wrote back a letter I will always cherish:

HENNESSY

AUTOMOBILE COMPANIES

3040 Piedmont Road • Atlanta, GA 30305
404-261-5700 • Fax 404-240-4496

MARK W. HENNESSY

November 1, 2002

Mr. Jim Warner
411 Pinetree
Atlanta, GA 30305-3416

Dear Jim,

I can't tell you how much your letter means. You were one of the first "adults" I had a chance to work with who treated me like an "adult". You were always very respectful of my input, would counsel when a 26 year olds ideas wouldn't work and yet always encouraged me to get the most out of our collective thoughts.

One of the great rewards the dynamic growth of Atlanta, a wonderful customer base and our very special employees has given me has been the opportunity to grow our business. I think I have had more fun envisioning, designing and building our new facilities than any other part of the business.

Your first design had a tremendous impact on our initial business and your friendship has had a lasting impact on my career. Thank you for your thoughts and please call on me if I can ever be of any assistance.

Sincerely,

Mark

Cadillac LEXUS JAGUAR GMC TRUCK
HONDA mazda LAND ROVER PONTIAC

6
JIMMY ROBESON. OUTSTANDING ARCHITECT.

Jimmy Robeson was a superb salesman. When I was working for Abreu & Robeson in Brunswick back in 1951, I was a camera nut. I took pictures of the local public housing, which for the time was not all that bad, thanks to good landscaping, and pictures of other architectural gems like run down unpainted wood houses (You know how unpainted wood attracts photographers). Robeson became aware of the pictures I had taken and had me put together a slide presentation showing public housing he had designed and how much better it was than the shacks.

He took me with him to St. Mary's one night to meet with a group of the city fathers to promote another Housing Authority and Public Housing project for the firm. His approach was to get the top men in a community together, tell them how great they were, how much public housing the town rated, set them up as the Housing Authority and fill out all the complex government forms for them.

When we showed the slides in St. Mary's he told how, before his getting public housing for Brunswick, the Boy Scouts in his troop came to the scout meetings in ragged clothes and unsmiling dirty faces. After he got the public housing for Brunswick to replace the shacks, they came to the meeting clean, well dressed and smiling. He forgot to mention that the pictures were all taken about the same time. He also forgot to tell them that he was never a Scout master and that the shacks were still there.

Abreu & Robeson made a fortune designing housing projects. There was a map in the office with little red pins showing the location of all the projects they had designed in Georgia. There must have been well over a hundred pins in the map.

During trips on which I accompanied him he would give me very sound advice. He took great pride in telling me how he made considerable money by buying up distressed property from poor guys, then later selling the property for a good profit.

He was always ready to give me guidance in the drafting room. I was doing the working drawings for an elementary school in Brunswick for minority students. The school was an "open corridor school". The classrooms were connected by a covered walk along the side of the classrooms. The end of a classroom wing was a blank red brick wall. In my innocence I was sketching an end elevation with a modest brick pattern to soften its dullness. Robeson walked by my drawing board, looked at the sketch and asked, "Did you do this?" I said, "Yes, sir". Then he gave me his kindly advice. He said, "I don't want to see anything like this in this drafting room again. If you can't do anything else, sit on your hands!", and walked out.

Robeson and Betty's dad played golf together frequently. One day just before Betty and I were to get married he told Dad, "Jim Warner will never amount to anything". That was so thoughtful of him. He was that kinda guy. Betty married me anyway, and Dad gave us his blessing.

Then there was the time I asked for a raise just before we were to get married. I was making $75 a week, and meekly asked Mr. Abreu for a $5 a week raise. He thought for a moment and said, "No. You're not worth it".

I was in the Naval Air Reserve. Shortly after we were married, I volunteered for active duty during the Korean "war". I felt it was less dangerous than working for an outstanding architect.

7
SIXTY PERCENT, WARNER?

While Summers and I gave 100% to Heery during our two month notice, we would go nights to our future architectural office at 5 Baltimore Place and try to get it in decent shape. We steamed layer after layer of wallpaper off the walls. We then put jute, that's cheap low grade burlap, on the walls (it looked better than the wallpaper) above the chair rail. We bought three pairs of sawhorses, three metal drafting stools and three flush doors, to be used as drafting boards, from FABRAP for $60 – we were thinking positive about expansion with that third drafting position. A card table served as a front office desk. So any correspondence that left the office would look legit, we dug up $600 and bought a brand new IBM Selectric typewriter. We also bought a cheap cardboard plan file in case we got a job.

The back door led to a parking lot that was about twelve feet below our floor level. Steps to the parking lot had long ago disappeared. Still, we were concerned about security. One night I suggested we test the lock on the door. I stood outside on an eight inch threshold twelve feet about the ground, in the pitch black dark and closed the door. I told Alex to lock it and I would check it.

I tried the door and the lock was secure. I said, "It's OK, Alex. You can open the door." No answer. "Alex. You can open the door now." No answer. After a third request to unlock the door, a small voice from inside said, "60%, Warner?"

Actually it was 50-50 all the way. On one occasion, for some reason I don't recall, the firm received a one dollar bill in an envelope addressed to Warner & Summers. When Alex opened the envelope he didn't say a word, he just tore the dollar bill in half and handed me half.

8
OUR FIRST DAY IN BUSINESS

It was our first day "in business" ... February 4, 1964. One of the secretaries at Heery's had a friend, a Mr. Lewyen (pronounced Loo-un), who had purchased several acres of land in partnership with five of his friends for the purpose of building their homes. The land was in beautiful rolling hills and woods.

Alex and I were going to meet with our first prospect the night of our very first day in practice. It felt like a good start. On the way to meet with Mr. and Mrs. Lewyen, we discussed how we would handle our first interview. We agreed that, no matter what happened, if either one of us didn't want to agree to something, we wouldn't have to discuss it. Whatever the one decided, the other would go along.

We had a nice visit discussing the scope of the Lewyen house design. When it came to fee talk time, we said our fee would be the standard, at the time, eight percent. Mr. Lewyen said that was too much and suggested a much lower fee on the grounds that we would meet the other five prospects and get a lot more work (an old ploy). We declined. Then he asked if we wanted to discuss his proposal with each other in private. We said we didn't have to. We couldn't take the project for less than eight percent. At that point we bid the Lewyens goodnight.

That incident set the tone for our thirty-year partnership, which was we would do nothing if one or the other was against whatever we were deciding to do.

When Summers and I started our architectural practice in 1964, we had a lawyer draw up a partnership agreement. When we sold the firm to three very talented hard working employees 30 years later, we had not yet signed the partnership agreement.

We didn't have to.

Summers was the ant and I was the grasshopper. When I wanted the firm to buy me a BMW, he wisely said no. Because he was a frugal person he managed the business of the firm so well that during our 30 year partnership we never borrowed a nickel to operate, and he never let me buy a BMW.

9
THE CONFERENCE TABLE

I left active duty at Quonset Point in December 1954 after my two year tour of duty. After WWII, I left active duty in December 1945 after my three year tour of duty. December was a good month.

My old Tech classmate, Van Vanover, was in Atlanta working at Vanover & Smith. The office was on Peachtree at Peachtree Place. It was just Vanover and Smith. Van asked me to come to work there with him. Smith was not able to really work at being an architect due to some physical problems, so Van needed help.

I took Betty to Brunswick to stay while I went back to the drawing board and looked for a place for us to stay in Atlanta. Just like when I got out of Tech and Van got me a job the next day, he got me a job almost the next day after I got out of the Navy.

Van was really snowed under with a couple of projects. We worked 'til almost midnight every night. We were so busy I didn't have time to look for a place to rent so I could get Betty to Atlanta. Van and Ruth had their son, Gary, in a two bedroom apartment in Colonial Homes, so I couldn't stay at Van's. As a result, I slept on the conference room table. I'd go to Van's to clean up and sometimes eat supper. This went on for over a month.

One day a manufacturer's rep, Ben Swift, from Beck and Gregg, the big hardware wholesaler, was in the office and he mentioned that there were two houses for sale near the Naval Air Station. They were selling for $11,500 on a 3 ½ % 25 year GI loan. Closing costs – $49! At lunch the next day I dashed out to look at the houses. The location was on Parkridge Drive, one mile west of the NAS east-west runway. I picked the one on the left.

I spent about 15 minutes looking at it and went back to the office, contacted the real estate company handling the sales, and bought 2889 Parkridge Drive. I finally got Betty to Atlanta, and no more conference room table.

10
BRASSTOWN BALD

The last project I was the architect on at Heery's was the observation tower and visitors center at Brasstown Bald in north Georgia. I was reviewing working drawings drawn by Tex Ritter (honest, that was his real name). Tex was one of those guys who were always having bad luck, like he's going home for Christmas and the trunk on his car leaks and ruins his entire little daughter's Christmas presents. Stuff like that.

I was going over Tex's detail of the ship's ladder that led to the observation tower. Summers walked by, looked at it and agreed that the detail didn't work. I told Tex why it didn't work and suggested that he go back to the drawing board and change it. He picked up the tracing and went back to his board. A few minutes later he came back and handed Summers a folded piece of scratch paper. It read, "To whom it may concern, I quit".

He had his check in five minutes and was out of there.

11
"WHAT DO YOU DO?"

The firm was selected to design several branch banks for the First Georgia Bank (which has been "absorbed" by one of the big banks). We were to make a presentation of our first design to the board of directors. The chairman of the board was former governor, Carl Sanders.

I took Jim Ditzel and Scott Ward, two of the brightest young architects in the firm, with me to the meeting. They had done most of the design on the project and were very familiar with it. Because I have always felt more comfortable one on one rather than before a large group, I decided to have Jim Ditzel make the presentation. He was great. I sat in the meeting relaxed and just watching.

As the meeting broke up, Carl Sanders turned to me and said, "What do you do?" I pointed at Ditzel and said, "I pay him."

12
ALL THE BEER HE CAN DRINK

I met Herman Russell at the Atlanta Airport when the Eastern Airline Cargo Facility, that Warner Summers designed, was being built by Holder-Russell. After it was complete, Herman called me to talk about designing a warehouse for his Coors beer distribution company to be built by his construction company. I liked Herman, who was a really nice guy, so I made arrangements to come to his office to discuss the project. The meeting was in his big conference room with big overstuffed chairs around a huge conference table. All the chairs were filled with his top people, average weight 300 pounds.

Shortly after the meeting started, Herman asked me to step into his office just off the conference room. When we sat down by his desk he asked me what my fee would be. I did some rapid mental calculations, which was my seat of the pants way to arrive at a fee; I pulled a number out of the air and came up with a lump sum. Herman said it was too much, so I pulled a lower number out of the air, and we had an agreement.

When we walked back into the conference room, Herman put his arm around me and said to the group, "Jim says he'll do the job for all the beer he can drink."

13
I DON'T PAY YOU ENOUGH TO BE PERFECT

John Sims was the head of the Georgia State School Building Authority. Any school or college built in the state came under his jurisdiction before and during construction. He was the client and paid our fee. John Sims did not like change orders. Before I opened my own office, I was with Heery & Heery, and on one occasion, I was the project architect on an elementary school in Athens.

After the job was under construction, a problem came up that I thought required a change order. When I requested Mr. Sims to approve the change order, he wouldn't approve it. He said that there were only three reasons for a change order. One - Unforeseen site conditions encountered during excavation. Two - The right of the sovereign, like the Fire Marshall ordering a change, and Three - The architect made a mistake. I bristled at three. He noticed and said, "Mr. Warner, if you make a mistake, admit it, and I will write the change order and I will pay for the change order. I don't pay you enough to be perfect." Later in my career, when I tried that line on Bob Vlasic, he didn't agree.

14
GONNA BE STRUCK BY LIGHTNING

Alan Salzman was a draftsman at Abreu & Robeson. On one of the projects he was working on he had drawn a sheet full of details and notes. Tucked away on the sheet he had lettered, "Help! I'm being held prisoner in Abreu & Robeson's drafting room." The job went out for bids with the note on it.

Alan and Jerry Cooper started their own firm, which later became Cooper Salzman & Carry. Then Alan spun off to work alone. Cooper Cary went on to do really good big work all over the country.

I designed three indoor soft courts for the Standard Club. When construction was complete I went one day to watch the tennis activity, and to see if the contractor had finished the punch list. Jerry Cooper was playing in a men's doubles match. I turned to one of the members next to me and said, "I didn't know Jerry could play tennis". The member said, "If you'll watch him, you'll see that he can't". Actually Jerry was a good tennis player.

One Easter morning, Charlie Jinks, David Blackshear and I were having trouble getting a fourth for our regular Sunday morning game at Cherokee. Charlie called Jerry who is Jewish and couldn't care less about playing tennis on Easter morning. As Jerry walked onto the court he said, "I can't believe I'm going to play tennis with three Christians who are gonna be struck by lightning!"

15
I DON'T THINK WE CAN AFFORD TO EXPERIENCE HIM

Warner & Summers had designed two Addressograph-Multigraph Distribution Centers – one in Dallas and one in Atlanta. Pat Dinkins built the one in Dallas, and Holder built the one in Atlanta. Holder's field superintendent was Junior Hales, just a good old country boy. He seemed too nice to be a field superintendent.

The project manager was Joe ---, Jr., a new employee at Holder's, and he was, to say the least, not very sharp. One day I was in the construction shack talking to Junior. I asked him, "How is Joe doing?" Junior said, "Well, Mister Warner, he just needs a little experience, (pause) but I don't think we can afford to experience him."

One other time I came out to the job and Junior was worried. He said he tried to get in touch with me to make an urgent architect's decision, but I was out of the office, so he had to make the decision. He briefed me, and told me what he had decided to solve the problem. I said, "Junior, I like it." Junior said, "Mister Warner, if you like it, I'm crazy about it."

Holder never sent Junior out of town on a project. Junior somehow convinced Holder that he was afraid to fly. Junior was a very cagey fellow.

Holder's corporate color was blue. Every superintendent was issued a blue company pickup truck. Junior always wanted a red pickup truck, but Holder insisted that he drive a blue one like the other superintendents did.

When Junior retired, Holder <u>gave</u> him a red pickup truck.

16
NOW THAT YOU EXPLAIN IT TO ME

When the Trust Company Bank built the TCB Tower near Five Points it had invested the max amount of money the Feds allowed to be invested in real estate. The bank needed more branch banks, but was restricted from building them. It was 1968. Bob Holder came up with a solution. Holder would build and own the needed branches and the Trust Company would lease them from Holder. I had designed several buildings for Holder and, if the bank went for his plan, I would design the prototype. The plan was to build twelve branches.

Enter Bud Taylor. Bud was the Senior VP in charge of Branch Acquisition. He was a great decision maker. I had made some freehand sketches to scale that I thought met the requirements, but Bud would have to approve them. I asked Bud to come by the office and look at the sketches. Bud breezed in that afternoon, took a quick look at the sketches for about two minutes and said, "That's good. Do it that way", and left.

I refined the plan and had a rendering prepared for approval of the exterior design. I had been requested to have the design recall (that's arch- talk for "look like") the main office tower. I said that it would be difficult to make a one story brick building recall a 26 story white marble building. Then I remembered the treatment of the 3 story element which housed the main banking floor at the tower. It had square marble elements around the fascia, so I designed repeating stucco elements on my fascia similar to the marble ones on the main office. I had the basic fascia design and two overlays showing alternate designs on a rendering. Bud liked the basic fascia design. Then he said, "I think we ought to present this to some of the branch managers for their comments."

He set up a meeting with twelve managers. I explained the plans and the comments were many – and negative. The meeting was getting out of control. After I had explained my reasons for the design, they all came around to agree that the plan was fine. Then I put up the rendering. I showed the three fascia designs and the group immediately divided into three different opinion groups. After a very active discussion Bud said, "Hold it. Mr. Stern (the top TCB guy) likes this one," and he pointed to the one with the stucco "elements". There was a pause and then a voice in the back of the room said, "Now that you explain it to me, I like that one, too." Everyone now agreed.

As we left the meeting, Bud turned to me and said, "I'm glad we did that. Now, if something goes wrong, I won't get all the arrows."

P.S. I retired in 1993. At the time of this writing it is 2007. The firm, Warner Summers Ditzel Benefield Ward & Associates, is still designing banks for The Trust Company a.k.a. SunTrust.

17
HOW TO RUN A DESIGN SESSION

The first project Warner & Summers did for Printpack was in 1965. It was a 20,000 square foot addition to their original 20,000 square foot office and production plant. It was a design-build project with Holder, the contractor and me, the architect. I remember the first meeting as if it were yesterday. We were in a small conference room next to the loading dock. The conference table was a folding table with a masonite top. Present were Holder, Erskin Love, Jim Smith (Printpack Art Director), Arthur Harris (plant engineer), and me. I remember Jim Smith didn't seem very friendly and I thought, "Am I gonna have trouble with him?" – we turned out to be very good friends. The first project went well from my standpoint.

Shortly after that first project Arthur Harris retired, and Gus Franchini became the Plant Engineer. As Printpack continued to expand, Gus became Director of Engineering with assistant engineers reporting to him. Gus had a great relationship with his engineers. I remember many design meetings with Gus' engineers and my engineers setting the criteria for a new plant. His engineers would argue a point with him, expressing their opinions very forthrightly – unafraid to disagree with their boss. After all sides were heard, Gus made the decision. That's the way to run a design session.

Over the years, Warner-Summers designed several plants for Printpack in Atlanta, Villa Rica, and Texas, and Gus and I became very good friends. I'm proud to say that forty years later, the firm is still designing plants for Printpack.

18
WE NEED THIS JOB DESPERATELY

Bob Holder and I flew to Chicago chasing after a proposed Brach candy "factory" in Nebraska. Brach's only facility at the time was a five story building in Chicago. After being shown through the entire operation (every desk in the place had a jar of assorted candies on it), we broke for lunch in the company cafeteria. Bob was sitting next to a Brach vice-president . The VP asked Bob, "How's business in Atlanta?" Bob said, "Business is GREAT, but WE NEED THIS JOB DESPERATELY." Typical Holder sense of humor.

We didn't get the job.

Some years later I did a lot of work in Georgia with First Atlanta Bank, later known as Wachovia. I worked for the facilities guy, Claude Head. Working for Claude wasn't work, it was fun.

I did a couple of new branch banks in Atlanta and a bunch of additions and alterations to existing branch banks in north and South Georgia. I would go with Claude, Larry Whaley, and Vic Granthum to analyze the situation. I would make a quick sketch of the floor plan and Larry and I would take measurements which I would be able to use to make a preliminary drawing for further study.

None of the branch managers had ever met me, but most of them knew Claude. During a visit, Claude and I would be talking with the manager about what changes were needed, when Claude would casually ask me, "How's business in Atlanta, Jim?" Then I would steal Bob Holder's great line and reply, "Claude, business is GREAT! – but WE NEED THIS JOB DESPARATELY! Claude and I pulled that line at every branch and had a lot of fun with it.

19
QUIT WHEN YOU ARE AHEAD

At Tech, Dr. Boris Bogaslavsky (Mister Chips with a Russian accent) was my professor in a "Strength of Materials" course. He frequently shared stories to illustrate things we should be aware of in life. One day he told us that we should always quit when we were ahead, and he told us this story:

Bogey, as we affectionately called him, was an expert witness for the defense in the Tacoma Narrows Bridge failure case. Trying to destroy an unfriendly expert witness, as bulldog lawyers always will, the opposing attorney asked, "Doctor Bogaslavsy, is it true that you were one of the structural engineers who designed the Tacoma Narrows Bridge that COLLAPSED!?" Bogey replied, "Yes."

This is when the lawyer should have quit when he was ahead. "And, Doctor Bogaslavsky, what part of the bridge did you design before it COLLAPSED!?" To which Bogey coolly replied, "The foundations, which were reused when the bridge was rebuilt."

Bogey left Tech to work for the Anglo American Oil Company in 1950. His students had a farewell dinner for him before he left. I remember he told us not to "waste". Always design economical solutions as we practice our professions. On his first visit back to the States we had a luncheon for him at the Farm Restaurant on Roswell Road (no longer there – replaced by a high rise condo). He returned to the States as a consultant to the Department of Defense, studying available Russian publications to advise the best way to destroy a Russian military installation (ironic).

As a kid, with his little brother on his mother's back, he escaped from the Bolsheviks via China where his mother did menial work to make enough money to get to this country.

At Tech, when the quarter started, professors would limit the number of students they would accept in a class to thirty. Not Bogey. He would take all comers, sometimes as many as sixty. At the end of the first week, he knew every student by his first name.

20
GUMMY ANDERSON

Abreu & Robeson's office in Brunswick was pretty small. Robeson, Gummy Anderson (an Associate and all around good guy), a secretary and me, a mere draftsman. I worked under Gummy, producing working drawings.

One day Gummy and I were discussing how to solve a particular detail problem. Our opinions were quite different. Finally Gummy said, "We'll do it my way. One of us has to be boss, and it might as well be me."

21
MISSISSIPPI PICKLE FACTORY

When we did the Mississippi "pickle factory", in Greenville. Bob Vlasic called me and said that the project would be financed with Municipal Revenue Bonds and an Owner Architect contract would be required. We hadn't had or needed a contract with Vlasic on previous projects. I said I'd send him a copy of the standard AIA Owner Architect Contract document.

When he got it he called me and said, "Jim, if I have my lawyer's look this over it will be months before they will get it back to me with all sorts of revisions. Let's not sign it and set it aside in case we really have to sign it". That was OK with me. He set it aside and we never signed it. Most of the work we did was done on a handshake or a simple one page letter describing the scope of the project and the amount of our fee.

We designed forty furniture stores for Haverty Furniture Company, from Texas to Virginia – never had a contract. There was a minor problem on only one of them. Our insurance carrier called Alex, the partner in charge of Haverty projects, and asked him to send them a copy of our contract with the Haverty Furniture Company. I remember Alex's reply verbatum, "Contract – with Rawson Haverty? We don't have a contract with Rawson Haverty. We do business like gentlemen in the South". That was the end of the conversation.

Summers was a really cool guy. We did several buildings for Aaron Rents (a furniture rental company). It was Design-Build with Aderhold Construction Company, the contractor. The fee was really cheap. The Aaron Rents project manager thought he would make some Brownie points with his boss, Charlie Laudermilk, by squeezing our fee some more. Summers wrote him a letter the body of which was just one sentence, "We have come to the conclusion that it is to our mutual best interest for you to get another architect". Is that cool, or what?

22
BERNIE ABRAMS

Warner & Summers designed a number of bank projects for what was then the Fulton National Bank. The bank always negotiated the construction contracts with A. R. Abrams Construction Company.

We always did a good job, and we hit it off with Bernie Abrams, the president of the company. One day Bernie asked me to design a big warehouse addition to his main facility on Jones Avenue in Atlanta. It was three stories and was about 50,000 square feet per floor. After describing the scope of the work, he asked me what the fee would be. I would furnish the architectural and structural design and Abrams Construction would furnish the electrical and mechanical design, using subs they worked with all the time. I thought for a minute and figured a fair fee would be about $50,000.

I said, "Bernie, let's make it $50,000 or 2% of the construction cost, whichever is the *lesser*." Then he thought for a minute and said, "No. Let's make it $50,000 or 2% whichever is the *greater*." Our contract was one simple sentence. We didn't even have to write it down. That's the kinda guy Bernie was.

The project went forward with no problems, and everybody was happy. It turned out that 2% was $5,000 *greater* than $50,000.

Bernie was a West Point graduate and went to Korea as a 2nd Lt. He got shot up so badly that they were going to amputate both his legs. His dad found out about it, pulled some strings and went to Korea to save Bernie's legs. His dad succeeded and Bernie's legs were saved. He got a medical discharge, and was able to walk, but with a limp, the rest of his life.

Fred Ellis was one of Bernie's project managers. Best I ever worked with. He had a rubber stamp that he would put on a drawing, just for fun. It read, "If this note is not on the drawing you are looking at, you are looking at the wrong drawing." ... I got one for myself to stamp on shop drawings.

23
THEY BOUGHT THE JET

When I was in practice I designed many industrial buildings and process plants with Holder Construction Company as a Design-Build team. One of the clients was Vlasic Foods. Bob Holder and Bob Vlasic were friends, having met in The Young Presidents Club.

How Vlasic Foods got started is an interesting story. Bob Vlasic's dad, Joe Vlasic, started out working for a Polish guy in Detroit driving a truck, delivering milk. One day it was so cold that Joe left the engine running for fear of not getting the truck started again if he turned the ignition off. His boss found this out and fired Joe for "wasting gas"... so Joe got his own truck and started a route of his own, getting his bulk milk from the Borden Company. When he got more customers than he could handle, he bought another truck and hired a driver. He got more and more trucks and hired more and more drivers as time went by.

One day some Corporate "suits" from Borden were in town and asked the local Borden people about all the little green trucks they had seen delivering milk. They were told that they were Joe Vlasic's and that he was buying his bulk milk from Borden.

On their next visit to Detroit, the "suits" became concerned about all the competition, so they bought Joe out. Joe, who was in his eighties at the time, told me this story as we drove to Imlay City in his convertible Mercedes. Then he told me, "They bought me out for five million bucks, and all I had was fifty trucks".

Joe had to do something else, so he started putting a Vlasic label on pickles he bought from a local "pickle factory". He began to sell lots of Vlasic Pickles to chain stores. One day one of his customers asked him if he had a pickle processing plant. He didn't, but he said he did, so he had to get one. He bought a beat up plant in Imlay City, Michigan, and became an honest man.

When his son, Bob, got out of college he began to expand the business. It became Vlasic Foods. Bob made a deal with MacDonalds and sold them all the pickles that went into their burgers. Business could only get better.

Enter Bob Holder and Jim Warner. Vlasic needed a big new plant, and, because he and Holder were buddies, Holder would build it and I would design it. The new plant was a state of the art pickle processing plant in Millsboro, Delaware. Bob Vlasic was very hands on during the design process and was a delight to work with. He could make a critical decision in about 30 seconds.

Next I designed another state of the art plant in Greenville, Mississippi, an addition to the beat up plant in Imlay City and Vlasic's corporate headquarters on 14 Mile Road in Detroit.

A little side anecdote – Holder had a Sabreliner corporate jet. I got to go places first class, and they paid me to do it. Bob Vlasic wanted to have his own corporate jet. His board of directors debated the question extensively. Old Joe was on the board and was dead set against it. When they asked him why he was against it he said, "Every time we make a corporate decision that will cost a lot of money we'll say, 'Well, why not? (pause) We bought the jet!" They bought the jet just the same.

After all this great expansion, Bob Vlasic sold Vlasic Foods to Campbell Soups for 40 million dollars and a seat on their board. I never saw him again.

24
SATTELMEYER

We designed ten industrial plants for Reliance Electric Company, from North Carolina to Texas. The CEO was Emory Orahood, a superb executive. His approach to management was – give a man a job to do and let him do it and leave him alone – and if he messes up, fire him and give the job to the next guy.

At one point in his career he left Reliance for a top position with another company, but was still sought after by Reliance, which had headquarters in Cleveland. They really wanted him back as CEO. He finally agreed to come back if he could continue to live in Atlanta and commute to Cleveland at company expense. It was agreed and he had long week ends in Atlanta and was in Cleveland in the middle of the week. Now to the point of my anecdote.

Emory put a guy named Bob Sattlemeyer in charge of site selection and new plant construction. The first time I met Bob was when Reliance was contemplating a building in Columbus, Ohio, that I would design and Holder would build if his price was right. I came away from that first meeting thinking there was no way I could work with this rough as a cob tough guy.

Orahood had given Sattlemeyer total authority on the project. Holder's price was too high, so we didn't do the Columbus plant, but Holder sharpened his pencil and we began to do more and more Reliance manufacturing plants. We did ten plants in the Sunbelt.

As I worked with Sattlemeyer, I began to appreciate what a gem he was to work with. He knew how to make decisions. When you asked him for a decision, you better be ready to write down the answer, because you had the answer instantly. He didn't have to check with anybody. He was out of his office one week when I was doing a plant for him in Texas. I had developed a list of ten questions on which he had to make a decision. I called him when he got back in his office and had the answers in about three minutes.

I learned a lot working with Bob Sattlemeyer. 1.) Don't be afraid to make a decision, and 2.) Don't judge a person by your first meeting. Bob and I became close friends and stayed in touch long after we both retired.

25
STEAK AND BURGER DINNER

I have a very good friend, John Stuart McKenzie, who was with Stein Printing Company, and was, at one time, an editorial cartoonist for the Atlanta Journal. He is a class guy. He makes sure that you spell it *Stuart* and not *Stewart*.

He always wears his kilts at Christmas functions. He told me that a lady once asked him what was worn under the kilt, and he replied, "Nothing, Madam. Everything is in perfect working order".

He was in my Kiwanis Club. Every year the club had a steak and burger dinner for poor black kids. The kids got the steak and the Kiwanians got the burger. At one of these dinners, John was sitting next to a little kid who was very embarrassed that he didn't know how to cut his steak with a knife. John said, "I did a very gracious thing. (pause) I ate the steak".

John was a Canadian and flew Wellingtons in the RCAF out of England. They did night bombing. He said their bombers didn't fly in mass formation bombing when the lead plane dropped its bombs like our B-17's did in the "precision daylight bombing" campaign. Each RAF bomber got to the target on it's own from different directions and altitudes. When there were large numbers on a mission he told me, "If the air got smooth, you knew you were lost".

26
THE CORPS

I made a trip to the Savannah Corps of Engineers hoping, in my ignorance, to obtain some work with the Corps. I had read in *The Commerce Business Daily* that prior work with the Corps was not a prerequisite. In my meeting with the top Engineer, I asked him if that were true. He was an honest man. He said that it wasn't true but that the Corps preferred to work with firms that had done work with them before and knew the way the Corps liked to do business.

I told him that I certainly understood that – no problem. As I left I gave him one of my business cards, on the back of which was a Daschielle Hammit quote in small print that was printed there just for fun.

> Associate with well mannered people and your manners will improve.
>
> Run with decent folk and your decent instincts will be strengthened.
>
> Keep the company of bums and you will become a bum.
>
> Hang around with rich people and you will end up picking up the check and dying broke.

About six months later I paid him a follow up visit to see if the Corps policy had changed. I walked in and introduced myself, "I'm Jim Warner". He said, "Oh, yes. I have your card right here". He reached over on his desk and produced my business card. I guess he thought the message on the back was worth saving. I had found a way to get a prospect to keep my business card.

I didn't get any work, though. It was just as well. I had been told by engineers who had done Corps work that you really lost money on the first few projects before you caught on to their system.

27
OUR DESIGN STINKS

When Heery's office was at Peachtree and 17th, I was approached by Tomberlin and Sheets to come to work for them. Their office was at Pershing Point, in the basement of an old house. I was flattered so I agreed to meet with them after work one day. When I saw their drafting room with rough stone walls and almost a dirt floor, I decided I didn't want to work in a place like that.

There was a drug store a couple of doors away from Heery's office. I would sometimes go there for an afternoon break (not every afternoon). One day a few weeks later, I walked in and saw Tommy Tomberlin and Frank Sheets sitting in a booth drinking coffee. They looked very depressed. They asked me to join them. I sat down and asked why they looked so unhappy. Tommy said, "Jim, let's face it, our design stinks. We need to hire a good designer". At least they were facing the truth.

Chuck Robisch who I had worked with at Heery & Heery was one of the most talented designers I ever knew. He was currently working for Tom Bradbury. I told Tommy about Chuck and suggested that he contact him. Tommy met with Chuck and offered him a position as their designer. Chuck made the change and went on to be a partner for the rest of his career.

28
WE ALWAYS HAD WORK

During the 30 years I was with the firm, we always had work. It was thin at first, but we grew as the years passed and were blessed with first rate clients – with only a few exceptions. We never had a problem collecting our fees, except from one lawyer client, and from Zayre. We were also lucky not to have had to "entertain" prospects. We never spent a nickel on "entertainment". Our work came through word of mouth.

At one time we had a very big work load. Ditzel (we had three Jim's working together at that time – Jim Warner, Jim Ditzel and Jim Finney. Everyone addressed the Jim's by their last name so, if somebody said, "Hey Jim" three people wouldn't stop working to answer) and I were discussing the situation, and I asked him, "How are we going to produce all this work?" He said, "We'll just have to work overtime". In the early days I worked seven days a week sometimes, and I didn't like to ask the guys to work overtime, because time with their families was too important. I told Ditzel, "I don't want to work overtime! I've done that!" Then he asked, "Why do you have to work overtime?" I said, "To set an example". Then he spoke the words that I will never forget. He said, "Let <u>me</u> set the example". That tells you the kind of terrific guy he is.

The firm became Warner Summers & Ditzel, and then Warner Summers Ditzel Benefield Ward & Associates, Inc. (WSDBW). Is that a mouthful, or what? ... Sounds like a law firm.

29
JIM WARNER MEMORIAL RAILROAD DOCK

We did a big manufacturing plant for Hoover Ball and Bearing Corporation (later known as Hoover Universal) in Athens, Tennessee. The plant produced steel seat frames for GM, Ford, Chrysler and Volkswagen. They had the market sewed up. I asked one of the Hoover VP's how long it took them to feel the effects of an auto manufacturer's strike. He said, "Three days".

Holder was the contractor, Fred Holbrook was his project manager, and Jim Wilkerson was the field superintendent. The plant had no storage areas to store the seat frames until they could be shipped. They didn't need any. A 400 foot long railroad spur came into the plant, and the frames were put directly into the railroad cars and shipped when all the cars were loaded. Hoover had a very efficient operation.

The loading dock was a 400 foot long, twelve inch thick, four foot high reinforced concrete "wall". Having designed buildings served by rail before, I knew all the standard required clearances (clear height was 22 feet from top of rail. Clearance on the dock side was six feet and on the opposite side eight feet from the centerline of the tracks); however, being the cautious person that I am (that's a laugh), I called the L&N Railroad office in Athens to double check. They confirmed my numbers.

About six weeks before the plant had to be operational, two Tennessee Public Service Commission inspectors visited the plant and informed Jim Wilkerson that they would not allow a train to enter the building. They had an obscure regulation that the dock had to be seven feet from the centerline. This was a major problem. The Hoover representative didn't want seven feet from the centerline. He said it would be unsafe to have that much space between the dock and the railroad cars. The PSC guys didn't care. It says seven feet in their regulations, not six feet. I missed the small print.

I was in big trouble. I went to an attorney in Athens to get him to request a waiver, the Hoover rep frantically pursued methods of pulling the train into the building without using railroad personnel and Fred Holbrooke calculated the cost (to Warner & Summers) to demolish and rebuild the reinforced concrete wall seven from the centerline.

The Public Service Commissioner happened to be running for governor and refused to grant the waiver for fear of antagonizing the railroad workers union, Hoover failed in the search for alternate methods to pull the train into the plant, and Fred came up with a figure of $47,500 to tear the dock wall down and rebuild it per the small print. It was the first (and only) Errors and Omissions insurance claim we ever had. Our insurance carrier approved $45,000 and expressed surprise that a contractor would come that close to their estimate. They paid the $45,000 with the provision that Holder would sign a statement that no further claim would be made. W. J. Blain, representing Holder, signed the statement. We had to pay our deductible, but I don't remember what it was. Problem solved!

The plant was finished on time and we sent our final billing to W. J. In spite of the fact that he signed a statement that there would be no further claims, he got his money simply by deducting $2,500 from our final billing to Holder Construction Co.

After all this, Fred and Charlie Smithgall threw a party at their place. Betty and I were invited to the party which was to celebrate, "The Jim Warner Memorial Railroad Dock".

You ain't gonna believe this. As time passed, and I didn't get a bill from the Athens lawyer for his services, I called to find out when he was going to send me a bill. He said he wasn't going to send me a bill, because *he was unable to get the waiver for me.*

30
I CAN'T SEE IT FROM MY HOUSE

It was a manufacturing plant in Corbin, Kentucky, for Certainteed-Saint Gobain. The plant produced sound insulation for hoods, roofs and doors for automobiles. Bales of scrap cloth discarded from textile mills were brought into the plant by rail. The scraps were chopped up and mixed with various resins, cooked in large ovens and molded into shapes for various car models.

We worked with the Miller Construction Company on a design-build team. "Bull" Miller and his project manager, Whitey Rollins, were both easy to work with.

All the lint from the process floated around in the air, collecting on the exposed steel columns, beams, girts, tie rods and vertical "X" bracing [wind bracing] members on the interior of the exterior building walls. Certainteed had similar plants which had to be closed down at frequent intervals to have the lint blown off the walls.

I had been using Inryco flush metal exterior wall panels on many of the industrial buildings we designed, mainly because I thought the usual corrugated panels commonly used on industrial buildings were ugly and looked cheap. So I thought, why not turn the building inside out? The structural members would be outside made of Cor-ten steel, which doesn't need to be painted, and lint wouldn't collect as much on the smooth flush panel walls on the inside. The plant would not have to be shut down as frequently, and the operation would become more efficient. Bull Miller and the Certainteed rep bought the idea.

On a monthly visit about the time the offices were being finished, I was upset to see that the colors I had selected had been changed, and a painter was applying the most godawful wall colors that clashed with the color of the floor tile. I told him he wasn't using the colors I had scheduled. He told me a Certainteed VP had changed my colors. I asked if it bothered him to paint such godawful colors. He just calmly kept on painting and said, "I can't see it from my house".

31
THE PAWN SHOP

We did a lot of work with Pat Dinkins on a Design-Build team. Pat was always getting involved in offbeat projects, but we always enjoyed working with him, even though he liked to play architect. He did teach us how to be practical architects. It was through Design-Build work with Pat that we got our first real project – Hennessy Cadillac.

Pat was asked to look at a burned out lease space on Whitehall Street, near Alabama Street. They have changed street names in Atlanta so much that I'm not sure where anything is any more. His man, Tony Gray, and I went to look the situation over and determine what needed to be done. The key to get in the burned out space was being kept by the owner of the pawn shop next door. It was a rainy day and Tony and I had worn our trench coats and felt hats to stay dry. When we arrived in the pawn shop, it was full of guys looking over the guns, knives, rings and stuff that had been hocked by the less fortunate among us.

We went to the back of the shop to get the key which the shop owner got out of his safe. As we turned to leave, I was surprised to see that there was no one in the place. It was empty. All the customers had suddenly left. I said, "Where did everybody go?" The pawn shop owner said, "They thought you were narcs".

Tony and I took the key and went through the burned out mess. It was hard to know where to start and what needed to be done construction-wise. I could see that I wasn't going to get any architectural design awards for this project. The good news is, I got lucky. Pat decided to not do the job.

32
WHAT TREE?

While working at Heery & Heery, before I opened my own office, I was the project architect on the Forest Service Research Lab at the University of Georgia. The topo showed a tree in what would be the front yard. I had to change the grades around the tree to position the building properly. I had to design an expensive retaining wall around the tree to save it.

Back in those days, a tree could not be removed on the campus without the express permission of the University president. The first time I went to the site was in the early grading stage. I was appalled to see the tree I had taken great pains and expense to the government to save was a misshapen scrawny dwarfed dogwood tree. The grading had not reached the point where the retaining wall had been built. I had to do something, and quick.

I sought out the grading contractor and quietly told him that, if his bulldozer operator happened to make a mistake and knocked the tree down, it would be our little secret. Before I left the site, the tree was gone. A change order would eliminate the expensive retaining wall, and I didn't have to get anybody's permission.

33
DRAW ANOTHER FENCE

Howard High was a four story brick building built in 1923, just east of downtown Atlanta. It covered a large city block, half of which was an athletic field. It was in line for a 36 movable classroom addition under some Federal Government program.

It was early 1964, and Warner & Summers was just getting started. Oby Brewer, Junior, was the president of the Atlanta School Board – and, just by chance, my friend. Oby told me he could get me selected as architect for a good school job, or he could get me selected as the architect for the 36 portables. I said, "We'll take the 36 portable classroom project".

Howard High was a tough school. All around the building there was an area about eight feet wide of broken glass from windows that had been broken by the "students". There were also a few old doors that had been thrown out the windows. Later that year, on another project, we designed efficient windows to replace the rusted steel awning type windows, most of which wouldn't close all the way.

One day Summers was talking about our project with Miss Jones, the assistant principal. She opened her desk drawer and Alex saw that it was full of Saturday night specials, knives, razors, and other deadly instruments. He asked where did all that stuff come from and she said, "We get it when we have open pocket book day". I told you it was a tough school.

Under the Federal Program the classrooms had to be "portable". The only way to do the project right was design 36 pre-engineered (Butler Buildings) connected by covered walks. A pre-engineered building ain't "portable" unless you take it apart and put it back together somewhere else. The school board wasn't bothered by that technicality. It was gonna be <u>pre-engineered</u> buildings – don't worry about the Feds. The two of us hit the drawing boards and in thirty days we had documents out for bids. The fee was $36,000 – not bad pay for thirty day's work (long days).

The site plan included a ten foot high chain link fence around the athletic field, one side of which was the back of the school. It seems that, by 10 o'clock in the morning, half the students had disappeared from the classrooms, so the fence had a gate with a teacher stationed at it to see that the students didn't disappear. I was showing Betty the plans one day, and I pointed out that the fence, which would cost $12,000, would generate about $700 of the fee, and I only had to draw three straight lines.

For long after I had told her that, any time household money was tight, she would say, "Draw another fence".

34
SHACK AT THE LAKE

It was through our neighbors, Philip and Harriett Gallion, that we were invited to join "Lazyfare" (a play on the French for "hands off"). Philip was one of a group of fifteen native Atlanta guys who had gotten together for the purpose of building a shack at Lake Lanier – sort of a hang out for the guys up at the lake. It didn't quite work out like that.

I was invited to join because I could draw the plans free. I don't remember all the names of the members, but I remember Philip (a banker), Trippe Slade (a bank trust officer at First National Bank), Stewart White (a realtor), Ronald Gann (a real estate trust officer at C&S Bank), Oby Brewer (insurance), Jim Stanfield (a lawyer), Dick Boyles (a Lockheed aircraft designer), Me (an architect) and, the guy we needed most, Syd Isenberg (a psychiatrist). We had all the talent we needed without paying any outside consultants.

Oby found a lot near Flowery Branch, right on a nice quiet cove. Oby found a rich old friend from whom we could borrow the money. We each paid $5 a month to pay it off.

In 1958, we decided it was time to find the money to build the shack. We went to the Gainesville Savings and Loan. We were told they wouldn't lend money on a shack. It had to be a structure that they could sell if we failed to pay off the mortgage. So I designed a very nice conservatively-contemporary two story house with a big screened porch and patio on the lake side. A good old boy local contractor said he would build it for $17,000. The Savings and Loan then lent us the money for 80% of the cost. Oby had another rich old friend who lent us the required 20% down payment on a second mortgage, plus the money to buy the furniture, including a record player and the condiments. Condiments on a second mortgage! Oby was a genius at getting things done.

After the place was built, we each paid in $25 per month. Trippe set aside a fund for taxes and maintenance, and we had a corporate meeting every year as required.

We had a bunch of rules. At one annual meeting we reviewed the rules and decided to eliminate all the rules and see what rules we really needed. We never made another rule.

I dropped out when we joined Cherokee and started playing tennis. A few years ago, Lazyfare was sold by the six remaining members, and each got $37,000 – *a shack at the lake!*

35
THE TRUTH WILL COME OUT

Back in the very early 60's, when I was working for George Heery, he was involved in a real estate development group. On one occasion the group was looking at the possibility of building a doctors' professional building in Baltimore. At the time, Sam Massell was an expert on how to manage professional doctors' buildings. George sent me with Sam to Baltimore to scope out the situation there. I would look at the site to see if it posed any difficulties and Sam would talk to real estate management prospects.

Sam and I flew to Baltimore on Delta (who else!?). We settled in our seats and Sam opened a beat up briefcase that was so full of newspapers that it wouldn't close all the way. He apparently was an avid reader of what was going on around Atlanta. As we taxied out we got to talking about architecture. I mentioned that I liked the Palisades building at Peachtree and Palisades, except the black exterior looked like waterproofing. At that he said good architecture was not good real estate, because it became too controversial and was sometimes hard to lease. Very interesting.

We got to Baltimore about sunset, checked into a less than plush hotel, and took a walk down one of the less than plush streets. We came to a shop that sold, among other things, hot dogs. Sam bought one and told me that he always bought a hot dog in any city he visited. He didn't say what this research told him about a city.

It was inevitable that we would come by a cocktail lounge. I should really say "bar". It was rather small, so we sat down at the bar and each ordered a martini. The bartender didn't know how to make a martini. When we told him he asked, "What's vermouth?" I told you it was a bar.

The next morning we visited the site, which looked like it would work without any serious drawbacks. Then we went to a real estate management company office where Sam was going to talk to a prospective manager for the building. As we waited to see the guy, Sam said, "Jim, if I make this guy angry when I'm talking with him, don't be alarmed. That's how I learn the truth". I thought that was pretty cagey.

36
SOLDIER COCHRANE

I started back to Tech after the war, in the spring of 1946. The first day all the new freshmen were assembled in the old Naval Armory for orientation. There must have been over 500 WWII veterans there and exactly ten high school graduate non-veterans. One of whom was John A. Cochrane from Augusta, Georgia. John wound up with me majoring in architecture.

When I started Co-op before I joined the Navy, I was majoring in mechanical engineering. After the war I decided M.E. would be too dull and decided to major in Industrial Design. Architecture had four options, Architectural Design, Architectural Engineering, Light Construction and Industrial Design. I had always liked to draw and I thought the Industrial Design option would be a good one. After the first year I discovered that, because there was no Industrial Design lab or professor, the option of my choice wasn't available, even though it was listed in the catalog. So I said to myself, "What the heck! I might as well be an architect".

Everybody was a veteran, except John Cochrane. Veterans didn't have to take ROTC, for obvious reasons, but Cochrane had to since he wasn't a veteran. He had to wear his ROTC uniform every Tuesday and every Thursday. Naturally he became known to the rest of us as, "Soldier Cochrane".

After graduation, life got interesting for Soldier Cochrane. He became a veteran the hard way, as a 2nd Lt. in a rifle platoon for a year in combat in Korea. He told me a few of his personal anecdotes, which I will relate here.

It was Christmas time and his platoon was entrenched behind two rows of barbed wire. He said on Christmas morning a fully decorated Christmas tree had been erected between the two rows of barbed wire, with a sign next to it that read, "Merry Christmas. Your girlfriend's tears wet your letters. We hope you live to see New Year's". It was pretty scary that the Chinese could do all that so close to our lines without anyone hearing a sound.

One night on patrol, his platoon was ambushed. He was near a big tree which hid the silhouette of a Chinese who had pointed a "burp gun" at him. He heard a click just before he shot the guy. It turned out that the burp gun had jammed and misfired. Cochrane had ordered, "Throw grenades!" He kept throwing grenades and suddenly realized he was standing up throwing grenades while all the guys in the patrol were flat on the ground handing him the grenades.

37
C. WILMER

When I worked for George Heery at Heery & Heery the office was in a grand old house on Peachtree near 17th Street. The office had a staff of about thirty people. C. Wilmer Heery, George's dad, had a two man office in Athens where the firm actually started. That office was C. Wilmer Heery and John Cochrane.

C. Wilmer was well known in Athens and had connections at the University. On one occasion he was approached by one of the sororities and asked to design a new sorority house. He didn't want to fool with a small, what amounted to be a residential project, so he quoted an outrages fee – fourteen percent – thinking they would not possibly pay that kind of fee. The normal fee for residential work at the time was a mere six percent. Guess what? They took him up on it. He was then obliged to take on the project.

He prepared a preliminary design for approval and it was accepted.

C. Wilmer didn't want to have to produce the working drawings in Athens. He had better things to do, so he brought his preliminaries to the Atlanta office. George had all the office staff come in one weekend, the various required working drawings were assigned to the draftsmen, and a miracle happened. A set of working drawings for a sorority house, plans, details and specifications was ready to be put out for bids on Monday morning. From that day on, we would joke that George thought bid documents for any project, regardless of scope, could be produced in two days.

When George got out of Tech, he went to work for his dad in Athens. After a while he asked his dad to make him a partner. C.Wilmer told him that, if he could make it on his own in Atlanta for a year, he could become a partner. George made it for a year in Atlanta. He said he made ten thousand dollars working for his dad and six hundred dollars the year he worked for himself in Atlanta. It became Heery & Heery. George built a great firm. When I went to work for him in 1957 as top dog draftsman, there were four of us in the Atlanta office, including a secretary who read the Saturday Evening Post every afternoon. When I left six years later to open my own office, there were thirty employees. When he sold to the Brits, there were 500!

When C. Wilmer got older and had heart trouble, the family decided that he should not drive his Cadillac any longer, so they took away his car keys. The next day, Wilmer went to the local Cadillac dealer and bought another Cadillac.

38
SVETLANA

When Warner & Summers started in 1964, the office was at 5 Baltimore Place, sometimes referred to as Baltimore Row, between Spring and West Peachtree near Crawford Long Hospital. We were on the first floor of a three story apartment group built in about 1917 that looked like Baltimore (Maryland) row houses, thus the street name. There was a basement area which was a beer joint known as *The Bottom of the Barrel.*

When Summers was at Tech, he lived on Baltimore Row with some Tech students. Lots of the architectural students lived there. It was a very Bohemian dormitory, to say the least. By the Sixties, the building had deteriorated badly and we were able to rent the space for next to nothing. If I remember correctly, it was $1.25 per square foot <u>per year</u>. That's cheap space. We fixed the office up pretty well – we thought so. In the front room there was an old marble fireplace and a folding card table we used as a secretary's desk on which there was our six hundred dollar brand new IBM Selectric typewriter. We wanted letters going out of the office to look first class.

On the second and third floor there lived a couple of writers, Priscilla McMillan and her husband George. Priscilla had spent some time in Moscow on an assignment during which she had met Lee Harvey Oswald. At one time she worked in Washington where she had met John F. Kennedy on an assignment. Small world. When in Moscow she also met Svetlana Stalin, old Joe's daughter.

When Stalin died and Svetlana wanted to get out of Russia, Priscilla asked her to come to the States and live at her father's estate on Long Island. [If she was so rich, what was she doing living on Baltimore Row?]. Svetlana brought with her a copy of Svetlana's book written longhand in Russian. Priscilla wrote a longhand translation in English for Svetlana.

Enter Warner & Summers IBM typewriter. Priscilla asked our secretary, who wasn't all that busy in those early days, to type the handwritten English translation on our IBM on our folding card table.

And that is Warner & Summers' claim to fame.

Footnote: The lady who owned 5 Baltimore Place, when a little girl, posed for the Buster Brown Shoe logo.

39
UNCLE EUSTICE

Betty and I were married June 14, 1952. I'm from a small square family. Betty is from a large colorful family. One of those colorful people was Uncle Eustice Butts. Uncle Eustice had been the captain of a machine gun company in France during World War One. One day, after he came back from the war, he shot and killed a man in downtown Brunswick.

It seems that a disgruntled, very disturbed ex-policeman went to the center of town and started shooting prominent people, lawyers, respected citizens and some innocent bystanders. Nobody could stop him until Uncle Eustice came on the scene. He dashed into the hardware store owned by his brother, Uncle Jay, grabbed a shotgun off the rack, a handful of shotgun shells (he claimed his brother wanted him to pay for the gun and shells before he left the store) and went after the madman. The guy was on his way up stairs to a law office intending to kill a lawyer. By this time six or seven people were dead and several others wounded. Uncle Eustice shot the man dead before he got to the top of the stairs.

There are a lot of great family anecdotes about Uncle Eustice. At one time he was a judge in Brunswick. Whenever a drunk came up before him, he would sentence the drunk to attend church every Sunday for six Sundays. Uncle Eustice was never known to have gone to church himself.

One day a lawyer before the bench disagreed with him. The lawyer said, "But, Judge, that's not the law!" to which Uncle Eustice roared, "To hell with the law! I'm the law!" He was like Judge Roy Bean who was the law west of the Pecos during the Wild West days. In Roy Bean's court and Uncle Eustice's court, the law was what they said it was.

He never married and he lived in a rustic house on Blythe Island just south of Brunswick, on Highway 17 to Jacksonville. He had all kinds of animals on a large piece of heavily wooded property and seven docks on the creek for fishing and boating. Rich and important Yankees who were some of his friends would visit, hunt, fish, play cards and drink a little (little?) whiskey.

One day when he was alone at home, he had a stroke. Betty's dad happened to drop by, probably to drink some whiskey, and found him helpless on the floor. Dad called an ambulance. As Uncle Eustice was being carried out on a stretcher, he rolled his eyes toward the kitchen and said, "The whiskey's under the sink, boys".

40
THE ANT AND THE GRASSHOPPER

Summers and I were 50-50 partners for 29 1/2 years. He was the ant and I was the grasshopper. I don't remember our ever having a serious argument. Luckily for me, Summers was the partner who handled the finances. He thought it was sinful to borrow money and pay interest. I had worked for one firm that once had to use contractors' plan deposits to meet the payroll. If I had been handling the money, we would have gone out of business in a few months. When I wanted the firm to buy me a BMW company car he said, "No way!"

One time soon after we started the firm I wanted to take Betty and the kids to Saint Simons for a long weekend. In a two man office, two-week vacations were a thing of the past. During the 29 ½ years, I never had a full two-week vacation. My '62 VW Beetle was too small for the five of us. Summers had a roomy Ford Fairlaine, so he was nice enough to let me borrow it for the trip. When I got back to Atlanta I had the car washed and vacuumed inside, and I returned it in good condition. That night his Fairlaine was stolen. It was never found. Summers said, "Warner, ...next time don't get the car washed".

As the firm got bigger, we had three "Jim's" in the office. We had to address each Jim by his last name so, if someone said, "Hey, Jim", three guys wouldn't look up and stop working. To this day, forty years later, all us Jim's are addressed by our last names.

Summers and I retired in 1993. It is now thirteen years later, and he has two BMW's, and I have a 14 year old Buick Park Avenue.

41
HIGH BAY

I am a lazy person and am always looking for the quick and easy way to do something. Case in point: The "high crane bay".

Manufacturing buildings frequently require a crane to move heavy stuff from one area to another, like from or to a truck door when receiving or shipping something heavy. The typical size of a structural bay in most industrial plants is 40' x 40' with more or less 16' clear below the roof structure. Crane bays are also about 40' x 40', but need more clear height depending on the type crane and "hook height" above the floor.

What this requires is raising the roof maybe five or six feet above the roof of the rest of the building. Picture this: The large expanse of roof (most manufacturing plants are large) has to change elevation at the crane bay. Also there is flashing between the low roof and the vertical exterior wall of the crane bay. Then there is flashing and gutters at the edge of the higher bay roof. Are you with me so far? This requires a lot of flashing and a lot of time detailing the way to build it all. Where there is complexity, there is the potential for trouble, like leaks. Nobody in construction likes leaks, especially architects.

I got to thinking in bed one night (I think a lot at night when there is nothing else to do) – why go to all that trouble and expense, just slope the roof up five or six feet from the far side of the adjacent 40' bay up to the high bay roof? This eliminated all the expense of the high bay exterior wall and the flashing and gutters. It made for a nice economical smooth flow of roof over the entire building.

I told you I was lazy. It was so simple I decided not to apply for a patent.

42
WHERE DID ALL THE PEOPLE GO?

When I was with Heery & Heery I became good friends with Bill Holland. Bill was hired from Lockheed at my suggestion, because I knew he was a specifications expert, as well as a very good designer, and we needed someone with those qualifications.

Bill and I would get together after work and talk about the possibility of opening our own office. We usually did this over a couple of martinis at the "14 Hundred Club" just in the next block from George Heery's office at 14th and Peachtree. We could get there from work in a hurry. Sometimes Andy Clement would join us. He had an engineering background and we thought he might be interested.

After many discussions about taking the plunge, Bill came up with a map of Georgia which had a little red pin showing where every architect in the state had an office. Bill pointed to an area in south central Georgia where there were no pins. He said, "This is where we should move to and open an office. No competition". I hated to burst his balloon, but I pointed out that there would be no competition in that area because there were no *people* in that part of the state.

As time passed, we remained good friends, but I realized that Bill and I were too much alike, and I would need a partner who was strong in areas where I was less talented. Sitting on East Beach watching the tide go in and out at Saint Simons in the summer of '63, I came to the conclusion that I needed a partner who was a lot different and smarter than I am. That's when I decided to approach Alex Summers to see if he would be interested in taking the plunge with me.

We opened the office of Warner & Summers on February 4, 1964. The rest is, as they say, history.

43
BEWARE OF DEVELOPERS BEARING PRINTS

I did an expansion of the First National Bank of West Point (Georgia). Batson-Cook Construction Company in West Point was the contractor. The head of the construction company, Cliff Glover, was highly respected in the construction industry.

After the project was completed, Cliff approached me to team up with him on a Design-Build hotel project in Charleston. The developer was Smith-Simmons with offices in Charleston. I immediately agreed because of my high regard for Batson-Cook and Cliff.

Smith and Simmons came to our office to discuss the project. They looked like well dressed business men. Smith was even wearing gold cuff links. I did notice that they had with them preliminary architectural drawings of a hotel project produced by two different architects. Red flag! I figured if Cliff was involved, everything must be OK.

I assembled a team of engineers with hotel experience and checked with my architect friendly competitor, Jack Summer, who specialized in designing hotels, as to what a fair fee would be. Our objective was to prepare a set of pricing drawings so Cliff could give Smith-Simmons an accurate construction cost.

Cliff could see that Smith-Simmons didn't know that when you design a hotel you need to know which hotel chain is going to run the hotel. They didn't have a clue how to go about this. All they knew was they had a piece of choice property tied up that would make a good hotel site. Through his connections Cliff Glover got them in touch with Marriott, and they were able to get Marriott to manage the hotel provided the design met Marriott's criteria, thanks to Warner-Summers.

Jim Ditzel came up with a design that met the criteria that was provided to us. The design team came up with preliminary working drawings which Batson-Cook priced. Jim Ditzel and I went to Washington, D.C., where Ditzel made a great presentation for Bill Marriott. Everything was approved. The next step was for Smith-Simmons to get financing for the project – with someone else's money.

They arranged a meeting in Atlanta with Prudential to get the financing. Smith, Simmons, Cliff Glover and I went to a meeting at Prudential. The meeting had gotten underway when I realized that Prudential didn't know the relationship between all the actors. I told the Prudential guy that he should know that I was working for the contractor, not the owner. The Prudential guy said that I would have to work for the owner, not the contractor. I said that was OK with me. No problem. The meeting then proceeded with no hitches.

After the meeting I told Smith I would work for Smith-Simmons for the same fee that I had with Batson-Cook. Smith wanted me to cut my fee. My fee was reasonable, in line with this type project, and it would be foolish to do a major project like this for less. I refused to cut the fee. To make a long story short, Smith dumped Warner & Summers, and got a cheaper architect. At that point we had spent $32,000, not counting what the engineers had spent, to get the project to a point which enabled Smith-Simmons to make the deal with Marriott, and we deserved to be paid. That didn't bother Smith. He dumped us anyway, and he didn't pay us one cent.

The moral of the story is, "Beware of developers bearing plans with other architects' names on them – and wearing gold cuff links".

44
DUST TO DUST

We designed two distribution facilities for Addressograph Multigraph Corporation. One was in Arlington, Texas, and the other in Atlanta. Holder Construction and Pat Dinkins Construction Company were the two bidders.

The Addressograph contact man was a very nice guy. He also happened to be an architect, which made our job easier. John Donaldson was our very talented young designer. He made beautiful colored sketches of his design solution on "trash" (the thin yellow sketch paper architects use to arrive at a solution to a problem) which was sent to our contact. He approved them immediately.

Holder got the Atlanta job and Pat Dinkins got the Arlington job. Arlington was interesting in that the site was an area of "active soil". This soil would shrink when dry and expand when wet. The foundations had to be designed to keep this soil condition from cracking up the footings and floor slabs in the building. This was accomplished with concrete drilled piers supporting grade beams that had material under them that would compress when the active soil expanded upward and keep the pressure off the grade beams.

On one of my early visits to the site, while it was still being graded, I was chatting with an old rough and tough Texas grading contractor. He told me you could tell where the active soil was, and where it wasn't, on a site by the type trees on the site. I suddenly became an expert then and there. I could look around and easily tell exactly where one type soil changed to the other type, just by looking at the difference in the trees.

While we chatted, we were sort of kicking at the dirt that was so dry it was like talcum powder. I made a comment about how dusty it was. The old grader said, "It sure is. Once we didn't have any rain for six years. It was so dusty that a five year old kid I knew had never seen rain. One day it rained, and when the rain hit his face he fainted." Up to that point he had my close attention. I told him I thought that was amazing. Then he said, "Yeah, we had to throw a bucket of dirt in his face to bring him to."

45
YOU GUYS HAVE ALL THE FUN

My first job after graduation was with a small A&E firm, Smith & Hobbs, in the Peters Building right next to the old Kimball House on Peachtree Street near Five Points. Carol M. "Bud" Smith was the architect and Emmett Hobbs was the civil engineer. Van Vanover, Cleve Cail, and I were the architectural draftsmen. Sandy Sander and Wendell Power were the engineering draftsmen, plus there was a surveying crew of about four guys.

It was 1950 and air conditioning was not yet with us. While drafting, we had to wrap towels around our arms to keep them from sticking to the tracing paper. To top it off, we had to keep the windows open, and the soot from the trains that went under Peachtree from the nearby Union Station blew into the drafting room.

I was stuck on the drawing board and envied the field crew being outdoors all day. I complained to them about it so much they decided to do something about it. They said they would take me out with them one day, if Bud approved. Bud was a nice guy and said it would be OK. After work the next day, Wendell and I, at his suggestion, dropped by the Kimball House for a beer. Then we had another beer – and so on.

The next morning the field crew picked me up on the way to one of their jobs. I was in bad shape. Too many beers – they planned the whole thing. They practically carried me to the car. They were surveying a line for the installation of a sewer south of town. The line was through an area of very heavy brush. We hacked our way through the brush with machetes all day long. It was hot hard work, but a strange thing happened. As the day went on, I began to feel better and the field crew began to feel worse. On the way home, I felt great and they were all pooped.

The field crew was a bunch of jokers. One afternoon I had left my drawing board for a moment. While I was gone they played a little trick on me. When I got back to my board I caught something out of the corner of my eye. It moved, it was alive, it was a snake. They had taped it to the edge of my board. Some joke!

46
WHY DID EVERYBODY STOP WALKING?

After we designed the two Vlasic state of the art pickle processing plants, one in Mississippi and the other in Delaware, we designed the Vlasic Foods corporate headquarters on Fourteen Mile Road in Detroit. It was a two story brick office building and, even if I do say so myself, it was good looking. Holder was the contractor.

The building was nearing completion in the dead of winter. On a routine "inspection" trip I took my structural, electrical and mechanical engineers with me. We got on the Delta flight and were told there would be a slight delay. It seemed the delay was caused by a problem in Detroit. We took off about an hour late. When we got to Detroit we saw what had caused the delay. There had been a blizzard the night before. We went to get a cab and the parking lot looked like a field of moguls. You couldn't tell there were cars there; they were totally covered with snow. There were no cabs or anything else moving.

Soon we saw a cab approaching. We were in luck. The cabby didn't have chains. He just had snow tires, but he managed to navigate pretty well. We finally got to the jobsite, which was deserted. I got out of the cab and headed for the building and was up to my knees in snow. Four of us had come all the way from Atlanta, at great expense, and the job superintendent had stayed at home. We turned around and headed back to Atlanta. Mission unaccomplished.

The next visit was in better weather, and we had the big man present for our inspection – Bob Vlasic himself. As we walked through the almost completed building, Vlasic was followed by Holder's people and my people. It happened that the second floor was supported by some very long bar joist spans. The building being not quite finished, the second floor was not yet as rigid as it would be on completion. As we trooped through the building behind Vlasic, I and others noticed that the floor was, shall we say – "flexible" – in a word, it "bounced". Apparently Vlasic was the only person who didn't notice.

Every time he stopped walking, everybody else stopped walking.

47
THEM SHOES, THEM SHOES

One of our projects for Holder was a three story office building for J. Mack Robinson on Peachtree Road near Oglethorpe University. Mack Robinson was one of the gentlest and nicest men I ever met. He also happened to be the richest man I ever met.

Mack was a patron of the arts and frequently went to artsy black tie functions. My partner, Alex Summers, also frequented artsy black tie functions. On one such occasion Alex had to borrow my patent leather "tuxedo shoes". He had never met Mack, but found himself in a conversation with Mack during intermission. Alex claimed that Mack said, "You must be Jim Warner's partner." Alex said he was amazed and said asked, "How did you know?" Mack replied, "Because you are wearing Jim Warner's shoes."

Yeah.

48
TOUCHÉ

When I was with Heery & Heery I was the project architect on the Castleview Town and Country Club on Pharr Court, south in Buckhead. It had a nice little club house, an adult Olympic size swimming pool, and a pool for loud teenagers. The club is gone and the site now has a humongous apartment (or could it be a condo?) development that totally fills the site.

Mr. Patterson of Springhill Patterson's Funeral Home on Spring Street lived on Andrews Drive where his property had a common back property line with the club property. Mr. Patterson was concerned that during construction there might be some damage to a blade of grass in his back yard. I had a surveyor clearly establish the common property line and arranged a meeting at the site between Mr. Patterson and the Castleview contractor, Howard Stillwell, the club manager, myself and Emory Schwall, a prominent Atlanta attorney and the perfect southern gentleman.

The meeting progressed on a very cordial basis. Mr. Patterson was assured that there would be no harm done to his grass. As the meeting was breaking up, Mr. Patterson made some snide remark inferring that lawyers made too much money. Emory turned to Mr. Patterson and in his typically gracious manner said, "But not so lucrative as being a funeral director, Mr. Patterson".

Emory Schwall has a great sense of timing and humor. He has a sign over his bar at home which reads, "Emory Schwall, the best lawyer money can buy".

49
LOOKING BACK

When I look back on my architectural career I marvel at how unusual it was and how lucky I was.

First off – I wanted to be an industrial designer "designing the products of industry" (that's the definition of Industrial Design). I was lucky enough to get accepted to Georgia Tech back when it was a lot easier to get in than it is now. After the first year, I discovered that Industrial Design, even though it was listed in the Tech catalog as one of the options in the Architectural School, wasn't available – no lab available and no faculty available.

Luckily, I said to myself, "What the heck! I might as well take Architectural Design and be an architect". I wasn't one of those guys who claimed he wanted to be an architect from the time he was two years old.

Most of all, luckily I got out of Tech. (You don't graduate from Tech. You "get out". Ask any Tech man what year he graduated.) As I've said many times, "The darkest years of my life were spent at Georgia Tech". From then on things only got better. Thanks to my Tech classmate, Van Vanover, I went to work in a good job with a small firm, Smith & Hobbs, the day after I got out.

When work ran out when the Korean War started, I was lucky to get a job in Brunswick with Abreu & Robeson, which was how I met Betty. Six months after we were married I volunteered for active duty, in December 1952 (to escape the mean Jimmy Robeson), and didn't get sent to Korea, but to NAS Quonset Point, R.I. where I got to fly the fantastic Grumman F8F Bearcat and the Douglas A-26. The only shots that were fired at me were from the five-inch destroyer deck guns when I towed targets in the A-26.

I was discharged on December 5, 1954, and went to work for Van Vanover at Vanover & Smith the day after I got out. During this time, Van and I studied for the Architect exam, at night in the office. When the time came to take the exam, I chickened and said I was afraid to try it. Van got all over me and insisted that I take it. The exam had seven parts and took five days. I only flunked one part, which I took over the next time, and luckily became a real sure nuff architect.

Times got tough again and through my Tech classmate, Dan Atkins, I got a job with Ayers & Godwin where I learned even more. I found myself doing the same thing over and over again and felt I needed to make a change and get "over my head" in another job. That is the best way to learn and progress. Through my Tech classmate, Fred Branch, I was lucky again getting to work with George

Heery when he was getting started and only had five people in the whole firm (except for Wilmer Heery and "Soldier" Cochrane in Athens).

After seven years and great experience, I got up the courage to open my own firm with Alex Summers, who was a perfect partner and a whole lot smarter than I was. He passed the Architect exam the first time and didn't even study for it. We were partners from February 4, 1964 to June 30, 1993. We never signed a partnership agreement. We didn't have to.

We started with nothing. Alex was a bachelor and I had a wife, three kids, a house mortgage, no money and no clients. But fortune smiled upon us and the firm grew and prospered. A major factor in what I consider to be our successful practice was we embraced the non-confrontational Design-Build concept early, when it was not popular with most architects of the time. We were blessed with quality clients and quality young architectural people working with us. Most of our work was done with clients on just a handshake – no contract necessary.

We only had two clients that we had trouble collecting our fees from. One was for four big K-Mart type stores for Zayre/TJMaxx. If you did over a certain volume of work for them, they put you on 120 days. When you sent your invoice, they would inform you of some minor mistake in the way you prepared the invoice, send it back and put you on another 120 days. The other client was a big time labor lawyer in Atlanta from whom it took us months to get our fee. He kept putting us off. We never got all the money – but who's gonna sue a lawyer?

We never had to do any marketing. The work just came in. Bill Holland, one of my architect friends, asked me how much we entertained prospective clients. I told him that we never entertained prospective clients. We didn't need to. He replied that he did a lot of prospective client entertaining, but never got any results. I told you I was lucky.

We sold the firm, which at the time had about twenty employees, to three young, very talented, long time employees who have continued to produce high quality architecture and interior design. The firm is known now as Warner Summers Ditzel Benefield Ward & Associates.

(You can check the web site of Warner Summers Ditzel Benefield Ward & Associates at www.warnersummers.com)

An afterthought – at the time of this writing I am 82 and retired for 13 years. I just figured out the reason I never had any work published in the architectural magazines and became famous. I always looked for the simplest most economical solution for my clients.

50
THE BATTLE OF PEACHTREE CREEK

It was the Summer of '42. I was elected president of the Georgia Tech Freshman Co-op Class. We were hazed by the Sophomore Co-ops. There was a tradition that there was a tug of war at Peachtree Creek, just upstream from where the creek goes under Peachtree Road, when half the quarter was up. The frosh and the sophs rode to the site in a big stake truck. The president of each class was at the front of the tug of war line when the war started. If the freshman pulled the sophomores into the creek, hazing was over. If the freshmen lost, they pulled the sophomores back to Tech in the truck, and hazing continued until the end of the quarter.

As president of the freshman class, I was the first to go into the water. That's leadership! "FOLLOW ME!" I will never forget pulling that great big stake truck full of celebrating sophomores up the steep Peachtree Road Race "cardiac hill". (Piedmont Hospital wasn't there yet, but the hill was.)

A little bit of family history: It was just about a mile downstream from the tug of war site that great-gran'pa Warner and great-gran'pa Klingler wisely surrendered at the Battle of Peachtree Creek during the Battle of Atlanta. Captain James Warner spent the rest of the war in Andersonville, and Matthew Klingler (First Bull Run, Gettysburg, Battle of Atlanta) was sent to a POW camp in Eufaula, Alabama.

The family legend is – a pig somehow got loose among the starving prisoners, and gran'pa Warner – got an ear.

51
THE ONE ARM MAN

You never know how you are going to get a project. The way we got the Schwinn Bicycle Distribution Center in Atlanta is an interesting story.

Bill Law was with a prominent Atlanta commercial real estate company. He sold big pieces of land to companies that built warehouses, distribution centers and the like. He was a very sharp young man. Through the grapevine, Bill heard that the Schwinn Bicycle Company planned to build a distribution center in Atlanta. Bill knew the company was headquartered in Chicago and Frank Schwinn was coming to Atlanta on a certain day. He knew the day, and he also knew that Frank Schwinn had only one arm.

How's that for homework? Bill went out to the Atlanta Airport on the known day and watched the gates where Delta flights arrived from Chicago. When a man with one arm got off one of the planes, Bill walked up to him and said, "Mister Schwinn, my name is Bill Law with Adams Cates Realty". Frank Schwinn apparently didn't know anybody in the real estate business in Atlanta, so Bill did a very gracious thing. He offered to help find land for the distribution center.

Bill and Bob Holder were good friends, and Bill would frequently steer work Holder's way. Holder now had a prospect with whom to negotiate a construction contract using Warner & Summers as the architects. A site was found in the Fulton Industrial District, but there was a catch. It turned out that the project had to be bid. Holder recommended that he and Pat Dinkins submit competitive bids for the construction. We were in good shape since we were the only architects the Schwinn people had ever met in Atlanta, so we got to design the facility.

The job was bid and Holder was the successful bidder; we designed the building and we never had to hit a lick at marketing. "It ain't what ya know – it's whom ya know" – and when you know 'em.

52
IF THE CLIENT AIN'T HAPPY, AIN'T NOBODY HAPPY

We did a branch bank addition in Rockdale County. We were referred to the president of the bank by our Atlanta Trust Company Bank contact. We had, and still have, a great relationship with the Trust Company. Our first "bank job" with Trust Company was in 1968. Forty years later, the firm is still designing banks for Trust Company, which has morphed into SunTrust Bank.

I went to meet with the Rockdale Bank president. He showed me a set of preliminary plans for an addition to one of his branches that had been prepared by a young architect with whom I was not familiar. The banker was not happy with the young architect's design and told me he had paid him for his time and dismissed him. (It's an architect ethics thing.)

He described the scope of the project, how the bank operated, and the bank's objectives. He hired me to submit a preliminary design for approval. When I submitted my design, he liked it and authorized me to prepare the construction documents. I did so and the project was bid within the budget. Abrams Construction Company was the successful bidder.

Construction proceeded smoothly and everybody, including the client, was happy. On one of my visits to the site during construction, the bank president and I were having a cup of coffee at a nearby short order joint. The president was a really nice guy and I felt comfortable with him. I asked him if I could ask him a question. He said, "Sure". I asked him, "Why did you hire me?" His answer was short – three little words, "Because you listened".

53
SOMEBODY HAS TO CHECK THE MAIL

Back in '62 George Heery was beginning to get more and more Federal work. He felt that he needed to have a Washington office, so he sent me and Vic Maloof to D.C. to set one up.

We flew to Washington to put it all together. It was fun. We went to a company that sold all kinds of architectural equipment and bought drafting tables, drafting equipment, desks and lots of good stuff. Cost was no object.

Actually it was set up there to let the Feds know that Heery was on the scene right in downtown Washington. Actually it was just a mail drop. George sent John Wurz from Atlanta once a week to pick up the mail. Now that is thinking big!

54
THREE LITTLE WORDS

Back when we first started the firm, we did a lot of Design-Build work with Pat Dinkins. Pat knew Heery and heard about our leaving to go on our own.

Pat got us into doing work with him for the Fulton National Bank. I worked very closely with Bob Whigham, who was Executive Vice President, Comptroller, and branch acquisition guy at the bank. Bob happened to be on the board of directors of the Haverty Furniture Company. After a board meeting one day, Rawson Haverty said to Bob, "I need to get an Atlanta architect. Every time I build a building outside Atlanta I have to educate another architect." Bob said three little words – "Call Jim Warner".

Rawson called to meet me. Summers and I went to his office to be interviewed. We didn't make a big pitch, mostly because we didn't have much to pitch at that stage in the firm's development.

He told us that, if he hired Warner & Summers to design his buildings, he wanted to work with the same partner on every project. At the time I was beginning to get involved in work for Bob Holder, so Summers was elected to handle the Haverty projects. It was a good choice for Haverty. Summers did 40 Haverty buildings form Virginia to Texas and did a superb job on every one of them. Summers always was a better detail man than I was.

Of those 40 buildings, there was only one little problem on one of them. Our Error & Omissions insurance carrier called and asked Summers to send them a copy of our contract with the Haverty Furniture Company. Alex said, "Contract? With Rawson Haverty? We don't have a contract with Rawson Haverty! We do business like gentlemen in the South." End of problem.

55
THE BEETLE

I met Miles Daly through a mutual friend, Dan Atkins, who was Miles' neighbor. Crain-Daly Volkswagen was the first VW dealer in Atlanta. The Daly's, Atkins' and Warner's went to dinner one night at the Top of the Mart restaurant. I was very impressed that Miles never once mentioned that he sold VW's. I was so impressed I bought a 1962 Sun top VW "Beetle" from him when his dealership was on Peachtree across from the "new" Piedmont Hospital.

Pat Dinkins knew Crain-Daly was relocating on Piedmont Road just a block from Hennessy Cadillac (now Hennessy Jaguar) which we had designed and Pat had built when Warner & Summers Architects first started in 1964. Pat got us to design the Crain-Daly building.

The Volkswagen people provided us with a "standard" plan. The plan had the show room up front, the service area next and the repair shop behind the service bays. The lot sloped down away from the street, which put the repair area well below the show room level. The plan was strung out and took up a lot of land. I suggested that the service bays be at the show room level and the repair area be under the service bays. This made the facility more compact and efficient. The Volkswagen rep said it wouldn't work because the service hydraulic lift cylinders would hit the roofs of the cars in the repair bays below. I told them all we needed to do was shift the lower bays so the hydraulic lift cylinders came down between the lower bays. We got approval and picked up a lot of land that was worth much more than the cost of the body shop.

In about 1966 I traded the Beetle for a beautiful convertible Karman Ghia, my first and, regrettably only, convertible I ever owned.

(The grading was done for the building with mule and a "scoop". It was the last time I ever saw grading done the old fashion way.)

56
A LIKE AMOUNT

Back in 1970, Warner & Summers was doing a lot of work with Holder Construction Company. Bob Holder had become a very good client and friend. He was a member and past president of the Cherokee Town and Country Club. It was the up-and-coming social club of Atlanta, formed in 1955.

Bob told me I ought to join, because it would be "good for business" – sounded like a good idea to me. Membership in the club is a personal membership. The membership fee cannot be paid by a business, the way it is done to this day. If your daddy ain't rich, there is another way. Your company pays you a bonus on which you pay the income tax, then you write a personal check for the initiation, provided you pass muster with the membership Committee. Initiation really only costs you the amount of the income tax you have to pay Uncle Sam. He ain't your daddy, but that's close enough.

Since Holder said it would be good for business, Summers and I agreed to each take a like amount (bonus) of $3,500 for my initiation fee. I don't know what Summers did with his like amount – he probably put it under his mattress*. When the club was formed in 1955 it cost $500 to join, and you had three months to pay it. Today (2007) it costs $70,000 to join.

I was lucky to get in for a mere eight hundred and seventy-five bucks paid to Uncle Sam. Interestingly enough, I never tried to get any "business" at the club. I didn't have to.

* He was the ant and I was the grasshopper.

[Cherokee is a great club. It is run extremely well by the Board of Directors. There has never been an assessment and the dues can only be raised by a vote of the membership. The Town Club has an Olympic pool and twelve tennis courts. The Country club has an Olympic pool and 45 holes of golf. Not bad.]

57
THE NEXT NIGHT, AND THE NEXT NIGHT AND THE...!

My last quarter at Tech was a bad time. I would have bet money I was going to fail at least three courses and never "get out". To make things worse, my GI Bill money was running out.

I got lucky. I squeaked through all my courses and entered the real world. I went to work for the small A&E firm of Smith & Hobbs. I had been living in a depressing room and board place on 15th Street just off Peachtree. I was also still flying in the "organized" Naval Air Reserve. I use the term "organized" loosely. It got more and more organized as the years passed.

Three of my squadron mates were "Kirby" Gordon Lawless, Cyd Bugden and Bob Turney. They rescued me from the boarding house and took me in where they lived on Emory Drive, you guessed it, near Emory University. It was an apartment in the back of a one story residence. There was a tiny living room, a tinier kitchen, a tiny bathroom with a four foot tub up on little lion feet and a bedroom just big enough for two double decker bunks. The best part was a screened porch which was furnished with a couple of nice chairs, floor lamps and a rush rug providing a pleasant place to relax in the summer, looking out on a back yard surrounded by trees.

Kirby was the only guy who could cook, I use the term loosely, and the rest of us had to do the dishes and clean house. He had some gourmet personal recipes. One night we would have his "American Pizza a la Kirby" which was a piece of white bread with a slice of cheese, a slice of tomato and a slice of bacon on top. The next night we would have his special "Tuna Fish Casserole" which was a can of mushroom soup, a can of tuna mixed, heated and poured over a piece of white toast. The next night we ate American Pizza and the next night we ate Tuna Fish Casserole. And the next night...!

Bob Turney was dating his future wife, Virginia, who was a dietician at Auburn. When she found out what we were eating, week after week, she sent Bob a standard weekly menu. A menu for Monday, a different menu for Tuesday, a different menu for Wednesday, and so on for an entire week.

Virginia probably saved our lives. Bob said she sent it so, "we wouldn't wind up too fat and couldn't see".

58
NO SMOKING

I was still working for Smith & Hobbs in the office building next to the old Kimbel House near Five Points when "Kirby" Gordon Lawless, Wes Chanell, Cyd Bugden, and I moved from Emory Drive to MacDonough Boulevard, in Decatur across the street from Agnes Scott College. Bob Turney had left the Emory Drive apartment and Wes Chanell took his place just before we moved.

It was a big two story house on what is now the present site of the Decatur High School. We had the first floor and three working girls had the second floor. The two floors did not have a common entrance. Right after we moved in, one of the girls from upstairs brought down a plate of home made fudge. The four girls were not ravishing beauties and we never took the plate back, not even empty. I always felt bad about our lack of courtesy.

To our good fortune, the Scott girls were not allowed to smoke on campus. At the time, I had a terrific record collection. Lots of classical music, movie sound tracks, plus stuff like the George Shearing Quintet. Through a contact at Scott, we let it be known that we had all this good music and anyone who was a lover of good music could come over to our permanent "open house" to listen to the music while they enjoyed a cigarette. Up until I moved to Brunswick I don't remember any Scott girl taking advantage of that neighborly offer.

We had more room than we had at Emory Drive so "Jug" Levison and John "What's his name" joined us to share the rent and the two supper recipes Lawless prepared.

Wes was from Saint Simons and had dated Betty when he lived there with his mother, "Fergie" Ferguson. One weekend Betty came to Atlanta to visit brother Bill Geiger, who was at Georgia Tech. During her visit she had a date with Wes, that was the first time I met Betty. When I first got to Brunswick I ran into Betty in Pap Andrews' drug store. I remembered Betty from her visit and asked her for a date. Betty didn't remember me, but she said yes. Before I got to her house to pick her up, she asked Dad to meet me at the door so he could come back to her room and tell her my name.

59
PROFESSOR REYNOLDS

In my first quarter Co-op Algebra class the summer of '42, the professor was Professor Reynolds. The classroom was in the Tech Tower, the old Admin building. He was tough, but fair. Every Friday we had a quiz and every Monday the graded papers were handed out. Near the end of the quarter when he was passing back the last quiz papers he said, "This is a very strange class. One week most of the grades are passing grades, and the next week mostly failing – except Mister Warner. He's consistent. He always fails" (his very words).

As I have said, I was not a brilliant student, but I managed to stay in the program, and in September I came home for my work term in the Steam Engineering Department of the TCI Ensley Works, one of the five U.S. Steel mills in Birmingham. It was like all the TCI steel mills – big – one mile wide and five miles long. It had four blast furnaces, two Bessemer Converters, six open hearth furnaces, a foundry, several coke ovens where soft coal was converted to coke and a rolling mill for rolling railroad rails. It was a big time operation.

My job was to go through the mill each day and change all the recording charts that measured flow of gas, water, air, steam, you name it, anything that flowed. I brought the charts back to the office where the engineers used them to calculate the cost of producing one ton of steel. I got to see the whole operation up real close. It was a very exciting experience for a teenager.

When I came back to Tech on the GI Bill after the war, I again had Professor Reynolds, this time for differential calculus which, true to form, I flunked.

60
PAY THE MAN THE TWO DOLLARS

I have always been a movie hound. I believe the young guys my age about to go into the service during WW II got some of their attitudes toward life and people from the movies of that era – a sense of sportsmanship, fair play, chivalry, if you will.

Stuff like Flynn and Rathbone in a fight to the death. Flynn knocks the sword out of Rathbone's hand. Flynn pauses, then with the tip of his shoe nudges the sword toward Rathbone and says, "Your sword". Rathbone picks up his sword and they continue to try to kill each other.

Or the scene in *Dawn Patrol* in which the German aviator who was captured after shooting down Flynn's best friend is brought in to be interrogated. He is introduced to Flynn as the one who shot down his friend. There are a few tense moments and the scene ends with the two "enemy" pilots drinking and singing together at the bar.

In 1959 there was a movie in which there was a sequence that pretty much was the way I felt about handling problems that might get out of control.

The scene opens with a rich old fellow played by Victor Moore and his lawyer played by Edward Arnold. They are on the subway in New York City. Victor Moore takes out a cigar, bites the end off and spits it out. Immediately a cop grabs him and says, "OK, buddy! It's against the law to spit in the subway. That's a two dollar fine!" Edward Arnold says, "Wait a minute. We'll take this to court". Moore quietly says, "Pay the man the two dollars".

Next scene is in court. The lawyer keeps fighting the problem and somehow the charges get more serious. The lawyer insists on taking the case to a higher court. Victor Moore pleads, "Pay the man the two dollars!"

This goes on until we find Moore in a striped convict suit clutching the bars of his cell begging Edward Arnold to, "PAY THE MAN THE TWO DOLLARS!"

61
IT DIDN'T WORK

I have always tried to be calm and polite to others, but this incident was an exception. When we were doing the Vlasic Foods Corporate Office building on 14 Mile Road in Detroit, Steve Fulford was the project manager for Holder Construction Company.

In my usual attempt to save money, I had specified that the stucco soffit remain unpainted. Unpainted stucco looks fine. It looks like exposed concrete and is aesthetically acceptable, especially two stories up.

Just before construction was completed, Steve called me to a meeting with him in his office. He told me that the stucco was going to be painted and he told me I was going to pay for it. That really got to me. I lost my usual cool and said (shouted), "I'm working for BOB HOLDER! I will pay for it when BOB HOLDER tells me to pay for it!" Steve decided I wouldn't have to pay for it.

I played tennis a few weekends with Steve to get to know him and find how to work with him better. It didn't work.

62
THE RESEARCH LAB

Our first job for Printpack, producer of flexible packaging, was a 20,000 square foot addition to the company's 20,000 square foot original manufacturing plant and offices in Atlanta. The next project was a large warehouse addition, then a project to enlarge the office spaces.

Printpack bought a small warehouse building on their street. It was to be renovated to create a research facility. My mechanical engineering consultant was Gene Anglin, with whom we had worked on some Atlanta Airport work. He was a good mechanical engineer and easy to work with – until ....

During construction of the research lab, some duct heaters were found to be undersized. Gene fixed them. After the building was occupied by the Printpack research people, there were many problems with the operation of the HVAC systems. Temperature control, humidity control, and office comfort are vital to the operation. The problems were serious and when asked to "fix it" ASAP, Gene refused to cooperate and walked out on me. To force him to fix the problem legally would take time, lawyer fees and no telling how long it would drag out *.

I had a very unhappy client and something had to be done quickly. I called in Derek Peters to recommend a solution. After studying the problems he said I should call in George Hightower, an outstanding Atlanta mechanical engineer and HVAC contractor. I had worked with George on some bank projects we did together. George agreed to help me and after examining the situation he made a list of ten corrective steps. Try step one, if that doesn't work, go to step two, etc. After step five the problem seemed to be solved and I "paid the man the two dollars" (actually it was more like $10,000) for Gene Anglin's mistakes. Even though I insisted, George would never send me a bill for his consultation services that solved the problems and saved my neck.

Shortly after that, Printpack made a major addition to the main offices up the street. Gus Franchini, the Printpack director of engineering, plugged for us to do the design, but we had the Research Lab cloud over our heads. The good news is Gus hired us to do the next manufacturing facility and the firm continued to work on several more manufacturing plants for Printpack, even 14 years after I retired from the firm.

63
THE DARKEST YEARS

Studying Architecture at Tech was great. It was studying the stuff that went with it (Calculus, Physics, Chemistry) that was so tough.

At the beginning of each quarter we signed up in the old Naval Armory for courses we needed that quarter. The first day of the quarter we would go to classrooms which had the course number posted at the door of an empty room. When we found a room with the right course number we would go in, take a seat and wait for the prof to come in. We didn't know who it was going to be.

On one occasion we had gone in a room marked "Calculus 102". Soon the prof entered. It was Professor Brooks, who many of us had had for previous math courses. He was not a very good prof. We called him Miss Brooks, behind his back of course. He addressed the students in his high pitched voice, "I am Professor Brooks and this is Calculus 102." There was stunned silence, then one brilliant guy in the back of the room got up and said, "Oh – I thought this was Calculus 101." At which we all got up and left the room.

In my first try at Tech as a co-op in the Summer of '42, I had Professor Reynolds for Math 102, Algebra. He was a tough old bird. I had him for some Calculus courses after I came back from WW II and started Tech over on the GI Bill.

Every Friday we had a test on the previous week's work. Every Monday Reynolds gave out the graded test papers. One Monday well into the quarter, he was giving out papers and remarked to the class, "This is the strangest class I ever had. One week everybody makes good grades and the next week everybody makes poor grades – except Mr. Warner. He always fails." That's why I started over after the war.

I was having trouble one quarter with Differential Calculus 101. I knew I didn't have a chance to pass it. If I flunked I would not pass enough hours to stay in day school and would have to go to night school and make at least a "C" average to get back into day school. A lot of guys who went to night school never got back in day school and never graduated.

In desperation, I went to the prof and said, "I know I'm going to flunk this course. If you will give me a 'D' I give you my word I will repeat the course next quarter."

He was a kind man and gave me a "D". I repeated the course – and flunked it – and went to night school.

64
ONE THING LEADS TO ANOTHER

Back in the 80's, Warner Summers Ditzel did a ton of work for Eastern Airlines at the Atlanta Airport. I don't care what they call it now, to me it is the Atlanta Airport. The first projects were not very glamorous. Stuff like a 10 by 20 line shack for the baggage handlers. As time went by, the projects got better. We designed the Concourse A and B Eastern Ionosphere Lounges, the Eastern Quarter Point Tunnel between Concourse A and B, as well as the Eastern Air Cargo Facility.

When RJR Nabisco moved to Atlanta, our Eastern connection recommended us to RJR to design their corporate aviation facility at Fulton County Airport. We were selected to design the architecture, engineering, and interior design. We had total design control of the hangar and the attached three story office building that housed the waiting rooms, three catering kitchens, pilot planning room, offices, and other amenities. It was an architect's dream job. The book *Barbarians at the Gate* called it the "Taj Mahal of corporate hangars", but most of the luxurious trappings are long gone.

When RJR left town, the facility was taken over by BellSouth. I think BellSouth sold most of the furniture and art work. Now twenty years later, AT&T has purchased BellSouth and feels it no longer needs the facility. It is sad that the Taj Mahal will end on the AT&T cutting room floor. The bean counters win again.

65
STRANGER THAN FICTION

Warner & Summers did several projects for a local large furniture rental company. Our client contact was a retired Army colonel. Retired Army colonels are not the easiest people to work for. Our fee was fair. More accurately, our fee was cheap. To make brownie points with his boss, who was the founder of the company, the colonel kept trying to get us to lower our fee. We finally got tired of the pressure and Summers wrote what was probably the shortest business letter ever written. It was just one sentence, "We have come to the conclusion that it would be to our mutual best interest for you to get another architect".

The First National Bank of Atlanta was one of our many great clients. The above mentioned founder of the rental furniture company acquired a well-known furniture dealership in Atlanta, and was a big depositor in the bank. He met with the bank president and told him, "If you don't give me all your furniture business, I will withdraw the $40,000,000 I have in your bank."

The bank president opened one of his desk drawers and took out a small slip of paper. Without saying a word he handed it across the desk. It was a withdrawal slip.

66
SPRAY THAT AGAIN

Jerry Provence was one of Holder's project managers. He was a tough, very down to earth guy. He used to call me "the best one-detail architect in Atlanta", because I would draw a typical wall section that would work almost over the entire building. I would supplement it with a few smaller details where the wall encountered some small differences.

I always disliked things on the exterior of a building that looked out of place or were distracting, like roof top units and annoying stuff like that. One day we were discussing something that I preferred would "go away". I suggested that we could "paint it out" so it would be less noticeable. He asked, "What do you mean by 'paint it out'?" I told him maybe we could pick a color that would make it less noticeable, paint it and it would "go away".

At that he imitated taking a spray can of paint, pointed the imaginary paint can at me and pretended to spray me so I would go away – and he would be rid of the troublesome architect.

67
"THERE IS NOTHING MORE STERILE . . . "

Here it is July 2007 and the new, at least it still seems new to me, Georgia Pacific Building is up for sale. When it was built in the 70's, it was a very big important building at Peachtree and Pryor, just a few blocks north of Five Points. The famous architectural firm of Skidmore Owings & Merrill was the architect. Little old Warner & Summers, Architects designed the large (all of two stories tall) branch bank in the building for the Trust Company of Georgia. Everything we did had to be cleared with S.O.M. (Remember the saying "There is nothing more sterile than Skidmore Owings and Merrill").

Let me tell you about S.O.M. They were a pain in the arse to work with. They were arrogant and slow to respond to our efforts to co-ordinate our design with them. The second level of the branch had a balcony served by an elevator and there was a big safe deposit vault on the first level with a parking garage just under it. A couple of parking spaces had to be given up to the required special structural support designed by our structural engineer. If you don't think that was a problem, think again.

Then there was the S.O.M. approval required for the Trust Company sign on the sidewalk in front of the entrance to the building, but that's another story. Believe me, big and famous ain't better. You seek approval at your peril from Skidmore Owings and Merrill.

68
I'M SANFORD AYERS

I went to work at Ayers & Godwin in December 1956 in the Bona Allen Building at Spring and Lucky Streets. The drafting room was just one big open room with eight standard drafting tables, eight metal drafting stools and eight reference tables behind the metal drafting stools. It was all very Spartan. It was very efficient. The desk in the front corner of the room belonged to Sanford Ayers. Jimmy Godwin didn't draw. He just chased after the work.

It was Ayers habit to go to lunch after all the draftsmen came back from lunch. While they were gone, he would go around the room and look at whatever each guy was drawing. Then he would go to lunch at Herrens on Lucky Street, near Forsyth, where he would consume numerous martinis. Ayers was probably the best English Gothic planner and detailer alive. Unfortunately for him, he was an alcoholic. You could hardly recognize his signature on the pay checks.

The last working day before Christmas, the old hands went out to buy the fixin's for the annual Christmas party – booze, paper cups and peanuts. For some reason, I was left alone in the drafting room with Mr. Ayers. I had never been introduced to him when I came to work there. Suddenly he got up, walked over to my desk, extended his hand and said, "I'm Sanford Ayers." No kidding?

If it wasn't English Gothic, Ayers only understood limestone, Flemish bond, and Hope steel casement windows. We did a lot of dormitory projects. Lots of Flemish bond brickwork. We also did all the work at the University of the South at Suwanee. I worked on the drawings for the stands at the playing field – granite, limestone, and English Gothic arches. I also worked on the drawings for the Darlington Chapel in Rome (Georgia).

I got some very good experience at Ayers & Godwin, but soon realized I was doing pretty much the same thing over and over, and it was time for a change. I got lucky. George Heery needed somebody to replace Fred Branch when Fred left to open his own office.

I went to work for George in September 1957, worked there for seven years and learned enough, thanks to George, to start my own practice with Alex Summers.

But that's another story.

69
WHO WERE THOSE GUYS?

I was sent out to a spot on Fulton Industrial Boulevard at Camp Creek Parkway to look at a site for a Trust Company branch. At that time, there was not another building anywhere in sight. I was to meet with a Georgia DOT engineer to discuss median and driveway cuts off Camp Creek Parkway.

I got there first. I parked on the side of the road. There was no one there but me until a stake truck with three black guys pulled off the road about 100 feet behind me. One of them got out and walked up to me and asked what I was doing. Not thinking anything of it, I said, "I'm just waiting for a D.O.T guy." I thought the guys in the truck were there to do some kind of work for somebody they were going to meet.

Then the other two black guys got out of the truck and all three of them came over and silently stood next to me. I didn't really think anything of it, because I was never afraid of black people when I grew up.

After a fairly long wait, the D.O.T. guy came along and parked in front of my car. I greeted him and took my roll of drawings, spread them out on the hood of his truck and we started to talk. It was then that I noticed the three black guys slowly walk back to their truck, get in, and drive off.

What would you have thought? I thought "That's odd. I better get a permit to carry a concealed weapon, if I'm going to be out on many lonely roads just waiting around for someone", and I did the next day.

70
DOVER, DELAWARE

Our first state of the art pickle "factory" design was for Vlasic Foods in Millsboro, Delaware. Holder's pilots flew me to Dover in his King Air corporate plane to get our design approved by the Delaware State Fire Marshall. The Dover airport was unbelievably small. The main runway looked like a poorly paved asphalt driveway. It was so narrow that when the plane turned around to taxi back to the "terminal" (I use the term loosely), the plane almost ran off the side of the runway.

I went into the building to a rent-a-car phone. I talked with an agent in the city and said I wanted to rent a car to go into town, please send one out to the airport. The agent said, "One of our cars is parked there at the airport and the keys are in it. Just take that one." Pretty loose.

I got to the capitol in Dover where I met a pleasant young fellow who was the state fire marshal. He quickly reviewed and approved our plan for the Millsboro plant. Then he said he wanted to have lunch at a great place near the water where the she-crab soup was wonderful. I had never had she-crab soup, but thought that might be nice. I would take him to lunch there.

We had a pleasant meal and the soup was terrific. When the check came, I reached for it and he pushed my hand aside and picked up the check. They sure did business differently in Delaware.

I got the car back to the airport and parked it with the keys in it as instructed by the rent-a-car guy in Dover. When we took off, the pilots had to make a no-flaps takeoff so as not to have the loose gravel on the runway damage the flaps.

71
HEERY AND PORTMAN

It was an AIA meeting at which John Portman was the speaker. George Heery introduced Portman. George gave John a glowing introduction – very complimentary. John stepped up to the rostrum looked at George and said, "I wish there was something nice I could say about you, George." I didn't make that up. I was there.

The best response to an introduction I ever heard was at a Buckhead Business Association meeting. The speaker was the British Consul. The introduction by the BBA president was very long and very good. The Consul came up to the mike and in a beautiful British accent said, "Of all the introductions I have ever had, that was the most – (pause) – recent."

ADVICE TO YOUNG ARCHITECTS
(What I learned in 30 years "in the business")

1. Every client should think that you have only one client.

2. Never, ever, have a lawyer for a client.

3. If the client doesn't like your design solution and you can't sell it in two tries – do it his way.

4. Never choose an engineer on the basis of fee. The engineer with the lowest fee may not be the best qualified for your particular project.

5. If you make a mistake, admit it immediately, and pay for it. Your reputation is worth more than the cost of the mistake.

6. Make the field superintendent your friend.

7. Once your fee is established, forget it, and give the project your best.

8. Always show respect for the tradesmen. They are the people who really create your building.

9. Don't waste time entertaining prospects. Spend your energy doing a good job for your clients and the rest will take care of itself.

10. If you are in the "business" to win awards (it's an ego thing), you are in the wrong business.

11. Do what you say you will do.

12. Don't be discouraged, if you're not selected for a project. It just improves the odds the next time.

13. Whatever you do, don't fall asleep at your drawing board.

SOME OF WARNER & SUMMERS / WARNER SUMERS DITZEL CLIENTS 1964—1993: (Many of the listed clients involved multiple projects)

Valsic Foods
Reliance Electric Company
Certaineed-Saint Gobain
KLM Royal Dutch Airlines
Eastern Air Lines
Delta Air Lines
Hoover Ball and Bearing Company
Schwinn Bicycle Company
K-Mart
Zayre
T J MAXX
BellSouth
Printpack
RCA
Federal Reserve Bank of Atlanta
Trust Company of Georgia
Hennessey Cadillac
Crain-Daly Volkswagen
First National Bank of Atlanta
Federal Savings and Loan
Haverty Furniture Company
Bank South
Guy Milner
Atlanta Public Schools
University of Georgia
American Home Foods
Equifax
Addressograph Multigraph
Rockwell International
Ivan Allen Company
Lathem Time Recorder
Chic-Fil-A
Office Building for J. Mack Robinson
Home Depot
First Union

First Georgia Bank
Toledo Scales
First National Bank of West Point
Davidson Buick
National Bank of Georgia
Fulton Federal Savings & Loan
Pepsi Cola Bottling Company
Atlanta Water Works
The Standard Club
Fulton National bank
Yokogawa Corporation
First National Bank of West Point
Atlanta Federal Savings & Loan
South Trust
National Bank of Warner Robbins
Wachovia
Bank of Bowden Carrolton branch
Davidson Buick
First National Bank of Dalton Georgia
Pepsi Cola Bottling Company
Wachovia
Hennessy Jaguar
Farmers Bank of Douglas Georgia
Abrams Industries
Cox Enterprises, Dayton, Ohio
RJR Nabisco Corporate Aviation
Facility, Fulton County Airport
Ackerman & Co. Olympia Building
Equifax
Towers Perrin
Peachtree Presbyterian Church
British Airways
Rome cable TV
H. J. Russell Company
Ziegler Tools

BUILDING TYPES 1964 - 1993

Industrial Buildings & process plants

Pickle processing plants
Auto seat frames
Auto plastic car accessories
Auto insulation plant
Turbine blades
Flexible packaging
Electric motors
Scales
Castings
Forges
Roofing materials
Fiberglas
RCA clean room
Distribution centers
Pizza processing

Banks

Trust Company Bank/SunTrust, Fulton National Bank, First Georgia, First National Bank of Atlanta/First Atlanta/Wachovia, Fulton Federal S&L, Atlanta Federal S&L, Georgia Federal S&L, NBG, South Trust, First National Bank of West Point Georgia, (and probably a few I have forgotten)

Other

Schools
Churches
Office Buildings
Residences
Warehouses
Car agencies
Furniture stores
Water treatment plants
Airport support facilities
Parking facilities
Corporate Headquarters
Corporate Aviation Facilities

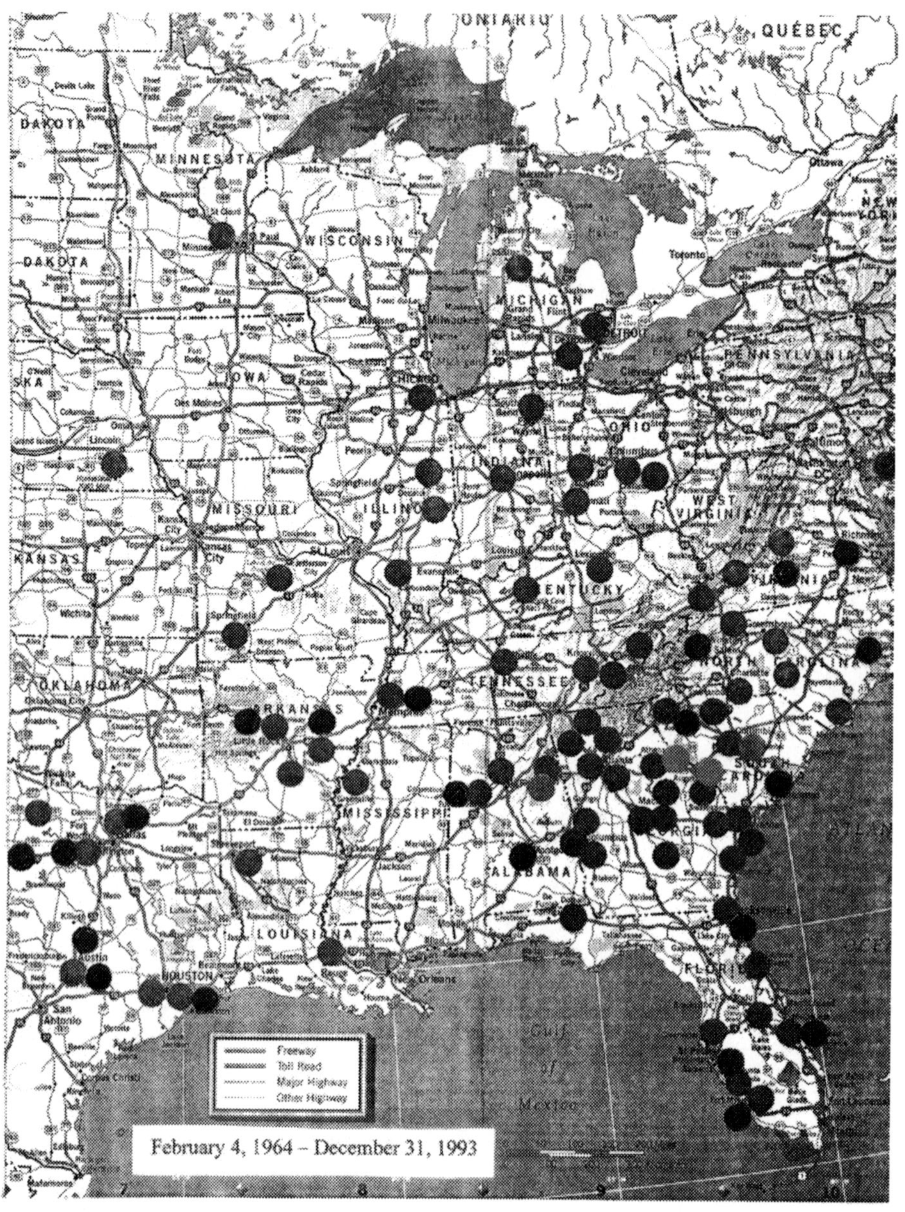

February 4, 1964 – December 31, 1993

WARNER REGISTRATION
1964 - 2003

Georgia
Tennessee
Alabama
Mississippi
Louisiana
Florida
Texas
North Carolina
South Carolina
Indiana
Ohio
Delaware
Maryland
Illinois
Michigan
Minnesota
Arkansas
Kentucky
Virginia

. . . and the District of Columbia

The darkest years of my life were spent at Georgia Tech

THE

FRESHMEN

From the Tech 1950 yearbook, *The Blueprint*

Jim Warner — Architect

THE

SOPHOMORES

Jim Warner — Architect

THE

JUNIORS

TECH
WARNER
"On the contrary, Fenwick. I found 'Our Heritage of World Literature' most enjoyable."

Saved from some cartoons drawn for the student paper, *The Technique*

"I'd cut English with you, Wadsworth, but I need the sleep."

COACH
PRES.
PRES ALUMNI ASSOC
APPLES
WARNER

HOW JOE COLLEGE LOOKS TO HIS.....
out to lunch —Joe.
...BARBER
...CREDITORS
...MOTHER
...GIRL FRIEND
...PROFESSORS
...SCHOOL
...ROOM MATE
...FACULTY ADVISOR
...BAR TENDER

"Of course you realize this means you flunk"

In small towns — most of them — life was self sufficient and pleasant — such a town was Gooneville. It was a time when a brick layer could live comfortably on his earnings.
BUTTER 3^{00} LB
EGGS 2^{00} Doz.
STEAK 5^{00} LB
FIS
Food was unbelievably cheap as measured by our present day stabilized prices.
Young People.
American individualism flourished and Gooneville's streets were lined with comfortable, well built homes.
Quiet Saturday evening gatherings spread a sleepy lull over the peaceful little town.

HNIQUE, ATLANTA,

"After all, Leibnitz, 94 is the next best thing to AA."

"Never mind the caustic remarks, Stumpwater; just hold the ball at the proper angle."

April 26, 1947

"Now, this next problem is so simple that you can work it in your head!"

Saturday, November 8, 1947 THE TEC

"Oh, no ma'am, it's not insomnia—I'm majoring in architecture."

"My God! I thought he fumbled!"

"I understand he's passing Physics."

GEORGIA Saturday, November 8, 1947

"The only thing I got out of chemistry was 25 cents when I sold the book!"

GEORGIA Saturday, October 25, 1947

HOW TO STAY AWAKE IN CLASS

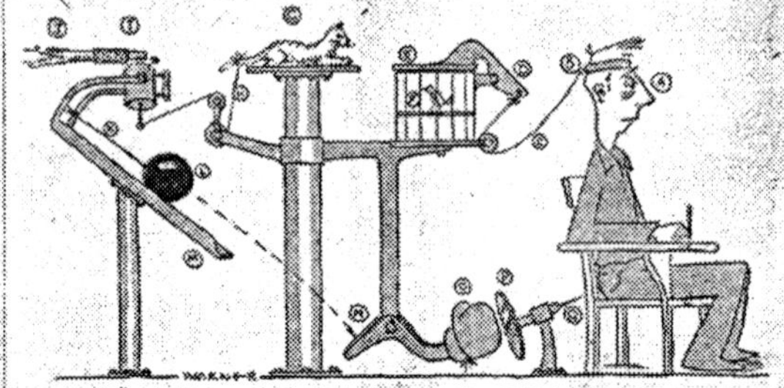

When head (A) nods as Prof. lulls class to sleep band (B) pulls string (C) which activates lever arm (D) opening lid (E) of bird cage allowing bird (F) to escape. This causes cat (G) to lunge for bird (F). When cat (G) lunges at bird (F) string (H) tied to tail of cat (G) tilts blow torch (I) causing flame (J) to burn string (K) thereby releasing cannon ball (L) down shute (M) cannon ball (L) strikes lever (N) causing boxing glove (O) to contact plate (P) causing needle (J) to contact student (ouch!).

PART III

And then I wrote …

1
THE STORY OF MY LIFE

"It was a dark and stormy night..."

At 8:45 pm on October 31, Halloween, 1923, in an unpainted wood frame house up on rock piers (sob), next to a marble quarry at Gantt's Quarry, Alabama (that's outside of Sylacauga which is outside of nowhere), Dr. Miller, a real country doctor, brought me into the world.

Dad had gone to work as an estimator for the Alabama Marble Company after he graduated from the University of Pennsylvania. I don't remember much at that early age. Mom did tell me about the time she had to go somewhere and left me with a poor ignorant country girl. When she got back she asked the girl if I had been any trouble. The girl said, "No'm, when he cry I jes' hol' him over de stove 'til he go to sleep". Maybe that's why I had such a tough time getting out of Georgia Tech..

"I used to live in Chicago. I did, but I don't anymore"

When I was about three years old, Dad was transferred to an office the company opened in Chicago. We lived at Blackstone Ave., Commonwealth and Surf Street, a high rise apartment looking over Lake Michigan. The apartment on Surf Street had one bedroom and a Murphy Bed in the living room wall. Dad's boss came to dinner one night. After dinner, the grown ups talked and talked. Finally the boss said, "Jimmy, isn't it time you were in bed?" I said, "I can't go to bed 'til you go home". I slept in the Murphy Bed. Mom told me that at one of the addresses we were a block from where the St. Valentine's Day massacre occurred – when it occurred. February 14, 1929. I was five years old.

I was about three years old when we moved to Chicago, and I clearly remember Mom taking me for a walk. I was in a leather harness on a leather leash --- just like a puppy dog. We lived within walking distance of Lincoln Park. She would often take me to the Lincoln Park Zoo to look at the animals. One time we got separated from each other in a crowd in the lion house. I guess that's when she decided to put me on a leash when we went out.

When it was time for me to start school, we moved to Glen Ellyn, just west of Chicago near Wheaton, where Red Grange became a college football legend.

Benjamin Franklin Elementary School was a mile from our house on Annendale Ave. There was no lunch room at the school so everyone had to go home to lunch. In the winter when it snowed, and, man, it SNOWED, I had to walk a total of four miles a day to and from school sometimes in three feet of snow (sob) --- really.

Glen Ellyn was on the Chicago Aurora and Elgin commuter train line. It was an electric train with a third rail, like MARTA but no guard over the third rail, and no fence. When we kids went from one side of town to the other, we just jumped over the exposed third rail. That was before OSHA. I was only in the third grade. If Mom had known that she would have fainted.

It was about this time that I realized Dad was very hard of hearing. When he was a teenager he had mastoiditis, an infection of the inner ear that left him very deaf. It turned out to be a lucky thing, because he was the perfect age for the World War I trenches, but considered 4F.

Back To Alabama

As the Great Depression deepened, the Alabama Marble Company retreated to an office in the Watts Building in Birmingham. Until we could find a house to rent, we moved into the LaSalle Apartments at Five Points on the south side of Birmingham. I was enrolled in South Highland Elementary School in the fourth grade. It was September, 1932. The kids in the fourth grade changed classrooms during the day and I was totally lost. To top it off, they took up long division. Dad tried to help me, but I just didn't get it. Homework was not a lot of fun.

After a few weeks we moved to Edgewood, a suburb south of Birmingham. Our house was on College Avenue, right across the street from Edgewood Elementary School. The school had a lunch room and no one was allowed to go home for lunch. Mrs. Weems ran the lunch room and made sure that each kid selected a proper balance of food from the cafeteria line --- none of this all desserts stuff. Mrs. Weems was a grandmotherly (at least she seemed grandmotherly at the time) type and we all loved her.

Believe it or not, in 1932 the Civil War, or, should I say the War of Yankee Aggression, was still very fresh in the minds of Southerners. Having lived up north during my early years, I had somewhat of a Yankee accent. As a result, plus the fact that I was not exactly robust, I got picked on a lot by the other kids (sob).

Living right across the street from the school, we rented a room to the eighth grade science teacher, Mr. Russell. He lived on the other side of Birmingham and didn't want to commute every day. He was a nice man and a good teacher. He lived with us and went home on week ends, but it didn't help my grades any.

Soon we moved to a house on Highland Avenue, the street just behind the stores in Edgewood..When we lived there, the Company (Alabama Marble) closed the Birmingham office and Dad was laid off with one week's notice after being with the Company for ten years. It happened that Wainwright Twing, a childhood friend of Dad's from Riverside, N.J., where he grew up, was in charge of the WPA office in Birmingham. Mr. Twing had come to the house one evening to talk to Dad about getting him a job as an engineer with WPA. That evening, about dusk, I was riding my bike home on Oxmoor Road when I got hit by a hit-and-run driver. My bike was totaled and I was bloodied up – no broken bones – and I dragged my bike home just in time to burst into the house, bloody and in tears, when Mr. Twing was talking to Mom and Dad. Dad did get the job and we continued to eat.

It was when we lived at Highland Avenue that one winter that we had twelve inches of snow in Birmigham. I think the year was 1935. From Highland Avenue we moved to Mecca Avenue, a couple of blocks farther away. Behind the house on Mecca Avenue there were a lot of woods and a hill that dropped off to the little pond and dam that held the water that went to the water hazards at the Jewish Country Club to the west. One day in February, about ten of us were playing around the pond. Some guy said, "Let's go swimming". In February?

So everybody started to take their clothes off. The guys jumped into the ice cold water. I wasn't going to be the only guy standing on the shore, so I took my clothes off and jumped in with the rest of them. That's what you call peer pressure.

When I started high school, I went to Phillips High in downtown Birmingham – September 1937. We moved to 1635 11th Place, south in Birmingham, so I could go to Phillips High. Shades Cahaba was the high school most kids in Edgewood went to. It was in Homewood and wasn't a very good school back then. I hear it's pretty good now. Phillips was a big school, still there, four stories high, and took up a whole city block. The teachers were superb. Pop Keller (Physics) a real Mr. Chips; Miss Saye (Math) I think I was secretly in love with her; little Miss Martin (English Literature); big Miss Martin (Math) kept a baseball bat in Study Hall to control the football players; Miss Senn (Latin) and Miss Hamilton (Latin and History).

Miss Hamilton was one of two teachers who came to our 50th class reunion. She looked so old and frail. I leaned down and said, "Miss Hamilton, I am so glad to see you. I'm Jimmy Warner." She asked, "What did I teach you?" I said, "Latin 101 --- three times." The first day I got to my "home room" late and didn't realize I was in a first period French class. When everyone started speaking French I thought to myself, "I'm never going to make it through high school". It didn't take the teacher long to figure out I was in the wrong place.

In my freshman year, Dad had left WPA and was working at the powder plant (gun powder) in Childersburg between Birmingham and Sylacauga. That was when Grandma and Grandpa Klingler moved down from Elgin, Illinois, to live with us for the rest of their lives. They were both wonderful people. (Grandma Klingler once told me, "Jimmy, it doesn't matter what happens to you in life. It's how you take it that counts.")

During this time, the house at 910 Saulter Road in Edgewood was built. Dad lived with family friends, the Dobbins, at Gantt's Quarry during the week and came home on weekends in our used 1935 Pontiac. It was the car I learned to drive on Lakeshore Drive after we moved into the Saulter Road house in August, 1938. I rode the street car to Birmingham and continued at Phillips. I found out years later that it cost Dad $10 a month for non-resident "tuition".

Here I need to digress to tell what a wonderful person Mom was. Grandpa Klingler had colon cancer. He was at home with Mom caring for him until he died. Grandma Klingler was bedridden with several maladies. Mom took care of her until she died at home. Dad had heart disease. Mom drove for him on business trips and she took good care of him. He died at home one day (at age 64) when he had come home for lunch. Mom lived to be 90 and lived alone until she died --- at home. She walked out the front door one afternoon and dropped dead with a massive heart attack. She had driven herself to the drugstore that morning. She, too, died at home.

Walking to and from school, I passed the YMCA. Mom and Dad got me a membership, and I would stop on the way home to swim or shoot pool. Then I got a paper route in Edgewood, delivering the Birmingham Post. The good thing was they didn't have a Sunday Edition, so I didn't have to get up early on Sunday. I didn't go to the Y anymore. I got out of school at about three o'clock, rode the trolley to Homewood, picked up the papers and rode my bike on the route that took me all the way to where Stanford College is now – on Lakeshore Drive. Things got worse. I sold the Bike for $10 and then I had to walk the long route. I'd get home just in time for dinner. I learned three things from my paper route: 1. The poor people always found a way to pay for the paper each week when I went around on Saturday to collect. 2. The rich people always had some excuse not to pay, or put it off 'til later, and 3. Don't sell your bicycle.

I delivered the Birmingham Post and my friend, Charles Wilder, delivered the Birmingham News. This was before I sold the bike. Our routes converged at Weaver's garage and gas station at Broadway and Oxmoor Road, near the lagoon, long gone, that fed Edgewood Lake, also long gone. We used to stop there, drink a five cent big orange and admire Mr. Weaver's Stanley Steamer. After the "break" we would deliver our papers up the hill on Oxmoor road and to Nancy Woodson's house. We would just hang around talking with Nancy, and trying not to be the first one to leave. The customers of both papers past the Woodson's always got their papers late.

Agnes Payne was one of the prettiest girls at Phillips High School. She lived in North Birmingham, several miles north of Birmingham. She asked me to take her to one of the high school Spring dances (I always thought she asked me to spite a boy friend she had had a spat with). The problem was, I didn't have my driver's license yet. So the chips were down. I had to take my driver's license test the day of the dance. Luckily, I passed. It was spring, and summer tux was the uniform. Agnes was not the kind of girl you would imagine in a used 1935 Pontiac in 1941, especially one that needed water in the radiator every ten miles. I had to be really careful not to mess up my tux. She took it very well, but we never had another date.

The Early War Years

In 1938, Hitler made his move into the Sudetenland and Life Magazine began to chronicle the events in Europe with great coverage. I remember the day in September, 1939, delivering the Birmingham Post on my paper route. The headline was, "Hitler Invades Poland". In the summer of 1940, while at Camp Cosby, the YMCA camp, we listened to the radio during the Battle of Britain. It all seemed so far away.

Camp Cosby was a great summer camp. The summer Dad lost his job, I wanted to go to Cosby (I had been told about it by one of my buddies who had been there). Two weeks cost $10.00. When I asked Mom and Dad if I could go, they said no. They didn't tell me that they didn't have the $10.00 to spare. The next summer, times were better and I got to go. There was a 26 acre lake above which, on a ridge, were six cabins. Every morning we would go down the hill to the lake with our bar of Ivory soap (it floated) in hand, and jump in the lake naked to take our morning bath. The water was really cold.

I remember checking out the 22 cal. rifle and going off to a designated area for target shooting with two of my best buddies from Edgewood, Roy and Robert Atchison, just the three of us. Little did we know then that two of us would be killed in the War. Robert became a Naval Aviator and was killed making a carrier landing in Tokyo Bay. Roy became a Marine lieutenant and was shot by a Japanese sniper while scouting a by-passed island --- both killed after the War was over. Forever young.

After we got into the War, Dad was in Youngstown, Ohio, working for duPont on some component of the Atom Bomb. Grandpa was in New Jersey working in a munitions factory, and I was in the Navy while Mom and Grandma kept the home fires burning, and hooked rugs. They used to jokingly refer to themselves as, "the happy hookers." They hooked some strikingly beautiful rugs. Mom also worked in the bookkeeping department at Sears in downtown Birmingham. They had to hire three people to take her place when she left after the War was over.

We moved into the 910 Saulter Road house in August, 1938. Dad had bought the lot the year before for $600. Dad could have bought the whole hill all the way to the creek at Broadway, enough for five residential lots, for a couple of hundred dollars more, but couldn't swing it. Dad drew the plans (I still have a copy of the blueprints) and had Mr. Clisby and his son, Vivian, build it for $6,000, under an FHA loan. The Clisbys were the best. The Great Depression was still going on and it was easy to get the best. Dad wanted the shutters mounted the correct way, louvers sloping inward when the shutters are open. Mr. Clisby, admitting Dad was right, begged Dad to let him mount them with louvers sloping out so people wouldn't think he had installed them wrong. Being an accommodating, nice guy, Dad gave him his way.

That summer I delivered groceries for the A&P that was in the little group of stores across from Doc Temerson's drug store at Broadway and Oxmoor Road. Doc didn't have any kids, but built three regulation clay tennis courts next to the A&P for us kids to play on. There was no sprinkler system and the clay got very dusty, ankle deep, if there wasn't much rain. There was a large grocery store there the last time I looked. After Doc died, it came to light that he had paid for the college education of several poor kids.

I had a big, really big, basket on the front of my Rollfast bike. The Rollfast replaced the bike totaled by the hit and run driver. One day I was riding through the school yard where two girls were swinging on the school yard swings. Luckily, I had no groceries in the big basket. Being the shy person that I was, I was averting my eyes just as I hit the tree. Humiliating! I also hit a parked car on Broadway while looking down to admire a new pair of shoes. Nobody saw that one. The real disaster occurred when I had a really big load of groceries and two girls were walking down the other side of the street (Broadway again). Just as I averted my eyes, I hit another parked car. Groceries everywhere.

Each time one of these "accidents" occurred, the bicycle fork was bent back and I would have to pull it into place again. This finally resulted in metal fatigue. One day I was riding down then unpaved Saulter Road toward the Saulter Road bridge. When I put on the brakes, metal fatigue did it's work. The fork broke, and I went head first onto the gravel. This was before people wore helmets. I picked up the parts and, semi-conscious, walked back up the hill to the house where Mom was washing clothes in the basement. That's when I came to and asked Mom, "What happened?" When she got a grip on herself, she called the doctor who came out to the house (this was before Medicare) and said I had a concussion, but would live. Another reason why Tech was so difficult.

Growing up in Edgewood was pretty good. Lots of woods and creeks to play in with buddies, plunking at cans with a .22, riding bikes all over, swinging on grape vines – a good time. It was a far cry from living in a high-rise apartment in Chicago.

When I turned sixteen, Dad taught me to drive in the used 1935 Pontiac which he traded our 1932 Oldsmobile for. We would go to Lake Shore Drive, which was a three mile straight stretch of gravel road then. It's pretty easy to learn to drive on a straight stretch of road with no other cars on it, but still a great thrill for a sixteen year old. The lake is gone now (the dam broke one night and it was never rebuilt). There is a lot of development where the lake was along the now paved four lane road with a median.

After I got out of high school, I worked at several jobs. The first was at the Claybecker Coffee Company. It was just me and Mr. Claybecker. His little place of business received large bags of coffee beans from all over the world. He blended and roasted the coffee beans and delivered them to some of the Birmingham restaurants (Mary Beard's Tea Room, the Tutwyler Hotel, etc.). The first day of the two days I was employed there he left me with a big gas fired roaster, roasting a large amount of expensive coffee beans. He told me how to tell when to turn it off. I didn't understand a word he was saying.

Luckily he got back before it was too late. The second day he let me deliver the coffee. At Mary Beard's I locked myself out of the car and "old" Mr. Claybecker (he seemed old at the time) had to walk six blocks in the hot July sun to bring the keys.

Then there was the day I worked for the Woodson Lumber Company. Mr. Woodson was Nancy Woodson's father. The Woodson's lived over the hill that was between our house and Oxmoor Road. I was secretly smitten with Nancy – puppy love. Mr. Woodson explained to me how to grade a truck load of 2x6's. I didn't understand a word he was saying. At the end of a very long day I told him I didn't think I was cut out for the lumber business. If I had played it right and married Nancy, I might have owned the Woodson Lumber Company. Mrs. Woodson's nephew, my good friend Earl Lackey, and I did yard work for her. One day we took down an eight inch pine tree very close to her house. We had to take it down by cutting three foot sections off from the top down and lowering them to the ground. Mrs. Woodson had a lot of confidence in us. Earl was with Patton all through Europe. After the War he died in a sailboat accident while on R&R in the Mediterranean Sea.

Following these two false starts in the real world, and always enjoying a good movie, I went to work as an usher at the Alabama Theater. It was very ornate – kind of like a small version of the Fox Theater in Atlanta.. I worked four on four off and four on. I learned to smoke in the ushers' locker room during the four off. I got 25 cents an hour. Street car fare was 14 cents a day and lunch was 25 cents for a chocolate malt and a ham sandwich at the drug store next to the theater. That left me with $1.61 a day, but look at the movies I got to see "free". I still like to see a good old movie more than once.

My next job was "mask out artist" at the Enterprise Engraving Company. It was just me and Mr. Mills, an ex-Marine sergeant who had fought the bandits in Nicaragua in the '20s where he contracted amoebic dysentery which he suffered from for the rest of his life. Mr. Mills had a deal with Loveman's Department Store to pick up Loveman's fashion ad art work, prepare it (that was me) for the photo engravers and deliver it to the Alabama Engraving Company around the corner. I got 15 cents an hour, but it was an easy job, except on Wednesday when everything had to be prepared for the Thursday newspaper ads. Every now and then a U.S. Treasury man would drop in to see if we were making any plates. With just me there when Mr. Mills was out of the office made it look a lot like a front. I read *"Gone With The Wind"* at the Enterprise Engraving Company.

And now for my last civilian job until I got out of Georgia Tech after the War (you don't graduate from Tech – you get out). I got a job in the Traffic Department of TCI, Tennessee Coal Iron and Railroad Company, a division of U. S. Steel, as a file clerk. The office was in the Brown-Marx building, the second tallest building in Birmingham, next to the Comer building. Brown-Marx was at the corner of 20th Street and First Avenue. I filed railroad bills of lading, there were a lot of railroads back then. This was not exactly creative work. I decided it was time to think about college and escape the business world. Dad was a graduate civil engineer, Tau Beta Pi, University of Pennsylvania, Class of '22. I was not exactly Tau Beta Pi material, but I admired my father so much that I wanted to go to engineering school.

In Birmingham, you either went to Auburn Polytech or University of Alabama. That meant Auburn for me. I went to the TCI personnel department in the building. The office consisted of the Director and one secretary. The Director said they didn't have a Co-op opening at Auburn, but they did have an opening at Georgia Tech. I said, "OK, where is it?" (Honest, my very words). So I was going to Georgia Tech, wherever it was. The only catch was, the opening was for the school term first. There was no work term first to make the money to pay the tuition and living expenses for the school term.

Since I had no money, and Dad had no money, he borrowed $600 (same amount Dad had paid for our lot) on his life insurance (I didn't know he had that much coverage), and off I went to Tech in "the Summer of '42" (great movie sound track). It was the first time I had been away from home for more than two weeks. On the first day at Tech I was getting to know my new Cloudman Hall roommate, Cub Culbertson, from Thomasville, Georgia. He was bragging about graduating tenth in his high school class. Having gone to Phillip's, which was huge, I was impressed. I asked him how many were in the class. He said, "Ten."

I was elected president of the Freshman Co-op class. We were hazed by the sophomores. There was a tradition of a tug of war at Peachtree Creek when half of the quarter was up. The Frosh and the Sophs rode to the site in a big stake truck. The president of each class was first in line when the tug of war started. If the Frosh pulled the Sophs into the creek, hazing was over. If the Sophs pulled the Frosh into the creek, the Frosh pulled the truck back to Tech with the Sophs in the truck and hazing would continue for the rest of the quarter. As president of the freshman class, I was the first to go into the water. That's Leadership The tug of war occurred at a point in the creek about fifty yards downstream from Peachtree Road. I'll never forget pulling that truck back to Tech, especially the part up the Piedmont Hospital hill.

Speaking of Peachtree Creek, it was just about a mile from the spot where we had the tug of war that Great-Grandpa Warner and Great-Grandpa Klingler wisely surrendered during the Battle of Peachtree Creek. Great-Grandpa Klingler was sent to a POW camp in Alabama, and Great-Grandpa Warner was sent to Andersonville.

Hazing in the Tech Co-op freshman class was relatively mild. Things like the Sophs sending a freshman to get some refreshment at the Varsity late at night. The expressway (it is now called the Interstate) wasn't there – just a big grassy field. One time they took us to Stone Mountain at 2 a.m. after removing all the money anyone had. One of the guys had hidden a couple of dollar bills in his shoe, and it was enough to get us back to civilization on the street car that ran from Decatur to Atlanta. Of course we first had to walk from Stone Mountain to Decatur. The whole class was involved except one freshman who had hidden in a closet when the Sophs came to get us. When we caught him, we gave him a Tech haircut – shaved his head except for a letter "T" on top.

In my first quarter Algebra class, the prof was Professor Reynolds. He was tough but fair. Every Friday we had a quiz, and every Monday the graded papers were handed out. Near the end of the quarter, when Reynolds was passing them out, he said, "This is a very strange class. One week most of the grades are passing grades, and the next week mostly failing – except Mister Warner. He always fails".

As I said, I was not a brilliant student, not even bright, but I stayed in the program. In September I came home for the work term in the steam engineering department of the TCI Ensley Works, one of the five steel mills in Birmingham. It was, like the other mills, big – one mile wide and five miles long. It had Bessemer converters, blast furnaces, open hearth furnaces, a foundry, coke ovens (soft coal was converted into coke) and a rolling mill. A big time operation. My job was to go through the mill each day and change all of the recording charts that measured flow of gas, water, steam, air; you name it, anything that flowed. I brought the charts to the office where the engineers used them to calculate the cost to produce one ton of steel. I got to see the whole operation up close, very exciting for a teenager.

While I was on this work term, I was walking down the street in Birmingham one Saturday morning in October 1942 when I came upon yellow footprints painted on the sidewalk. I followed them around the corner right into the Navy recruiting office. What the heck – I took the screening test the Navy had for the Naval Aviation Cadet flight training program. I passed, but I had to get my parent's permission to enlist. Mom and Dad didn't want to sign the papers, but I told them I was going to have to "go" sooner or later anyway so let me go into the Navy where I wanted to go. I had seen *All Quiet on the Western Front* years before and it made an indelible impression on me – anything to avoid the infantry. They finally were convinced and signed the papers. They probably saved my life by letting me stay out of the infantry.

The next step was going to the Naval Aviation Cadet Selection Board in Atlanta, in the Capitol Cadillac show room and repair shops across West Peachtree from the Biltmore Hotel. GM was making tanks and torpedo bombers that year, not Cadillacs. The mental and physical tests got serious here. The minimum weight for the program was 124 pounds. I weighed 123 pounds, but I guess they needed pilots and made an exception for me. Later, during flight training, my cadet buddies told me that the reason for the 124 pound minimum was that if you bailed out and weighed less than 124 pounds the chute wouldn't open. I passed all the tests, even though I was a 123 pound weakling. Those who passed were sworn in (it was November 4, 1942) and sent home to wait for orders. I went back to the Ensley Works to wait. When my work term was up, I had not yet been called. The head of the steam engineering department was a great guy. He said I could continue on a second back to back work term until called up. I got the orders to report on March 4, 1943. I can remember as if it were yesterday walking down the woods path to catch the streetcar to WWII with Mom waving goodbye from the front door.

Flight Training

I got off the streetcar at 3rd and 20th and walked about eight blocks to the Terminal Station where I got on a Pullman car full of Cadets from other towns west of Birmingham. We arrived in Columbia, South Carolina and were bussed to the University of South Carolina where we were assigned to a dorm, which the Navy called a barracks. It looked like a dorm to me. I was in the 3rd Battalion in "Flight Prep". Who should I run into the first day but my childhood buddy, Robert Atchison, who was in the 2nd Battalion? Since most of us were just high school graduates, the classes involved instruction in math, dead reckoning navigation, Morse code, blinker, semaphore, aeorolgy, aircraft engines, recognition, and a bunch of athletics (and a bunch of athletics and a bunch of athletics and...)

After three months of Flight Prep, the fun started. We were sent to St. Petersburg, Florida for what they called WTS, War Training School. Sort of an odd name since we were learning to fly a Piper Cub ("...and a beautiful thing it was, but not much use in a fight"). It was half day flying and half day athletics – on the beach at St. Pete. Not bad. My first instructor, Mr. Lindsey, was an old (he looked old to me), crop duster, and he was mean as a snake. He looked like the Western movie villain Lee van Cleef. We had to have eight hours of instruction before we could legally solo.

On my first flight at St. Pete (I had never been in an airplane before in my life), his note under "Remarks" in my log book was "TENSE". On the second flight, the remark was "APPREHENSIVE", and on the third flight he wrote "RELAXED". On my eighth hour, I was making a landing approach while another Cub was in take off position. Lindsey yelled, he never spoke he always yelled, "Go around!" After I went around and made the landing he yelled, "Let me out. You're not safe to fly with!" It's obvious to me now that was his way of saying, I mean yelling, "You are safe enough to solo now". It was a great experience soloing, but no match for 60 mph on the Lake Shore Drive gravel road in a 1935 used Pontiac.

At St. Pete, occasionally a Russian Mine Sweeper would dock near our airport, which was right on Tampa Bay. The epaulets on a cadet uniform had just one star. Stripes were added as you advanced in rank. When Russian sailors passed us on the street, they would salute. They must have thought we were very young brigadier generals.

We ate at the nearby Merchant Marine cooks and bakers school. They had a two week course. The food was not all that great the first week of their course, but by the end of the two weeks it was pretty good, especially the baked goodies. The next two weeks started with a new class and we had to get used to the first week cooking all over again.

St. Pete was great fun, almost like summer camp. I remember it as if it were yesterday. The big adventure was with Mac MacMahan (biggest guy I ever knew), Fighter Williamson (his nickname was "Fighter" because he wanted to be a fighter pilot more than any cadet I ever knew – he probably got orders to Torpedo Bombers when he got his wings), Lou Helms (I am in touch with Lou after all these years), Tojo McClellan (Tojo because of his slanting eyes. His father was an Army officer stationed in the Far East at one time), Glenn Pugh and Henry Livingston (both killed later in training) and many others, all young and eager.

Next came the really tough part – "Athens Preflight" at UGA. More "half day ground school, half day athletics". Celestial navigation was added to all the usual subjects. The athletics were very much like what you saw in the movie *"An Officer and a Gentleman"* except the athletic instructors didn't use foul language, and none of us had motorcycles, we had to walk everywhere. The Marines that drilled us would use a mild expletive now and then, but nothing really bad.

Athletics involved a series of two week periods during each of which we would engage in two different athletic activities. For example: football and boxing, jiu jitsu and tumbling, track and basketball, wrestling and obstacle course, swimming and swimming, etc. Swimming was a big thing in the Navy. If you couldn't meet the rigid standards, you were considered a "sub-swimmer" which meant no Liberty until you were no longer a "sub-swimmer".

We lived in another barracks that looked like a dorm. The barracks were all named after aircraft carriers. Ours was "Essex". Years later, when it was a dorm again and named "Mary Linden Hall", my architectural firm was commissioned by the Board of Regents to design the remodeling of what to me would always be "Essex".

Preflight was tough, but most of us survived to go on to Memphis for "Primary Flight Training" (sometimes referred to as "E Base", "E" for Elimination from the flight training program) flying the wonderful N2S Stearman, the most beautiful open cockpit two-seater biplane ever designed. This is where we really started flying – it separated the boys from the boys, so to speak – most of us were only 19 years old. We became proficient (those of us who weren't washed out) at precision landings, formation flying, aerobatics (Chandelles, wingovers, precision spins, the falling leaf, slow rolls, snap rolls, Immelmans, formation take-offs and night flying – talk about confused!). It was great fun except for the fear of washing out and becoming a Seaman 2nd Class at Great Lakes Training Center in Chicago. Seaman 2nd Class is the lowest rank in the Navy.

Air Corps cadets who washed out of flight training could go on to become officer navigators or officer bombardiers. Since most Naval Aviators do their own navigating and bombing, the Navy did it differently. If you washed out flying, you went to the bottom of the pecking order. I never met a Navy cadet who was afraid of being killed, and a lot of them were killed, but we were all deathly afraid of washing out. By the time I retired from the Navy I counted up the number of guys I knew during my flying career who were killed in just training accidents – 35.

My Primary flight instructor at NAS Memphis was Ensign Ed Brown, the exact opposite of my crop duster instructor at St. Pete. Ensign Brown was a kind and patient man. I found out years later that I was his first student. He was from Birmingham. Right after the War we got together and rented an SNV trainer at the Birmingham airport. We proceeded to buzz the hell out of 910 Saulter Road. Mom and Dad were in the front yard waving bed sheets. When we got back to the airport, the guy who rented us the plane ran out to the plane and hollered, "What the hell did you guys do? The phone's been ringing off the hook ever since you left!" Unbeknownst to me, a Civil Aviation Authority employee lived not too far from our house. It was right after the War was over, so nothing ever happened to us. Things were still loose – so loose that we didn't even have to prove we could fly the airplane when we rented it.

It was at Memphis that I almost washed out. At the end of B-Stage (the precision landing phase), I had a check ride which involved slips to the circle, S-turns to the circle, and figure eights at 500 feet around pylons. A slip is a way to lose altitude on the approach to landing if you are a little too high. It involves right rudder and left aileron which puts you in a left bank attitude but flying straight ahead, lined up with the runway. Just before you touch down you neutralize the controls and land in a three point attitude. I got a "down" at the end of B-Stage.

If you got a "down" you had to go before a board of three Instructors who decided if you would get what was called "Squadron Time" which was two extra hours of instruction after which you had to fly two "ups". I went before the board and it was decided I was worth saving. I got the extra time. They asked me if I wanted a different instructor and I said I wanted to keep Ensign Brown as my instructor.

Ed took me up and concentrated on slips to the circle, the most difficult maneuver. He would pick out a cumulus cloud top and show me how to do it right. I slipped to the top of a lot of cumulus clouds for two days. Then came the moment of truth – the first of the two check rides.

On this check ride I had a notoriously tough check pilot, LT Shelton. It was a clear afternoon and the air was smooth. I did the routine climb out at 60 knots and making 90 degree timed turns (three degrees per second). The smooth air made it easy. I did it perfectly. To make a long story short, all went just right. I had never flown better. The slips to the circle were perfect. As we started back to the home base, LT Shelton was looking at me in the mirror over his windshield with a puzzled look on his face. Then he said, "Go back and do some more slips to the circle". I thought that was odd, but I went back to the field we had been using and I did some more perfect slips, recovering just as I touched down. He said, "Take me home".

When we got back to the schedule board, Shelton asked me to show him my dog tags. That was odd. Ed walked up and said, "How'd my boy do?" Shelton turned to the chalk schedule board and marked a down arrow. He gave me a "down"! Ed asked him why, and he said my slips were dangerous and that I didn't fly like a student. They were too good."(ENS) Shelton just rubbed his LT collar bars and walked off. I didn't get much sleep that night, but the next morning Shelton had changed the down arrow to an "up". Ed must have done some fancy talking that night to get me through. I think what happened, not too long before this, some instructors dressed an instructor as a cadet to play a trick on Shelton. The next day I flew the second "up" required, and the rest is history.

Primary at Memphis was in the winter of '43-'44 and flying in the open cockpit Stearman was pretty cold. I flew one hop a day, but poor Ed flew all day long. I can still see him talking to me through chattering teeth after a flight.

Next stop Pensacola, the birthplace of Naval Aviation a mere 30 years earlier. First was Saufley Field for what was called "Basic", flying the SNV "Vultee Vibrator" like the one Ed and I rented after the war, a low wing monoplane with fixed landing gear and – A RADIO. The radio was for the back seat instructor's use only. They used it to shout at cadets for doing something stupid while flying formation or making precision landings. On solo flights the cadets would have fun, unauthorized, on the radio. "Basic" involved precision landing, touch-and-go landings (the British called it "circuit and bounce"), cross country formation, and (gasp) more night flying plus ground school and athletics.

The food was good at Saufley. We went through a cafeteria line with real plates, not the usual metal trays, and sat at tables with white tablecloths and silver. We thought this must be like being an officer except for the cafeteria line.

From Saufley we went to Whiting Field, part of the Pensacola Training Command near Milton, Florida. There was South Whiting for Instrument Flight training in SNJ's and, separated only by hangars, administrative, and classroom buildings, there was North Whiting for advanced multi-engine training in the twin Beech SNB (we called it the Small Navy Bomber, get it? – SNB). Nobody wanted multi-engine. Everybody wanted to be a fighter pilot.

As a cadet I hated Instrument Flight training. It was hard. (Jimmy Doolittle had made the first successful instrument approach and landing barely ten years earlier). It was no fun at all just flying around staring at a bunch of instruments that would tell you what attitude the plane was in relative to the horizon, which you couldn't see, while your inner ear played tricks with your senses. This was coupled with low frequency radio navigation of the most primitive kind and with flying precise patterns – so many seconds on one heading, then so many seconds to change altitude and 90, 180 and 270 degree standard rate timed turns (turns at three degrees per second) while changing altitude, etc. Not exactly fighter pilot stuff. As always, unpleasant experiences come to an end.

On to "Bloody Barin". Barin Field was near Foley, Alabama, where we went through training that was called "Advanced" or "Final Squadron" flying the SNJ with – a radio and RETRACTBLE landing gear. You couldn't see the gear come up, but you could just picture in your mind how hot you looked on take off. Training at Barin involved more precision landings, six plane formation with six planes in two Vs of three during day and NIGHT flying – at night no running lights, just exhaust flares and good night vision – strafing, bombing, and air to air gunnery (great fighter pilot stuff), over water navigation, plus the usual ground school and athletics. It was called "Bloody Barin" because at one time an average of one cadet a day was killed in a training accident. A nephew of Walter Winchell was one of those fatalities. Winchell raised so much hell in Washington that things were tightened up flight safety-wise and we only lost one cadet per week, on average.

During this period the cadet load was so great that my "flight" of six cadets, (me, Bob Warner, Bob Scales, Elmo Parker, Lindsey and Smith, the same six throughout this phase), and many others had to go to ground school half day and athletics the other half – no flying because there were not enough planes. The choice of athletics was left up to the cadet – tennis, baseball, swimming, etc. I picked tennis. Bob Warner and I played tennis half a day all of August 1944. The brass came to the conclusion that a certain percentage of cadets needed to be washed out. We called it, "the Purge". Since my flight wasn't flying, we couldn't be purged. Soon the brass realized they had washed out too many, and we got to start flying again with less chance of being washed out. Timing. Lucky again!

Navigation and gunnery were flown over the Gulf, south of Mobile Bay. A gunnery flight consisted of one of the cadets in our six man flight towing a target sleeve and the other five flying in echelon about 200 feet above the tow plane. The five in echelon would peel off in turn (just like in the movies), make a gunnery run on the sleeve, pull up and join up as last man in the echelon until his turn came again. A flight instructor would chase behind and score each cadet's runs, etc. After half the period was up, the tow plane would do a 180 and head back for land.

At the start of the exercise, the tow plane would orbit over the beach at the head of one of the five ranges that extended out over the Gulf and wait for the rest of his flight to approach to make a positive identification. Sometimes there would be more than one flight assigned to a range. We would fly from Barin Field to the range in V formation. When the flight leader spotted a tow plane orbiting at the head of the assigned range, he would put the flight in step down column (line astern), head for the tow, fly under the tow plane slightly to the right to check the side number, and, if the ID was positive, the tow plane would head out over the water.

The flight leader would then climb up 200 feet above the tow, putting the flight in echelon, and the runs would start, each plane pealing off in turn to make a run. We had a .30 caliber machine gun mounted on the cowl. There was no gun sight. You just lined up the target with the third rivet on the cowl just left of the gun. I don't know if we ever hit the sleeve. The form of the run is what we were being taught.

On a final check ride at Barin in an SNJ, I had a particularly tough check pilot. The check ride went fine, then I almost messed up. Well, I did mess up, but the check pilot missed it. On the final approach to the field I came in a little short. There were two little scrub pines close to the approach end of the runway. I had my eye on them and was concentrating on the one on the right. The right wing barely hit the top of the tree. The instructor said, "You just did miss that tree." I figured he must have been watching the pine tree on the left, which I did miss.

Midair collision

Leading the flight one day, I was about to approach a tow plane for I.D. when another cadet formation was starting an I.D. approach on the same tow plane. To give the other flight some time, I took my flight in a 360 turn to be in position to I.D., if the other flight and tow didn't match up. As I came out of the 360, I saw the other flight leader fly over instead of under the tow plane. Each plane in step down column came closer to the tow plane. When flying formation in column, each pilot in the formation is intently focused on the plane ahead. The last man in the column, not aware of anything but the plane ahead, collided with the tow plane. It turned out to be our tow plane flown by Cadet Lindsey.

The tow plane went into a graveyard spiral and the other plane went into a normal spin. It all seemed to be in slow motion. It seemed like forever, but finally both cadets bailed out and survived. Lindsey got his Pararaft out and waited for a PBY to come pick him up. When the PBY taxied over to him, one of the wing floats hit him and knocked him back into the water. Before all this happened to Lindsey, he was a very quiet introvert, laid back type guy. After the midair he was a changed person, very outgoing and sociable – a complete personality change.

Speaking of collisions: night practice landings were without landing lights, and the runway was lit with three flare pots spaced about 100 feet apart. We were supposed to land between the first two pairs of flare pots on each side of the runway. One night I landed where I was supposed to land, but the cadet landing behind me was coming in hot and long. As I started to turn off the runway, he caught up with me and his prop cut the tail off my plane. He was overtaking me slightly to my right. If I hadn't started turning to my right, his left wing would have hit my tail and his prop would have hit the cockpit. No one was hurt. Lucky again.

Night formation was interesting. Before we went up we waited in the ready room which was lit by red light bulbs to preserve our night vision. The formation flying at Barin consisted of two Vee's of three planes each in tight formation.

No running lights, just the flare of the exhaust stacks. The closer you held your position, the quicker you could detect any slight movement out of position, and make a correction. This really focused the mind. One of the dangers in flying formation at night is "Auto Kinetic Hypnosis". Flying formation and staring at the only light source, the light begins to appear to oscillate when actually it isn't, and you are actually maintaining your position. If you start correcting for the perceived relative motion you can get vertigo, lose control and spin in.

Getting the bird (the long coveted gold wings)

After Barin we went to Pensacola "Mainside" (Chevalier Field) for a two week course in "Naval Customs and Traditions" plus check out in the Dilbert Dunker. The Dilbert Dunker in the movie *An Officer and a Gentleman* looked like, and probably was, the very same one we used. We went to the tailor shop in the San Carlos hotel in Pensacola and ordered our officer uniforms. We got a $300 uniform allowance with which to buy Aviation Greens, Blues, Khakis and a really neat grey trench coat.

In late 1944 at "Mainside", 300 cadets were commissioned and designated Naval Aviators every Tuesday and every Thursday, every week. I got my wings on October 3rd, 1944 and was ordered to Ft. Lauderdale for operational training in Torpedo Bombers. My orders included 30 days leave prior to reporting. The next day I was informed that my orders had been changed, and I was to "report without delay" to Instrument Flight Instructors School (IFIS) at NAS Atlanta. "Report without delay" means what it says – NOW! I caught the train for Atlanta that night.

IFIS

NAS Atlanta did not have quarters for all of the officers going through IFIS. Families in North Atlanta would take in an officer, providing room and board. I lived with the Simonton's on Alberta Drive, just a few doors off Roswell Road at The Peachtree Presbyterian Church. Years later, my architectural firm designed an eight million dollar expansion, and later an eleven million dollar expansion to the church. The Simonton home was like a home away from home. Nicest people you would ever want to know. Mrs. Simonton treated me like her own son.

At IFIS we flew the NH-1 Howard, a high wing monoplane with fixed landing gear. It looked non-aggressive, to put it mildly, but a lot safer than a torpedo bomber. It had dual controls in the front and one position with controls in the back, along with a bunch of instruments and radio navigation gear for the student. The two in front were the student instructor and the instructor. The guy in back was the "student". Along with the basic instruments course and radio navigation work we did aerobatics under the hood in an SNJ. This was to teach us how to get out of unusual attitudes on instruments. The whole idea of instrument flying is to ignore your inner ear sensations that will give you false sensations and that cause you to think the plane is doing one thing when in fact it is doing another. If you believe your inner ears, they will kill you. If you believe your instruments, they will save your life.

One of the pilots in Flight 3 when I got to Whiting was George "Sandy" Sander who later became a close friend and now, in our 80's, lives just around the corner from me. We ran into each other at Tech after the war, joined the Naval Air Reserve in September 1946, got jobs at the same A&E firm after graduating, both rose to commanding officer of a Reserve squadron.

To Whiting Field

After completing the IFIS training I was ordered to Flight 3 – Squadron VN3D8 – at NAS Whiting near Milton, Florida. That's where I met Sandy. There were eight Flights with about 16 instructors each. We flew three 1 ½ hour flights per day in SNJ's with the cadet under the hood in the back seat. The syllabus was basic instruments, precision patterns (timed climbs and turns), low frequency radio range navigation, and recovery from unusual attitudes, with the cadet under the hood, plus ground school lectures. When I gave a lecture I didn't feel any older than the cadets. If a question was asked that I didn't know how to answer I'd say, "We will get to that in the next lecture." Never did.

After a few months, the syllabus was changed to add a Basic phase instructing the student flying VFR (Visual Flight Rules as opposed to IFR, Instrument Flight Rules – blind) in formation and practicing the usual precision landings. The theory was that if the cadets flew the plane VFR they could better visualize the plane's attitude relative to the horizon while under the hood, which is the objective of blind flying. The Basic instruction was fun, especially the formation flying, even if the instructor had to ride in the back.

In Flight 3 we tried to give the cadets every chance to stay in the program. If a cadet was not doing well on a check ride and it looked like he should get a "down", we would stop the check ride and start instructing the kid on things he was weak in. When the hop was over we would write it up as an incomplete check ride, which gave the kid another shot at it. I don't know of any Flight 3 instructor ever giving a "Down".

When the war was over in August of '45 the flight program began to wind down and I was mustered out in December. I instructed Instruments from December '44 to December '45.

Back to Georgia Tech

I started over as a first quarter freshman. Since I had pretty much flunked out before I went into the Navy, I was getting my second chance. Most of the students were veterans. We had to take a math "placement" test in the old Naval Armory. It was the only place they could accommodate the large number of vets. Only ten guys in the group were non-veterans. There were about 1,600 veterans that "got out" of Tech in the Class of '50. All the veterans wore parts of their old uniforms. We weren't getting that generous military pay now. You could tell the pilots (but you couldn't tell them much), because they all wore their flight jackets – proudly.

The way it worked was the school got $500 for tuition and supplies for each veteran who passed a minimum of 12 hours per quarter. Most of us took as many as 20 hours. If the vet took a major that required less than $500 per quarter, the school got the difference. If the major required more than $500, the school ate the difference. Architecture required a lot of supplies, more than any other major. I think Tech got well on the $500 for the other courses.

I had some good profs and some bad profs. We had weekly exams for ten weeks in almost every course, except Architecture. You could tell what your grade was going to be, knowing you had to get at least 600 points to pass the course. Near the end of the quarter, you could pretty well tell if you weren't going to make it. I was flunking Calculus one quarter. If I flunked it, I would have to go to night school (you had to have at least a "C" in everything you take in night school to get back into day school). I went to the prof (he was one of the good profs) and said, "If you will give me a 'D', I give you my word I will repeat the course". If he did I could stay in day school. He gave me the 'D', and I repeated the course, and – flunked it. And so to night school. It wasn't much fun, but I did get back into day school. Many who went to night school never got back into day school.

At the beginning of each quarter we stood in line at the old Naval Armory, waiting for the doors to open so we could rush in and get our preferred schedule for the quarter firmed up as to subject and time the class met. The next day we would report to the classroom we had signed up for to find out who the professor would be. A group of us reported to a Calculus 102 classroom. We took our seats to wait for the prof to come in and introduce himself. Who walks in but Professor Brooks. Many of us had had him in previous courses. Brooks was a very effeminate, boring professor. He walked to the front of the class and announced, "I am Professor Brooks and this is Calculus 102". There was a silence and then a guy in the back of the room said, "Oh (pause), I thought this was Calculus 101". At that, everyone in the room got up and walked out. That's what I call quick thinking.

I made poor grades in the non-architectural subjects, and I made top grades in the architectural courses. That pulled my overall point average up to the point where I squeaked through and "got out" of Tech – with a 2.0 point average – and so the darkest years of my life, March 1946 to December 1949 were over.

Into the cold cruel world

The day after I got out I went to work for Smith and Hobbs, a small A&E firm in the Peters Building near Five Points, right next to the Kimball House. The hotel and the firm are long gone. This was before air conditioning and the office was practically over the railroad tracks that served the Union Station, also long gone. (Pretty soon I'm gonna be long gone). In the summer we had to keep the windows open and the soot from the trains was a problem. We also had to wrap towels around our arms so the sweat wouldn't make us stick to the drafting paper.

My good friend, Van Vanover, was working for the firm while at Tech. Carol M. Smith, the architect, was very crippled from infantile paralysis that he had when he was just a teenager. He wasn't able to do any drafting and Van really ran the architectural part of the firm, even while he was still in Tech. We had become friends at Tech and Van got me the job.

Van was in the inactive Air Force Reserve, and I was in the Active Naval Air Reserve. When the Korean War started, Van was recalled to active duty. I was dating an Emory nurse at the time. We both liked classical music. I figured I'd be recalled to active duty too, so I gave her my entire collection of 78 rpm classical records – and then I wasn't recalled. Van could never understand why I was getting paid by the Navy and he wasn't, but he got recalled. I think he has since forgiven me inasmuch as I went back on active duty two years later.

After the war started, business began to drop. Building materials were hard to get and that affected the commercial building industry. Cleve Cail and I were the only architectural draftsmen. It was obvious that one of us would have to go. Cleve had a wife and two kids, and I was single, so we would go to a different architect's office at lunch every day – to find me a job.

One day we went to the office of Griff Edwards, on the second floor of the old Leows Grand theater building. George Hampton was alone in the office eating his lunch at his drawing board. I asked him if Griff needed a draftsman. He said no, but he had heard that Abreu and Robeson were looking for one. So the next day we went to the office of Abreu and Robeson. This was when my life changed.

Matt Jorgenson was in the reception room talking to the secretary. I asked him if they needed a draftsman. He said, "Mister Abreu is here. I'll let you talk to him." Everyone in Atlanta mispronounced it Abrew and Robeson, when the correct pronunciation was A-bray'-uh and Robeson. I was a little nervous and didn't realize I was going to talk to the top dog.

He asked me, "How would you like to live in a bachelor's paradise?" I guess I looked so young he knew I was single. I asked him, "Where's that?" He said, "Sea Island" (He lived on Sea Island – the office was in Brunswick). I asked him if I could think about it. He said, "I'll give you five minutes". I was at a fork in the road. I had always kinda gone with the flow and taken the easy way. All my friends were in Atlanta, and I really didn't want to leave. It happened that I had been to Saint Simons the previous Labor Day weekend with Kirby Lawless and Wes Chanel, two of my roommates. Wes Chanel was from there and his mother, Fergie Ferguson, ran Sadye's dress shop. Leaving Atlanta was the tough choice, but I took that fork in the road and said, "Yes".

Brunswick and Saint Simons

My first day on the job was a Monday after a drill week-end. I caught the night train from Atlanta. I got off the train and checked the phone book for the office address. It was a few doors from the drug store near the train station. I ate breakfast there and went to report for work right on time.

There was nobody in the office, so I waited in the corridor for someone to show up. I waited and waited and waited, and I kept thinking they either have banker's hours, or it's some kind of off beat holiday. After waiting longer than I should have, I went downstairs and asked somebody what the deal was. They told me the firm had moved recently to a new office on Union Street, just a few blocks away. So I arrived very late, inexplicably in a uniform and very embarrassed.

Fergie let me stay at her house, Belvedere Cottage on Saint Simons, 'til I could find some place to live. She was a great old gal. She was a good mother

– she taught Wes how to drink and play poker at an early age.

Wes had dated Betty (my future wife) a few times. Fergie knew her and would have given anything if Wes would marry her. Fergie loved Betty. I had met Betty once when she was in Atlanta visiting her brother, Bill, so I knew what she looked like. She looked great.

Wes Chanel, Kirby Lawless, Jug Levison, Cyd Bugden and I lived in a house on MacDonough Blvd. caty-corner from Agnes Scott College. We each chipped in $50 a month for rent and food that we cooked for ourselves – they cooked and I washed dishes. The first time I met Betty was when Kirby and I got home from a Navy drill week-end (in our Blues). Betty had a date with Wes while she and Dottie Dedwyler were visiting Bill at Tech.

So, when I walked into Pap Andrews drugstore shortly after I arrived in Brunswick, I ran into Betty and asked her for a date. She didn't remember my name, but said yes. I hoped she remembered the uniform. I didn't have a car, so Fergie let me use her 1949 Plymouth – bless her heart.

Our first date was at the Oasis near the airport on Saint Simons, where the famous Washboard Band played. We double dated with George Betsill, who was a landscape architect with the Sea Island Company, and his date. We had a great time and I asked her for another date. You ain't gonna believe this – I asked her to marry me on that second date. She thought I was crazy, and it took me fourteen months to get her to say, "Yes". I wasn't crazy. I just knew right away that this was the girl I wanted to spend the rest of my life with. We began going steady.

I didn't have a car and rode the bus to work from Saint Simons to Brunswick. Sometimes, if the bus was late, I had to hitchhike to work (sob). I had to get a car. Fergie heard that there was an old couple in Savannah who wanted to sell their 1942 Ford coupe for $300. I didn't have $300, in fact I owed Rich's that much for records, but it sounded like a great opportunity. I went to Betty's Dad's bank, he was Executive Vice President of the American National Bank, to borrow $300. I didn't have any collateral, but he lent me the money anyway. When I look back on it, I realize he must have co-signed the note to satisfy the loan committee, but didn't mention it to me.

So, it was the Greyhound to Savannah the next weekend. When the old couple showed me the car, it was not the mint condition old folks Ford coupe I had visualized. Their son used the car and he was a painter – house that is. The car was close to what would be called a "heap", but I had to have a car. For the only time in my life I dickered with someone on price, and I got it for $250 and headed back to Brunswick. I remember that drive back on Highway 17 so clearly. I kept thinking, "What have I done?"

On the first date after I got the "heap' I parked in front of the vacant lot next to Betty's house. I didn't want to embarrass her folks. She got in that car as if it were a Cadillac. Never batted an eye when she saw how bad it was. That was Betty – she always had class. Still does.

Working at A&R was no picnic, and my inexperience didn't make it any easier. The only time I got to take a break was when the Red Cross bloodmobile came to town. It was a small office, with Robeson (a first class S.O.B.), Abreu (colorful but rarely there), Montgomery "Gummy" Anderson (a really good guy), a secretary and two draftsmen – me and Margie Tindall. The bigger main office was in Atlanta where they did tons of highly profitable public housing projects.

I need to explain why I thought Robeson was an S.O.B. On those rare occasions when I accompanied him on one of his evening visits to a small town to show the town fathers how they could create a Housing Authority and get public housing (which he would design for a fat fee), he would tell me how clever he was. He bragged about how he had made a lot of money by buying real estate cheap from some person in financial trouble and later selling the property at a big profit. He seemed to have contempt for anyone who he thought was not as clever as he was.

Robeson and Betty's Dad played golf together on a regular basis. Robeson knew that Betty and I were going to get married. Betty's Dad told her one day on the way to school that Jimmy Robeson had told him that, "Jim Warner would never amount to anything". Betty said, "Tell Jimmy Robeson to go to hell!" She had never spoken to Dad like that before – or since.

As the weeks passed, I did some "moonlighting" to supplement my draftsman's pay. I'd work in the office after supper until the wee hours drawing house plans for people who couldn't afford an architect. I had my home-made record player under my reference table and played my favorite classical music. After giving my 78's to the Emory nurse, I had started a 33 1/3 collection. The good music made the time pass. One of the houses I "drew" was for Stewart Tuten on Palmetto Avenue. They were great clients and I got $300 for the plans. I had already paid off the $300 car loan at the bank and was able to buy Betty's engagement ring for $300 at Cunningham Jewelers. Three hundred dollars keeps cropping up in my life.

When we were about to get married in June of '52, I went to Mr. Abreu to ask for a raise. He happened to be in the office on one of his rare visits. He was poring over some papers at his desk. I said, "Mr. Abreu, Betty Geiger and I are going to get married next month, and wonder if I might get a raise." He didn't look up. He asked, "How much are you making now". I told him fifty dollars a week. He asked, "How much raise do you want?" He still wasn't looking up. I gulped and said, "Five dollars?" He thought for a minute and then he said, "No. You're not worth it." He never looked up.

We got married on June 14, 1952, at the Presbyterian church in Brunswick. We were going to go to Gatlinburg for our honeymoon. We didn't make it there for the wedding night. We spent the first night in Glenville, Georgia, in a dinky little tourist court. Betty's dad had graciously let us use his new 1952 Buick for the trip. As we drove away from the reception, which was at Betty's home, Dad called after us, "Take good care of the car."

Six months after we got married I volunteered to go to Korea. I figured it would be better than staying at the offices of Abreu and Robeson.

NAS Atlanta - Thirty Day Refresher Course

Having escaped from the big bad architects, I was happy to report for active duty (again) on December 5, 1952 at NAS Atlanta. NAS Atlanta was a great place. I felt at home, having gone through IFIS and flown in the reserve from that very familiar field. It is now PDK and is now all general aviation.

On reporting for active duty, aviators underwent a thirty day refresher course. For those of us who had been active in the reserve, it was a piece of cake. We flew Corsairs in which I had lots of hours. (See, I didn't end that sentence with a preposition). We didn't fly as a group like in a squadron or "The Class of umpty-ump", we just bored holes in the sky to get the prescribed amount of stick time.

Since I had only been making $75 a week, I didn't have much money to finance the early expenses involved. The Navy, in its wisdom, had a great program for personnel returning to active duty short of funds. It was called, "drawing a dead horse". You were advanced $900 which they took out of your pay a little each month. I was rich!

Betty came with me, and we lived in the old Piedmont Hotel at Peachtree and Forsyth near Five Points. I had fun flying all day, but poor Betty was by herself with no friends to pass the time with (oh, oh – sorry about the preposition, but I don't know how else to say it). Of course we ate breakfast and dinner at the hotel, so there wasn't any house to take care of. She was lonely just the same.

When the thirty days were up, I flew to Norfolk to get my orders. The three guys who got their orders before me got carrier night fighters and the possibility of going straight to Korea. By some twist of fate I was assigned to a Utility Squadron on the East coast. I had a choice of VU-4 at NAS Chincoteague, Maryland, or VU-2 at NAS Quonset Point, Rhode Island. Betty was five month's pregnant. I asked which base had the best hospital, and I was told, "Quonset Point", so that was my choice. I flew back to Atlanta with a few days leave so I could take Betty to Brunswick to stay with her folks until I got settled at Quonset.

I hit the road for Rhode Island with my fingers crossed. I had traded up to a 1946 used Oldsmobile that used more oil than gas and wouldn't go over 55 miles per hour. I drove 12 hours the first day and 11 hours the second day. I watched the oil pressure gauge, not the gas gauge. I stopped for oil when I saw the oil pressure drop several times, even when I didn't need gas. I made it to downtown Providence and spent the night there. I checked in to VU-2 the next day. Beat the hell out of being in Korea.

Utility Squadron Two

I checked in with the SDO at VU-2 and got a room at a BOQ where I would stay until I could find housing for Betty and me.

VU-2 was under the operational control of COMDESLANT (the Commander of the Atlantic Destroyer Fleet based at Newport just across Narragansett Bay from NAS Quonset) and under the administrative control of UTWINGLANT (headquarters in Norfolk for all Utility Squadrons in the Atlantic Fleet).

The mission was to provide aircraft services for destroyers training exercises which involved towing targets for destroyer firing their five-inch deck guns, providing aircraft for the CIC schools at Newport and Boston where shipboard fighter director officers were trained to direct fighter intercepts, photo missions photographing destroyer surface firing exercises (photographing hits on a target sled towed with a sea -going tug), ship radar calibration, coordinating submarine exercises (subs out of New London), and making simulated attacks on destroyers from various directions and altitudes to train the gunners to pick up targets and train their guns when under aerial attack.

Our operating area was south of the shipping lanes for ship training exercises, between Block Island and Martha's Vineyard for the CIC school at Newport and the boondocks of eastern Massachusetts for the CIC school at Boston. A training exercise was referred to as "an Event". The typical daily flight schedule, which as Flight Officer, was my job to prepare based on COMDESLANT training requirements, typically had about 18 EVENTS a day and looked like this:

EVENT	TIME	PLANE	PILOT	AREA	MISSION	FREQ	ACTIVITY
201	0930 1200	JD	WARNER	N/W cor. 10	Z-56-CC 1-N-22	7500 253.8	ISHERWOOD DD-520

(and so on)

We had 21 pilots plus supporting administrative and maintenance personal. All pilots had to remain proficient in all different type aircraft we flew regardless of their collateral ground duties (like Personnel Officer, Administrative Officer, Operations Officer, etc). We had the Grumman F6F "Hell Cat" (carrier fighter in the Pacific War), the Grumman TBM "Avenger" (WW II torpedo bomber like the one George Herbert Walker Bush flew), the Grumman F8F "Bearcat" (hottest prop fighter ever built), the Douglas B-26 "Invader" (single pilot twin engine attack bomber later designated the A-26 – the Navy called it the JD) and, of course, the SNB Twin Beech for pilot instrument proficiency checks and night GCA.

Soon after arriving I found a duplex in a community called Yorktown Manor. Betty left Brunswick and joined me in February. She was seven months pregnant. On checking in, it is the custom to pay a call on the C.O. and a call on the Exec so Betty and I did our duty. The C.O. was Commander Soderholm. He was a cagey guy. When an officer made his call, Soderholm would serve the drinks in aluminum "glasses". He would drink water and ply his guest with the hard stuff. This gave him a very unfair advantage getting to really know what kind of person his new pilot was.

When we visited the Exec, Lieutenant Commander "Shakey" (he was a very nervous fellow) Fuller, he asked me as we were leaving if I had ever had chicken pox. It seems his twin boys had it. I had never had it. As a result, I spent two weeks in sick bay with the worst case of chicken pox the Medical Officer had ever seen.

In April, Betty checked into the Infirmary (it wasn't a hospital like they told me at Norfolk) to have Jimmy. It was rather Spartan but inexpensive. Jimmy cost $10.50 for Betty's food while there. When we got home, and for the rest of my two year tour of duty, Betty had to do all the "up-at-night" stuff taking care of Jimmy. I told her, since I was flying all day, I needed eight hours sleep – honest. We did fly a lot, because we had all the exercises with COMDESLANT that twenty one pilots could handle, but it was fun flying – at least when I look back on it.

After Jimmy was born on April 22, 1953, there was a lot of laundry Betty had to wash in the bathtub since we didn't have a washing machine. One day she was under the weather and couldn't do the laundry, so I had to wash it in the bathtub. The next day I bought a washing machine.

Some Flying "Experiences"
(Flying: "Long hours of boredom punctuated by moments of stark raving terror")

The first plane I checked out in was the F6F Hell Cat. Since I had a fair amount of time in the Corsair, checking out in the F6 was easy. Checking out in a single-seater plane consists of a pilot who has flown it before leaning over the side of the cockpit and explaining what all the instruments and levers are for. Then, after reading the pilot manual and studying the stuff in the cockpit, you get a "blindfold cockpit checkout" during which you are blindfolded and asked to touch and name each instrument and control lever. Having done that successfully, you are on your own.

The next plane was the TBM – single pilot with two airmen in the back – used to tow targets, looking for lost practice torpedoes fired by submarines, photo missions and fly "Bogey" between Block Island and Martha's Vineyard on CIC training exercises. At the time it was the largest airplane controlled with a joy stick rather than a yoke (wheel). It could fly for six hours, which sometimes we did when working with a submarine exercise, and it landed like a feather.

Next came the F8F Bearcat. When asked in an interview what his favorite airplane was, Neil Armstrong said, "I never saw a plane I didn't like, but my favorite was the Bearcat". A Hellcat was to a Chevrolet as a Corsair was to a Buick as a Bearcat was to a Maserati.

The reason it was so hot was the Navy needed a fighter that could protect the ships from the Kamikazes in the Pacific War. Early in the War a German Focke Wulf 190, the best fighter the Luftwaffe had, was captured intact. A Naval Aviator and a Grumman rep studied it and Grumman designed a fighter with the biggest engine available, in the lightest airframe possible. It could get to 10,000 feet in 92 seconds, a record for the fastest rate of climb for prop planes that still stands. It weighed 13,460 pounds max weight (7,650 pounds empty weight) and had a twin-row 18 cylinder air-cooled Pratt & Whitney R-2800-30W 2,250 Hp (Horsepower) radial engine. That's a lot of Hp per pound.

After getting qualified in the F8, the JD was next. It was an attack bomber and handled like a fighter (but not like the F8 – nothing handled like the F8). We used it primarily for CIC work and target towing.

The check out was usually by a Chief AP (Chief Petty Officer Aviation Pilot – because they were the best pilots in the squadron), in the jump seat next to the pilot while practicing landings. I had never flown a twin engine plane bigger than a Twin Beech, so this was a big deal for me. One of the things you had to do was make a simulated dead stick landing. The Chief checking me out pulled one on me over the field at Charley Town. The JD dropped like a rock. There he was, with no controls, telling me how it was supposed to be done. The tricky part was flaring at just the right moment. We made it and I thought he was the bravest pilot I had ever known.

[The following episodes are not in chronological order, but I remember them very clearly.]

Lieutenant Commander Gerry Colleran, the Exec who relieved Fuller, was a really neat guy. He was a real leader – the kind of guy you would follow anywhere. He was just the opposite of "Shaky" Fuller who had been transferred to another squadron, and was killed in a midair collision. Every month we had to get two hours of night flying and three GCA approaches. Most guys did it in the SNB Twin Beech. Gerry and I frequently did our night flying in a two plane section of F8's. Since he was senior to me, I flew on his wing.

One night at the end of the period we were doing the GCA approaches. We took turns flying safety pilot for each other. When making the approach the safety pilot flew close astern keeping an eye out for any other planes while the other pilot was making his approach "under the hood". When Gerry lowered his landing gear and full flaps (45 degrees) at "100 feet and a quarter mile" on his first GCA approach, I dumped full flaps so as not to overrun him.

The F8 went into a violent uncontrollable 90 degree bank to the left. Only the right flap had extended. I immediately pulled the flap handle to UP. The plane went into an immediate uncontrollable 90 degree bank to the right. The right flap had come up and the left flap had gone full down. Some mechanic had hooked the flaps up "cross ways" when the plane was in for a routine check before I took it up that night. With no time to think, I automatically put the flap handle half way down. The right flap went half way down and the left flap came half way up.

Sometimes when flying you do the right thing without thinking. This was one of those times.

"Winelist" – Winelist was the call sign, as in, "Anthony four zero, this is Winelist. Vector two seven zero, angels eight...." for the CIC fighter director school at Newport. VU-2 call sign was "Anthony", followed by the plane's side number, as in, "Hello, Winelist, this is Anthony 47 over Block Island at angels eight (8,000 feet)....".

The way the exercise went was like this: A VU-2 TBM (as "bogey") flew from Block Island to Martha's Vineyard and back to Block Island – back and forth and back and forth. An F8 was at each end of the course. While one F8 orbited at its end, the other F8 was vectored on a series of headings so as to be positioned to make a gunnery run on the bogey. This went on for 3 ½ hours, morning and afternoon, every day that weather permitted. It was very monotonous, like reliving the same moments day after day for two years – it could drive you nuts.

One day I was orbiting Martha's Vineyard waiting for my turn to be vectored on an intercept. I decided to break the monotony by doing some aerobatics – much more fun than orbiting. I was at 8,000 feet. I started an Immelman. An Immelman is a half loop followed by a half roll. Max Immelman invented it in World War One. He used it to get on the tail of an enemy plane flying in the opposite direction and above him.

When I got to the top of the half loop I ran out of airspeed – there I was, flat on my back at 9,000 feet. The plane stalled upside down before I could complete the half roll. I went into an inverted spin, which means I was in a tailspin upside down. Inverted spins were prohibited in the F8F Pilot's Handbook. That's when I found out why.

In flight training we were taught how to recover from an inverted spin in a Stearman. The recovery is just the opposite of the recovery from a normal spin which is a tail spin right side up. Do you follow me? I did all the right things, but the F8 was not responding. Finally it did, and I recovered at 1,000 feet. Close! Someone once wrote, "Mastering the prohibited maneuvers in the Pilot's Manual is one of the best forms of life insurance you can get". The next time I did an Immelman. I went into it with plenty of airspeed.

We lived next door to Sally and Dick Bowers. He was a LTJG Civil Engineering Officer. One evening we were having drinks, and Dick mentioned that he was taking a work party to "No Man's Land" the next day. "No Man's Land" was a little one square mile island about five miles west of Martha's Vineyard and was used for bombing practice. You can barely find it on the map. The work party was going to do some target repair work.

I told Dick I was checking out in the F8 the next morning and I would give him a buzz. I headed straight for "No Man's Land" the next morning and could see a small boat approaching the island. I pushed over in a dive and came roaring down toward the boat. Every man in the work party jumped over the side, except Dick – he hadn't told them I was going to give him a buzz.

We towed targets with the JD for the destroyers' five-inch deck gun firing exercises. The JD was a great twin engine single pilot attack bomber rigged so that two ordnance men aft of the bomb bay could deploy a six foot diameter, twenty-six foot long, bright red nylon target (the nylon sleeves came in very handy when we traded for mahogany in Haiti while we were in San Juan for winter maneuvers). The target was on a quarter inch steel cable and was 2,000 feet behind and 200 feet below the plane. We made various patterned runs on the ships during the exercise.

On one exercise I felt the plane surge forward. I knew the ship had shot the target off. I told the ordnance men to reel in the cable and stream another target so we could continue the exercise. They said, "Mister Warner, we only reeled in 100 feet of cable!" I told them to deploy another target. After all, a miss is as good as a mile. I didn't want to abort the exercise because the ship would have to steam all the way back the next day to complete it.

Every winter VU-2 sent a detachment to San Juan to provide services to destroyers on maneuvers from Newport. I was on the detachment the winter of 1954-55. We operated out of the San Juan civilian airport. On one exercise I was towing a target in a JD for a destroyer in an operating area about 80 miles north of Vieques. That's where the ocean is 35,000 feet deep. (We used to say, "If you ditch, you'll be fish s—t before you hit the bottom.)

As the exercise progressed, the ship kept requesting me to make lower and lower passes. I obliged. On my final pass the ship radioed, "You just carried away our radar antenna". I never heard an official word about the incident. I guess the skipper never reported it, since he was responsible.

When my tour in Puerto Rico was up, I was assigned to fly a JD back to Quonset Point. Our guys always flew from San Juan to Miami, refueled, RON (remained over night), then flew to Quonset the next day. Everyone hauled a load of cheap booze back (a fifth of V.O. was 85 cents). To clear customs with no sweat they knew how to slip a bottle or two to the right Customs agents. Being a short timer I wasn't up on that procedure, so I decided to fly direct to NAS Glynco at Brunswick. Betty and Jimmy were at Betty's folks while I was on detachment.

Since the JD only had one set of controls, the crew was me, the plane captain (crew chief) and two ordnance men aft. I would still have to be inspected by Customs at Glynco, so the day before I left I passed the word that I wasn't going to allow any booze on my airplane. Just before we took off the next morning the plane captain said, "Mister Warner, there is something I need to tell you". I asked, "What is it?" He confessed that he had some whiskey hidden in the airplane. I said, "I told you guys – no whiskey on the airplane!" to which he replied, "They'll never find it". I had to trust him because it was too late to do anything about it, since we had already been cleared by Agriculture (no bugs back to the States).

My plan was to make landfall at West Palm Beach and fly up the coast to Brunswick. It was a five hour flight over water at the west side of the Bermuda Triangle. Maybe that's why I couldn't make radio contact with any station to report my position for the five hours over water.

When I made the approach to the 1,800 foot runway at Glynco I was surprised at how short it looked. The shortest runway at Quonset was 5,000 feet and the longest was 12,000 feet long. I put the JD down on the very end of the runway and finished the roll out at the very other end. The crew had to be impressed – I know I was.

A Jeep with an officer in it came rushing out to the plane. He said, "Who the hell are you, and where are you from?' When a plane leaves for a destination an "Inbound" is sent from the field of departure. Glynco had never gotten an Inbound on me.

I had to wait for a Customs agent to come from Brunswick to check me out. I showed him my Agriculture clearance. After inspecting the plane, everything was OK. He didn't find the whiskey. I spent the night, and the next morning I put Jimmy's high chair (it had been Betty's father's when he was a baby) in the bomb bay and took off for Quonset. It just happened that Mom and Dad were in Brunswick on the way back to Birmingham from one of Dad's business trips to Florida. They got to see their "little boy" fly the big airplane.

We had an air show at Quonset. There were several flyovers, and since the scheduled Blue Angels couldn't make it, four guys from one of the fighter squadrons put on the same kind of show flying F9F Cougars. They were almost as good as the "Blues". I asked the NAS Quonset Operations Officer if I could demonstrate an unrestricted take off to 10,000 feet in an F8. At the time an F8 could beat an F9 jet to 10,000 feet from a dead stand still. It still holds the rate of climb record for props (10,000 feet in 92 seconds). He OK'd it, but because of the timing of some of the flyovers, I would have to make it quick and come right back and land. I said, "The crowd needs to see something more exciting than the take off. I'd like to do a roll on the 180 turn onto the downwind leg". He said, "Can you do it?" I assured him I could (I had plenty of practice doing rolls a lot lower than the Quonset 500 foot traffic pattern when working - playing – with destroyers in our Op area). When I think about it, there was no way this guy could know if I could do it. He had never seen me before.

Betty was watching the show from a friend's house on the base. I got to 10,000 in 98 seconds from "wheels up", came back and did the roll on the break. When I got home that night I asked Betty, "Did you see me?" She said, "No. I was changing Jimmy's diaper". My 15 minutes of fame and Betty was changing a diaper.

There is an old quote: "There are rules and there are Laws. Men who think they know how to fly your airplane better than you make the rules. The Laws (of Physics) are made by the Great One. You can, and sometimes should, suspend the rules, but you can never suspend the Laws. If you deviate from a rule, it should be a flawless performance (i.e. if you fly under a bridge, don't hit the bridge)"

Another of my collateral duties was Hurricane Evacuation Officer. It was my job to have pilot/plane assignments and cross country flight plans all ready to go on a moments notice if the balloon went up. During hurricane season in 1954 we had three "flyaways". Our evacuation base was Albany, New York.

The first blow that year was Hurricane Carol, a bad one. It went up Narragansett Bay at high tide washing 300 cars off the base into the bay. Luckily, my car was spared. Downtown Providence was under nine feet of water.

We flew the F8's, F6's and JD's to Albany on such short notice that most of the pilots and crew members had no money. Some were airborne when the order came to evacuate, only had their flight gear on when they got there.

I was the last one out and I flew an F8 (being the schedule officer gave me the advantage of flying whichever plane I wanted to fly). I felt very important when, what seemed to me, the whole damn town turned out to see all the planes land. We were quartered at the Ten Eyck Hotel – the best hotel in Albany. The Supply Officer told us to just sign the check for any food (and drinks) while we were there and the Navy would take it out of our pay later (the Navy never got around to it).

We were there three days while they cleaned up the runways at Quonset so we could land. It was the best squadron party I ever attended. When I drove in the driveway at home, which was about a mile from the field, the house was covered with a spattering of leaves and dirt. The power had been off for three days and happened to go back on just as I drove in. Betty was not happy. She said, "You save the planes and leave the wives behind!"

The second flyaway was not so much a novelty to the citizens of Rochester, and the crowds there to see us land were much smaller. We were quartered in the second best hotel. It wasn't bad, but no Ten Eyck. The drinks would be at our own expense while there this time.

The third flyaway was really a letdown. Nobody showed up to see us land and we were quartered in a third rate hotel. The Supply Officer was getting smarter. Having been spoiled by previous luxuries, all the pilots checked out and then checked in at the Ten Eyck, at our own expense.

Hurricanes being unpredictable, this third hurricane came closer to Albany than to Quonset. The pilots went to hear the Concertgebouw Orchestra of Amsterdam at Renselear Polytech, a short bus ride from town. Nobody back at Quonset believed us.

LT Milt Pugsley was straight out of central casting. He looked like a fighter pilot and had the fighter pilot's personality. Of all the pilots in the squadron, Milt was the most gung ho.

Pug and I were scheduled for a "Battle Problem" Event. We flew to the Op area at about 1,000 feet in a two plane section of F8's, Pug on my wing. When I spotted the ship I started a diving turn to make a low pass in order to identify the ship by its side number. Expecting Pug to stay at 1,000 while I confirmed that the ship was ours, I came out of the turn right on the water, headed for the ship and did a barrel roll up over the ship, rolling out right on the water.

Unbeknownst to me, Pug had followed me down on my dive and caught up with me just as I was upside down over the ship. Spectacular, but unintentional! The guys on that ship must have thought we were the hottest pilots in the Navy.

When we got back to Quonset, Pug said, "Gee, Warner, I had no place to go". Most pilots would've raised hell with me for not letting them know what I was going to do, but Pug thought it was pretty neat.

Don Hayes was the exact opposite of Pug. Don was a quiet laidback "by the book man", but loved to fly the F8. On one occasion we were scheduled for a battle problem in two F8's working with a troop transport – slightly bigger than a destroyer. We conducted the exercise in the prescribed manner, and when we finished we decided to put on a little show for the guys on the ship, so we chased each other around the ship at deck level, having a great time.

When we got back to the VU-2 Operations Office, Harry Hicks, the Ops officer, said, "Did you guys know there was an Admiral on that ship?" I figured we were in real big trouble. Then Harry said, "The Admiral sent a message, "Thank you for the excellent aircraft services".

During the winter of 1953-54, I was on detachment to San Juan, Puerto Rico, We flew from the San Juan commercial airport before the big new commercial airport was built east of the city in about 1955. On one occasion I was working with a submarine on a live torpedo firing exercise. Just north of Vieques is a small island named Culebra – mostly rocks. The subs used the rocks for targets. My job was to fly around the rocks to make sure there weren't any fishermen dumb enough to fish in the vicinity of a known live torpedo target (see, we really cared about the civilians). We flew the TBM on these Events because it could stay on station for six hours. I couldn't believe how long it took a sub to fire one torpedo at a big stationary rock. Maybe it was for training new Ensign submariners. I can hear the skipper now, "OK, five hours are up. Fire One!"

Commander Schultz was the new skipper who replaced Commander Brown – a slight improvement. The UtWingLant Commander in Norfolk, Commodore Fox, thought it would be a good idea for us to deploy to NAS Roosevelt Rhodes on the east end of Puerto Rico for our Winter '54-'55 deployment. He wanted Schultz's evaluation of Rosey Rhodes as an operating base for us. The skipper took me with him to look the place over, since I had been on the previous deployment.

When we landed at Rosey Rhodes and realized how far it was from San Juan, we decided before we even left the airplane that Schultz would recommend San Juan for the next detachment. It would have been a long ride to San Juan in a broken down "Publico" (native taxi). Of course we were thinking only of the welfare of the men.

I flew mostly fighter types where, if I screwed up, nobody knew it but me. Some of my time was spent in TBM's and some in JD's. The TBM had two ordnance men aft, and the twin engine JD had two ordnance men aft plus a "Plane Captain" (which was like a crew chief) next to the pilot to keep a lookout for anything on the side that the pilot couldn't see well. Sometimes this position was occupied by a radarman when the plane was used for certain exercises.

When I look back on it, I often wonder if the crewmen, who had to fly with whatever pilot they were assigned to that day, thought they were flying with a hot pilot, a good pilot, a poor pilot – or a crazy pilot. These guys had nerve, in my opinion. While most of the pilots were having fun, some of the aviation ratings flying with us probably weren't having much fun.

I remember one time when I was making a low pass on a destroyer to check its side number, one of the men in the back picked up the mike and said, "Mister Warner, water is splashing on the bomb bay". I guess he thought I was one of the crazy pilots.

When I was leaving to go back to the hum-drum world of architecture the men in the line crew gave me a letter that read:

> *"Mr. Warner, upon your separation from the Naval Service, we of the line crew wish you to know that we have enjoyed working with you during your tour in Utility Squadron Two, and all of us are sorry to see you leave. As a token of our esteem, please accept this small token of friendship and our best wishes to you and your family on your return to civilian life."*

There were 33 names at the bottom of the letter. Then they presented me with a Waring Blender, which I humbly accepted, even though it was against Naval Regulations. The Wimbeldon Trophy couldn't have looked better. That letter means more to me than anything that ever happened to me in the Navy.

And then there was the time . . .

December 1954, back to civilian life where I had to work for a living.

Just before I left Quonset, I had flown to Atlanta to talk to Van Vanover. Van was back from his two year Air Force Reserve recall and was in practice with Bud Smith. Bud was in poor health, so Van was really practicing solo. We thought it would be good if we could work together again. I got off active duty in December 1954. After driving to Brunswick with Betty and Jimmy in my two tone green 1950 Olds hardtop convertible that I bought from Johnny Butner for $300 (there it is again), I left Betty and Jimmy with her folks and drove to Atlanta to start work with Van immediately.

Van had enough work to keep us busy 12 hours a day. I didn't have time to find a place to rent. Van didn't have a spare bedroom, so I slept on the conference room table (sob). After better than a month of that, I heard from Ben Swift, a Beck and Gregg hardware rep, that there were two houses for sale in Ashford Park, in Chamblee, on Parkridge Drive. The next day at lunch I dashed out to take a look.

Both houses were 1,000 square foot, one story with basement spec houses built by the Parker Realty Company. All the houses on the street were the same floor plan, just opposite hand and different paint jobs. Ben told me that they qualified for a VA loan, 3 ½ % 30 year loan, with $49 closing cost (nothing down).

That would be cheaper than renting, so I picked the one on the left, went back to the office and called Parker to buy 2889 Parkridge Drive.

Alice and Bill Hooper were our neighbors on our right and Toby Road, as yet un-graded, was on our left. There was nothing but woods in back. The house had a full basement at the back yard level. We had a lot of privacy.

We had moved in early in 1955 and Betty was pregnant with Madeline. Madeline was born on June 4, 1955 at old Piedmont Hospital which was located about where the old Fulton County Stadium was built (and which has now been destroyed to make room for Turner Field – or whatever they call it). About that time the Gallions, Philip and Harriet, lived three doors on the other side of the non-existent Tobey Road.

Betty met Harriet and Suzanne while out walking with Madeline, and they struck up a friendship. They would visit in their back yards and watch the kids play, Madeline with Suzanne and Jimmy with Suzanne's older brother Flip.

Lazyfare

It was through the Gallions that we were invited to join "Lazyfare". Philip was one of a group of native Atlanta boys who had gotten together for the purpose of building a "shack" at Lake Lanier – sort of a hang out at the lake for the guys (it didn't quite work out like that). I was invited in because I could draw the plans for free. There were a total, including me, of fifteen up and coming young men. I don't remember all the names, but there was Philip (a banker), Trippe Slade (a trust officer for the First Atlanta bank), Stewart White (a realtor), Curtis Cheshire (Trust Company Bank), Bennett Whipple (a member of National Association of Security Dealers, now a self regulating organization for NASDAQ and the NYSE), Ronald Gann (a real estate trust officer for the C&S bank), Jim Stanfield (a lawyer), Oby Brewer (an insurance executive and politician – and all around good guy), several others and me (just a lowly architectural draftsman).

We had all the talent we needed without going to outside consultants. Oby found a vacant lot at Flowery Branch on a quiet little cove. I don't remember how much it cost, but Oby probably found a way to get the money and the fifteen members paid $5 per month to pay it off.

In 1958, we decided that it was time to find the money to build the "shack". It turned out that Gainesville Savings and Loan wouldn't lend us the money to build a "shack". It had to be a structure that would sell, if we defaulted on the loan, something with bedrooms, baths, kitchen and stuff like that. The result was a very nice conservatively contemporary two bedroom, two bath, two level (main floor at grade at the entrance and full basement at grade with a patio on the lake side). There was a great screened porch the full width of the main level looking out toward the cove. In architectural school we had been told that facing west was not good, because of the setting sun. The porch faced west, but the setting sun was filtered through the trees and was very pleasant.

A good old boy local builder said he would build it for $17,000. The Savings and Loan gave us about an 80% loan which was signed by 15 co-signers. Oby Brewer had an old rich family friend who lent us the rest on a second mortgage, which was sufficient for us to buy all the furniture, the dishes, the record player, and (I'm not making this up) – the condiments. Oby was a genius at getting things done.

Vanover & Smith

I worked with Van for about a year. Carol (Bud) Smith never came into the office. He had been stricken with infantile paralysis as a teen ager and was very crippled. He was a very nice person and a good architect, but had lost interest in architecture.

After we got the jobs out that had required such long hours, I got Betty and Jimmy up from Brunswick and settled in the Parkridge Drive house. It was in June, 1955, that Madeline was born in the old Piedmont Hospital on Washington Street near the future location of the Fulton County Stadium.

Work at the office started to drop off. Pretty soon there wasn't any. I stayed in the office to answer the phone that never rang, and Van was out looking for work he never got. Things were bad. Again somebody had to go, and it was me. I heard through my Tech classmate, Dan Atkins, that the firm of Ayers & Godwin was looking for a draftsman.

Ayers & Godwin

I went to talk to Jimmy Godwin about getting the job. The office was in the Bona Allen building at Spring and Luckie, right next to the YMCA.

The office was relatively small, but had steady work thanks to Jimmy Godwin's salesmanship. There was Sanford Ayers, Berlin Pless, Dan Atkins, Cliff Nahser, Freddie James, and Tally Piper (a field inspection type), plus a secretary.

Ayers was probably the finest English Gothic design expert anywhere. He designed the Cathedral of Saint Philip. The firm did Wesleyan colleges all over the Southeast as well as school buildings and all the buildings at Suwanee (The University of the South).

Each of the architect types was capable of producing the working drawings of any project. On a large project two or more could work effectively together. It was a good set up.

One day in early 1957, my Tech classmate Fred Branch, who was George Heery's number one guy (total staff of five) called to let me know he was leaving Heery to open his own office with Lou Swazey. Fred wanted to know if I would talk to George about taking his place. I wasn't ready to go anywhere at the moment, but I was flattered. Later that year, I realized that I was doing the same type work over and over. I was bored, so I called George and said, "If Fred's job is still open, I'd like to talk to you".

I met with George the next Saturday morning in his office in the old house on Peachtree at 25th Street. He fixed me a gin and tonic – the first and last drink I ever had in that office. I was hired and started a very good seven year stint as Heery's number one guy.

Enter Alex Summers

It was in September, 1957, right after I started with George that Leslie was born in the new Piedmont Hospital on Peachtree at Collier Road. In the office there was George, me, two other draftsmen and Nora Baker. Nora was the secretary. Business was slow, so she read the Saturday Evening Post at least half of the day. As business improved we needed to add another draftsman. George had known Alex Summers from his days at Tech. I talked to Alex and hired him for $75 dollars a week. He never forgave me for hiring him so cheap.

I was head of production and Alex became George's right hand man, draftsman and administrative assistant. As the firm prospered and grew, Heery & Heery moved to an old house on Peachtree at 17th Street. George's dad, Wilmer Heery, had his office in Athens where the firm started. He had one draftsman, John "Soldier" Cochrane. Time marched on and pretty soon we had 30 people on the staff in the Atlanta office.

Alex and I became Associates in the firm in about 1963. We had a contract with George which went from February to February. Each year the contract was reviewed, renewed, adjusted, or terminated with two month's notice. I had never thought I would have my own office, but would always be an employee. I began to realize I was producing work for George that I could produce on my own. In our first talk that Saturday morning in 1957, George had been up front with the fact that it would always be Heery & Heery, a father-son partnership. Fair enough.

If I was going to take the plunge and open my own office, I would need a partner. Alex was a lot smarter than I was and, since I would need all the help I could get, I figured Alex would make a great partner. I really wasn't that close to him, but I approached him with the idea of forming a partnership. He accepted my offer right off. It would be "Warner & Summers, Architects" a fifty-fifty partnership.

When time came to renew our contract with Heery we agreed to give our two month's notice. We also decided that we should both tell him at the same time and not change our minds, even if he doubled our salaries, which he didn't.

George was really surprised that we were going to leave him. I'm pleased to say we left good friends and faithfully worked out our notice working for George 100%.

Baltimore Place

While we worked out our two months we rented a place at 5 Baltimore Place between Spring and West Peachtree, near Crawford long Hospital. Number 5 was, like all the other units there, a dump. We would go there at night after work and try to get it in shape. We steamed layer after layer of wallpaper off, and by the time we opened for business, it was in pretty decent shape. We didn't have any money or any clients, but it was a very exciting time and the beginning of a thirty year association.

We bought three flush doors, three metal drafting stools for the two of us from FABRAP for $60, plus one cardboard plan file just in case we got a job. Somehow we dug up enough money to buy a brand new IBM Selectric typewriter so anything that went out of the office would look professional. We put it on the card table that was the "reception room" desk.

My good friend Oby Brewer happened to be the president of the Atlanta School Board. He called one day and said he would give us a good school project when the next good one came along, but he could give us a not-so-good project immediately. I said we would like to have the not-so-good project so we could eat. The project was a 36 "movable" classroom addition to Howard High School, near downtown Atlanta. There was a federal program that would fund removable class room additions. It was decided to use pre-engineered metal buildings, even though they would be hard to make movable. The idea worked. From the time we got the job until we put it out for bids, it took us one month. The fee was $36,000. We could eat.

Pinetree Drive

At this point the family was getting too big for out little 1,000 square foot house on Parkridge Drive. We started looking for something closer to our office. We would look at different houses on weekends, none of which I could afford. The Gallions had moved to Garden hills, about six miles from Baltimore Place in downtown Atlanta. We would visit them from time to time and noticed a beautiful house for sale at 411 Pinetree Drive. A doctor owned it and had it on the market for $42,000. My banker friend, Trippe Slade, once told me, "When you make an offer, make it ridiculously low. It doesn't cost anything", so I offered $32,000. The real estate lady, Trudy Greene, said the doctor was insulted.

We really liked the house, so I got my pencil out and figured how much I could seriously afford to offer. I came up with $35,000. I told Trudy that was my max and I wasn't playing games. That Thanksgiving we went to Brunswick. While we were eating turkey, Trudy called and said, "I have good news. He'll take $36,000". I was crestfallen. I said I wasn't kidding, $35,000 was my absolute max. An hour later she called back and said he would take $35,000.

I went to the Atlanta Federal Savings and loan at Piedmont and Peachtree to get a loan. I hadn't been in business for a year yet, but they gave me a verbal agreement for a 30 year 5 ½ percent mortgage. I needed $8,000 down, which I didn't have. I went to Philip Gallion at the First National Bank of Atlanta. Banking was loose in those days. He gave me an $8,000 loan on the spot and we bought 411.

Design Build

After a few years we had outgrown Baltimore Place and moved to 1800 Peachtree, near Palisades. The firm had acquired many first rate repeat clients because of our relationship with two general contractors, Holder Construction Co. and P.C. ("Pat") Dinkins.

Holder heard we had left Heery. He called me one day and asked if I had a problem working for a contractor. In 1964, it was considered unprofessional for an architect to work for a contractor. I believed it was a free country and I told him I had no problem with that. We designed a little 20,000 square foot warehouse for him in the Fulton industrial District, southwest of town. We did it fast and made it look better than most warehouses, without it costing a lot of money. Holder was impressed. From that humble beginning, most of the important work we produced spun off from that first job. That led to projects for SunTrust, Reliance Electric, Toledo Scales, Eastern Air Lines, Hoover Universal, Vlasic Foods, RJR Nabisco, Printpack – on and on.

Pat Dinkins had known us when we worked at Heery & Heery. He knew we had gone out on our own and needed work. Pat somehow got in with Bob Hennessey, who was about to build a dealership on Piedmont Road near East Paces Ferry to compete with Capitol Cadillac, the only Cadillac distributor/dealer in Georgia. We would be working for Pat, the general contractor. Bob Hennessey was one of the nicest clients we ever had, and we had a lot of nice clients during our thirty year partnership. Hennessey Cadillac was a really class job for us beginners.

Warner Summers & Ditzel

As the firm grew, we had many great young architectural aspirants work for us. Jim Ditzel came to us from Heery & Heery. Heery was getting bigger and bigger, and Jim probably wanted to be with a smaller firm. He was a talented, hard working, clean cut guy. During a period of heavy work I said to him, "How are we going to produce all this work?" He said we would just have to work overtime. I always tried to minimize overtime for the staff, because people need to have a family life and not work all the time. I said, "I don't want to work overtime. I've done that (a lot when it was just me and Alex)!" He asked, "Why do you have to work overtime?" I said, "To set an example". Then Ditzel said, "Let me set the example". I knew then that he would be our next partner.

As the years passed, we added an Interior Design group. It was a very smart thing to do. It turned out that work would frequently spin off from Interiors to Architecture and vice versa. Linda Benefield came to us from Allen Ferry's interior design firm. He was the top Atlanta interior designer. Linda was an unusual interior designer. She was highly intelligent, had great talent, and had a good business head. I don't think she ever blew an interior design budget.

Another outstanding addition to the firm was Scott Ward. I had flown in the Reserve with Scott's dad, "Skootz" Ward, the smartest pilot I ever flew with. Years ago Skootz told me that his son wanted to be an architect. I gave him the standard "break his fingers" reply. As fate would have it, Scott went to Tech and then to work for Niles Bolton. We were lucky Scott left Niles to come with us. He developed into a young architect who understood the practice of architecture better than any young architect I knew. I could send Scott to meet with a client and never worry about him making anything but a perfect impression for the firm.

If I had any talent, it was a talent for delegating. For example, we were selected to design branch banks for First Georgia Bank. Scott, Ditzel and I went to a presentation meeting before the board of directors. I was always uncomfortable before large groups. I preferred one-on-one meetings, so I had Scott do the presentation. I was sitting next to the Governor, Carl Sanders, who was the chairman of the board, listening to the whole thing. When the meeting broke up, Carl Sanders asked me, "What do you do?" I pointed to Scott and said, "I pay him".

Doctor Blincoe

In the fall of 1988, I was playing tennis on court #4 at Cherokee. During the warm-up, I had a funny feeling in my throat. It was like my throat felt when I was a kid and had run too fast in cold weather. After we started to play, the feeling went away. I didn't think any more about it. It happened again a few days later, and it went away again when play began.

A couple of mornings later, I was getting ready to go to work and sensed that something wasn't quite right. No pain, just not quite right. I told Betty I thought I ought to go to the hospital. It was September 30, 1988. When I got to the hospital it was determined that I had had a mild heart attack. They stuck me in the hospital and did tests and watched me for a few days. Andy Abernathy was my internist. Ten years prior to all this, I had a treadmill stress test and had no problems. I asked Andy, shortly before the mild attack, if I should have another stress test. He said, "Your heart was so strong on that last stress test, you'll never have a problem". Wrong!

The morning I was sent home, all the medical people had left the room except a nurse. She lowered her voice and said, "Get another internist". Nurses know what the score is, so I switched to Doctor William "Bill" Waters as my internist.

As luck would have it, the first day in the hospital after the diagnosis was the first day I was eligible for Medicare, so Medicare and my Warner & Summers supplemental coverage paid for ever penny.

While in the hospital, just by chance, Doctor William "Bill" Blincoe, M.D. became my cardiologist. After my release, he checked my heart from time to time and monitored my medication. He would watch over me for the rest of my life.

The Knife

In late 1989, it was discovered that I had a couple of blockages, so my first open heart surgery, double by-pass CABGx2, in medical-speak [coronary artery by-pass graft – pronounced "cabbage"], was scheduled for February, 1990. Five days before the operation, I went to Ft. Benning on a V.I.P. trip with David Blackshear and Charlie Jinks and even rode the drop from the parachute tower.

The "CABG" was a piece of cake. My tennis friend, John Teltsch, had hit tennis balls 27 days after his CABG. I was determined to beat that. I was hitting balls with Betty 26 days after mine.

Not the Knife again!

In 1997, it was determined that I had another blockage(s). I had a choice of angioplasty or open heart surgery. Blincoe said the angioplasty would do the job, but it doesn't last as long as open heart surgery. The first operation in 1990 was so easy I figured, what the heck, I'd go for the CABG. CABGx3 was performed in February 1997. This time it was not a piece of cake. Recovery took longer this time, and it was determined that I had 50% left ventricle dysfunction, probably caused by a heart attack during the surgery.

I finally had to quit trying to play tennis. Blincoe continues to watch over me and has got the medication very fine tuned. I have no pain, just no stamina, and I have shortness of breath after any physical activity. Walking is uneasy. I can't hear and I can't walk steadily. Thank God I can still drive. Lucky for me, Betty is in great physical shape (same weight and same "shape" as she was when we were married in 1952). She takes very good care of me.

And Then There Were Five

In June 1993, "Warner Summers & Ditzel" became "Warner Summers Ditzel Benefield Ward & Associates, Inc., Architecture and Interior design".

Alex and I had been partners for thirty years. When we first started we had a lawyer draw up a partnership agreement. Thirty years later we hadn't signed it yet. We didn't have to. It was always fifty-fifty all the way. One day years earlier an envelope addressed to Warner & Summers arrived, from I don't remember whom. It had a one dollar bill in it. Summers opened the envelope, took out the bill, tore it in half and handed me my half.

I stayed on until December 1993 to wind up projects I was involved in and hand off some of my long term clients to Ditzel and Scott. SunTrust (then Trust Company) and Printpack had been clients since 1968. As of this writing (2007), the firm is still designing buildings for both – and they answer the phone just "Warner Summers" – period.

Unemployed

After leaving the firm in good hands in December, I became totally retired. I had asked my tennis partner, George Burke, who had been a buyer for Rich's, how he liked retirement. His answer was, "How do you like Saturday?" That sort of hits the nail on the head. Many of my retired friends complain they are busier than when they were working. They must not have been working very hard.

Summers did some residential remodeling projects for some of his Brookwood Hills neighbors, but gave it up after a short time, because, after doing a fine labor intensive architectural service, they would complain about his modest fee being too high. No good deed goes unpunished, as the saying goes.

I spend a good bit of my time now going to medical appointments and taking Betty to her appointments. We sold Betty's mint condition 1985 Olds 98 since we need only one car and moved to St. Anne's Terrace the first week in February, 2007.

Saint Anne's Terrace

Gran'ma Geiger lived at St. Anne's after she was attacked by an intruder in her home in Brunswick. She was not injured. When the culprit forced her into the bedroom, she grabbed a can of hairspray and sprayed it in his face. That scared him off, but he was never caught. She moved to Atlanta just a few weeks after the incident.

While she was here we would visit with her at St. Anne's and consequently became very familiar with their facilities – so, when it came our turn to downsize and move, we decided to follow in her footsteps. We checked Lenbrook (a high rise) and Canterbury Court (not a high rise – more like a stretched out big building), both on Peachtree just north of Lenox Square. Both were too big and too expensive. It takes $300,000 to $400,000 just to get in and then you pay about 5,000 bucks a month rent. Forget it. We ain't got the 3K to 4K and don't want to pay 5,000 bucks for all the amenities we wouldn't need or use.

When we went to look at St. Anne's, the common areas, corridors, entry lobby, etc., looked as nice as the expensive places and only cost $500 to get on the waiting list. A one bedroom-den unit only costs $3,000 a month rent, including one meal a day, housekeeping, and many simple amenities.

Goodbye 411

When an apartment became available at Saint Anne's in January 2007, we signed up for it, paid the first month rent and put 411 Pinetree on the market. The word got around and a guy on East Wesley called me and wanted to make an offer dealing with me direct. His wife had played in the house with a friend who lived here and liked the house and her childhood memories. The guy also happened to be a real estate agent. His offer was, I thought, too low. Then I decided that I needed the help of a professional.

CiCi Harris was a real estate agent who lived in Garden Hills and had sold homes in the neighborhood for as long as I could remember. I called CiCi and asked her to help sell the house. She was great. She said we wouldn't put a sign in the yard and she had thee couples quietly come by and look at it. Two couples came by who I thought were just curious and weren't serious about buying. The third prospect was Michael Barstch. His wife works at the International School [old North Fulton High School] just a few blocks away, and he is Chief Operation officer of Porches Cars North America. They were so nice I had a good feeling about them. I wanted them to be the kind of people who would live in my house. To make a long story short, they bought the house.

On the way to the closing, he came by for "the walk through". He brought Betty a dozen and a half roses and a bottle of Australian wine. Now that's a class guy. Everything went very smoothly at the closing.

The plans for 411

The Brastch's have four children and needed two more bedrooms than we had. They planned to expand the house to get the extra bedrooms and make some other additions. They loved the look of the house. I think the term is "curb appeal". After studying the possibilities, they decided that the needed expansion would be too expensive. They decided that it would be cheaper to demolish it at and build the needed space new. I hated the thought of tearing down my home. We lived there for 42 years and I knew every square inch of the place, but when I thought about it I decided he had made a very wise decision. I was told that he intended to build the new house with the same "look" as the original. He will have a house with the look they loved and a house with everything brand new and in perfect working order. I'm lucky he had the big bucks to buy it and the big bucks to tear it down and rebuild it brand new.

We bought it in 1965 for $35,000 and sold it in 2007 for $800,000. Everybody says it was a good investment. I didn't buy it for an investment. I bought it because I liked it and loved living there.

On to the Old Folks Home

The move was really difficult. Downsizing 3,500 square feet to 800 square feet is not easy. We couldn't have done it without the hard wok and great help of Leslie, Madeline and Lewie, and wise investment of the proceeds of the 411 sale by Mike.

I had made ¼ inch scale cardboard cutouts of all our furniture and studied the way we could arrange what we could take with us to the smaller place. The only way I could make things fit right required some partition "adjustments" which were permissible – at my expense. I finally came up with a plan that would require about $16,000 worth of partition changes. The new layout fits just right.

When a resident moves out, Saint Anne's Terrace totally re-does the unit – new paint, new carpet new appliances, new everything. The standard colors are perfect. I made one color change. I had the den painted a color that comes close to the color of our paneled den at Pinetree. It has the same "feel" even though it is painted and not paneled. All and all it is very comfortable and the 'included in the rent evening meal' food is out of sight delicious.

The residents here are all very friendly, all very nice, and mostly all very OLD.

I Never Can Say No

One of the residents is the Reverend Bill Schotanus, a retired Presbyterian minister. He is 90 years old and in better shape than most 80 year olds. He is the president of the Saint Anne's Membership Association and conned me into being the "recording secretary". He is the kind of guy you can't say, "No" to. Being the secretary can be a pain in the neck, but it is probably a good thing.

Betty 911

On the morning of March 23, 2008, Betty had some dull chest pains that wouldn't go away. She had some similar pains a few weeks before, but they didn't last long. I remembered a nurse telling me when I was in the hospital after my first heart attack not to worry about the sharp pains, worry about the dull pains.

I decided I'd better call 911 and get Betty to the Piedmont Emergency Room, only about four miles from Saint Anne's. Three fire fighters from the nearby Fire Station were there in no time. The pains were finally going away. They checked Betty and said that they thought she would be O.K., but there was an ambulance on the way, if I wanted one. They didn't think we would need it.

I felt we should play it safe and told them to radio the ambulance to come on. The ambulance got here soon after and the firefighters briefed the ambulance attendants. Betty got all hooked up and put in the ambulance which I followed to the ER.

At the ER the routine tests were performed – EKG, blood work, etc. The blood work showed that Betty had in fact had a heart attack, so they put her in line for the cath lab. The heart cath indicated a blockage in a major coronary artery. The cardiologist put in a stent and Betty went to recovery. After an overnight stay, she was released to go home. She had been at Piedmont for exactly 48 hours. She was back to normal in no time – but it was a big scare for me.